THE GIFT OF MISSION

THE GIFT OF MISSION

YESTERDAY, TODAY, TOMORROW

The Maryknoll Centennial Symposium

JAMES H. KROEGER, MM
Editor

ORBIS BOOKS
Maryknoll, New York 10545

Founded in 1970, Orbis Books endeavors to publish works that enlighten the mind, nourish the spirit, and challenge the conscience. The publishing arm of the Maryknoll Fathers and Brothers, Orbis seeks to explore the global dimensions of the Christian faith and mission, to invite dialogue with diverse cultures and religious traditions, and to serve the cause of reconciliation and peace. The books published reflect the views of their authors and do not represent the official position of the Maryknoll Society. To learn more about Maryknoll and Orbis Books, please visit our website at www.maryknollsociety.org.

Published by Orbis Books, Maryknoll, New York 10545-0302.
Manufactured in the United States of America.

Queries regarding rights and permissions should be addressed to:
Orbis Books, P.O. Box 302, Maryknoll, New York 10545-0302.

Maryknoll Centennial Symposium (2011)
    The gift of mission : yesterday, today, tomorrow : the Maryknoll Centennial Symposium / James H. Kroeger, editor.
        p.   cm.
    Includes index.
    ISBN 978-1-62698-012-9 (pbk.)
    1. Catholic Foreign Mission Society of America History—Congresses.
I. Kroeger, James H. II. Title.
BV2300.C35M37 2012
266'.2–dc23   2012036319

Contents

Part III
Pivotal Areas for Mission Today

Part IV
The Mission of the U.S. Church

Part V
Rewards and Challenges of Mission

Introduction

James H. Kroeger, MM

The "Maryknoll Century in Mission" (1911–2011) was commemorated by a wide variety of events, both in the United States and in the local Churches where Maryknoll serves around the globe. Diverse mission symposiums, thanksgiving masses, mission promotion events, publications, reflection days, and renewal of friendship among Maryknoll's mission partners are just a few of the events that expressed the gratitude that the Maryknoll family felt for God's generosity and graciousness in granting this humble mission community the opportunity to serve the coming of the Kingdom—for a full hundred years.

One of the pivotal mission events held in the United States was the mission symposium that Maryknoll sponsored in conjunction with the Catholic Theological Union (CTU) in Chicago. In welcoming the participants in the October 6–8, 2011, event, CTU president Donald Senior, CP, noted how "the Maryknoll community has brought its characteristic sense of mission to the school . . . [and] greatly enriched our preparation of men and women for the worldwide mission of the Church." In speaking of the event itself, Maryknoll superior general Edward Dougherty, MM, noted that "we all feel the presence and guidance of the Holy Spirit in the presentations and discussions of these days." This book is an attempt to capture and share the essence of the joyful, fruitful CTU symposium.

The symbol, or logo, that the Maryknoll Fathers and Brothers adopted for the centennial year bore the words: "The Gift of Mission: The Maryknoll Journey." The word "gift" captures the feelings and experience of missioners of all ages laboring in the Lord's vineyard around the world. Evidently Maryknoll does not originate or own mission; it is freely given by a loving God who generously shares this gift, calling missioners to participate in witnessing and proclaiming God's overflowing love.

The response of the missioner to God's gift can be captured in three words, all beginning with the letter "R." Mission is all about profoundly *recognizing* God's inestimable gift in sending his Son for our salvation.

With a deep awareness of God's love, the missioner focuses on *receiving* the gift and personally integrating it into one's life. The recognition and reception of the gift issues in concrete efforts to transmit one's faith and love to others, indeed, in *reciprocating* God's love through missionary service. The CTU experience captured well the three "R"s of holistic mission.

Within this volume of the materials presented in Chicago one discovers a wide variety of insights: the theological underpinnings of mission, various approaches to the tasks of mission, concrete experiences of mission in diverse geographical locations around the globe, special questions and concerns (for example, migration, peacemaking, Islam, care of creation). One may validly assert that this volume represents well the comprehensive, yet diverse, nature of the Church's contemporary mission of evangelization.

The Maryknoll Centennial Symposium was much more than a series of lectures and presentations. It brought together several hundred persons with a heart for mission, including Cardinal Archbishop Francis George, OMI, of Chicago, who made a presentation on the third day of the symposium. This writer recalls an elderly Maryknoll priest who never tired of repeating: "Mission is people." His time-worn dictum again proved true as the CTU gathering was certainly a "people-event," drawing together bishops, laity, religious, priests, students—all at the service of mission. The joyful, celebratory atmosphere of the event was infectious, and one CTU professor quipped that the Maryknoll Centennial Symposium was among the very best that CTU has ever hosted.

A brief perusal of these materials will readily reveal that all mission is dynamically interconnected: the historical notes (past) become alive for us today (present) and are readily seen as beacons to move the missionary enterprise forward (future). Savor the individual insights, be they from Africa, Asia, or Latin America. Appreciate the synergistic interaction seen in the areas of theology, proclamation, dialogue, and inculturation. Hear the voices of women and men tell the story of God's love. Discover the pathways that the "Maryknoll Journey" has traversed over the past hundred years.

The "Maryknoll Century in Mission" is almost equally divided between the period prior to the Second Vatican Council (1911–62) and the era of renewal initiated by the profuse outpouring of the Holy Spirit in Vatican II (1962–2011). Maryknoll has tried to be a faithful witness to the Gospel of Jesus in both halves of this century. Understandably, the majority of the material in this volume will reflect a "Vatican II missiology," always seeking to appreciate that "the pilgrim Church is missionary by her very nature" (AG 2).

In celebrating a century of mission, Maryknoll is very aware that concomitant with its involvement in mission, particularly *ad gentes* mission, other great mission efforts were underway, springing from the dedicated faith of many women and men who departed from these shores to witness to the Gospel. Maryknoll, moreover, will always treasure its intimate connection with the local Church in the United States. Maryknoll was born from an April 27, 1911, resolution by the archbishops of the United States to establish "an American Seminary for Foreign Missions." Already on June 29, 1911, Fathers James Anthony Walsh and Thomas Frederick Price received the necessary authorization and blessing from Pope St. Pius X to begin this holy endeavor.

In the lengthy planning that went into the Maryknoll Centennial Year, the superior general asked Society members for their ideas and feedback. One elderly Maryknoller, a missioner in China, gave this advice: "Keep a proper focus to the centennial commemoration. No more than 25 percent of the activities should be focused on Maryknoll's past and her contributions to evangelization. At least 75 percent of the effort should be directed toward the future, discovering new pathways for continuing mission in the future, exploring the meaning and challenges of mission for the third millennium." The materials presented here attempt to preserve this focus with a clear emphasis on the future of mission. If that "future-focus" emerges, then the October 2011 CTU event will have achieved its purpose. One symposium participant termed the gathering as a "great mission renewal weekend." Hopefully, such enthusiasm is captured in the diverse contributions found in this volume!

The Maryknoll Centennial has now passed and the Society has begun its second century in mission. With the Psalmist Maryknoll can ask: "What return can I make to the Lord for all the good done for me? (Ps. 116:12). Maryknoll has known its limitations and successes, it has its share of heroic witnesses of the Gospel, it has successfully pioneered the establishment of local Churches around the world, and, although not formally canonized, Maryknoll has its many martyrs who gave their lives in fields afar. What return can Maryknoll make for the abundant blessings it has received? The simple answer is: continued fidelity to its charism of witnessing to the Kingdom of God in all situations and contexts. Fidelity to the motto of cofounder James Anthony Walsh remains a constant call: *Primum Regnum Dei*—seek first the Kingdom of God!

Finally, as editor of this volume, I wish to thank the scores of generous persons who contributed their material for the symposium (and thus for this book); their names and brief biodata have been included. However, there is one person to whom special gratitude is due, and I express my heartfelt appreciation to Susan Perry, the Orbis Books editor and friend who marvelously assisted me—with such great skill and dedication—in guiding this project and bringing it to a fruitful conclusion. Sincere thanks to everyone!

Manila, Philippines
June 29, 2012

Part I

Mission *ad Gentes:*
Maryknoll's Journey

1

The Maryknoll Journey: Coming Home by a Different Route

Stephen P. Judd, MM

One of the clearest examples—although by no means the only one—of how to access the scope and the depth of the hundred-year Maryknoll journey is to retrieve and recover the unparalleled experience of Christian witness at the beginning of World War II. Almost from the beginning of our history Maryknollers have accepted commitments in the United States to work among the growing population of Asian immigrants on the West Coast, especially in Seattle and Los Angeles. In the patriotic fervor of the time after the attack on Pearl Harbor anti-Japanese feelings ran high. So when President Franklin Roosevelt issued Executive Order 9066, which called for the displacement and the eventual internment of American citizens of Japanese ancestry, numbering over a hundred thousand, little or no overt opposition met what today would be termed a draconian decision.

With little or no reflection, Maryknoll priests, Sisters, and Brothers from parishes in Los Angeles and Seattle accompanied people, many of whom were U.S. citizens, to the various camps in isolated places throughout the American West, including Manzanar in Death Valley, California; Heart Mountain in Wyoming; and Minidoka in Idaho. The decision of these Maryknoll women and men to go to the camps was a natural one in what remains a traumatic and shameful chapter in American history and one largely omitted from history textbooks. Fortunately, well-documented oral and alternative histories of that period exist. The 1988 reparation act did not fully erase the terrible memory for the children and grandchildren of the interned, but at least it made the story better known.

Nonetheless, even now, over sixty years later and even within Maryknoll circles that could benefit from advances in historical research, scant knowledge of this extraordinary witness of solidarity is available except for those scholars willing to plumb the documentation available in the Maryknoll archives. However, thanks to the extensive research carried out by Maryknoll Sister Joanne Doi, herself the daughter of parents interned in two different camps, her master's and doctoral dissertations provide valuable insights into the vital and critical role played by Maryknollers in the everyday lives of those interned in the camps.

By virtue of these accounts we have a better idea of how Japanese Americans endured this ordeal with courage and resilience, and later they began to rebuild their broken lives. No Maryknoll witness to this grave injustice remains so we can only conjecture about the enduring effect it had on the interned. But we can certainly point to this as a pivotal moment, every much as pivotal as Walsh and Price's "Montreal moment" (meeting at the International Eucharistic Congress) in the life of our mission movement.

Fifteen years ago in Seattle, thanks to the courageous initiative of then Archbishop Thomas Murphy, Maryknoll leadership and Maryknollers in the area held a first reunion of the survivors of the camps and their children and grandchildren, all with ties to the now extinct Queen of Martyrs Parish. Two of the Maryknoll Sisters who worked in the camps, Regina Ann Johnson and Mary Rosario Greaney, were able to attend this powerfully moving reunion. All present that day basked in the glow of a common shared experience of displacement, suffering, resilience, redemption, and reconciliation. All that survives of Seattle's Queen of Martyrs Parish, later converted into a parking lot for the Sisters of Providence Hospital, is a painting depicting the martyrdom of Japanese Catholics. It has hung for years in the parlor of the Maryknoll Society Promotion House in Seattle. For several years, women from the parish continued to meet every week at the Maryknoll House to pray the rosary. They preserved not only the historical memory of the parish but also the memory of the injustice of the internment experience. The solidarity of Maryknoll Sisters, priests, and Brothers found a permanent place in their collective memories.

While this unique pilgrimage experience unfolded in their homeland, Maryknollers throughout the Far East suffered another kind of pilgrimage experience, a different kind of displacement because of the upheaval of war. Many Maryknollers were interned in camps in the Philippines, and others met the fate of martyrdom. A large number assigned to the Asian and Pacific regions experienced repatriation and involuntary exile back to the United States aboard the Swedish ship *Gripsholm*. At the same time, in 1942 and 1943 Maryknoll launched its first missions to the Latin American continent. And immediately after the war, in 1946, Maryknollers arrived in East Africa in yet another daring kind of mission pilgrimage. All in all the wartime years were defining moments and left a unique indelible mark on the Maryknoll spirit. Only now, in retrospect, can we begin to appreciate how these episodes shaped our identity and set the stage for postwar growth.

Journeys into Particularity

Some readers may wonder why I begin my reflections by evoking this largely unknown and often forgotten piece of Maryknoll history as a way to describe our century-long mission journey. What relevance might it have as we reflect on the future of our mission project in the twenty-first century? What could the retrieval of this episode possibly say to people of this and future generations? You might rightly wonder why I settled on this example when hundreds of others might just as easily serve the purpose of capturing the spirit of the Maryknoll journey.

Likewise, many other examples could describe the courageous witness of Maryknoll. The stories of Lay Missioners Susan Nagele and Liz Mach in the war-torn Southern Sudan powerfully illustrate the living out of the Maryknoll spirit in adverse conditions. And does not Bob McCahill's mission of presence among the Muslim Bangledeshi people serve as an example of the paradigmatic Maryknoll experience? Do martyrdoms in the past in Asia, and in recent memory the deaths of Bill Woods in Guatemala and of Carla Piette, Maura Clarke, and Ita Ford in El Salvador, underscore the unconditional self-sacrifice and dedication in giving up one's life for others in faithfulness to the Gospel mandate? Bishop Patrick Byrne's martyrdom on the Korean death march at mid-century and Navy chaplain Vince Capodanno's self-sacrifice on a battlefield in Vietnam are sagas of heroic proportions worthy enough to be a fitting starting point to tell the Maryknoll story. Surely every Maryknoller could come up with many more examples.

No single expression of the Maryknoll story, however, or no one experience can possibly exhaust the full meaning of this journey. At best we can approximate it with partial interpretations and a herme-neutic of the power of the intercultural encounter that connotes a life-defining transformation. In the final analysis, it remains fundamentally a grace-filled narrative marked by mysterious twists and turns, detours and midcourse adjustments, along with as yet unknown pathways into the future.

Capturing the fullness of the Maryknoll story lies largely in high-lighting the subversive power of historical memory and belief in the surplus of meaning behind symbolic actions of solidarity. It is also found in the provocative sociocultural and religious significance of pilgrimage, in the transformative power of alterity in discovering the face of Christ in the faces of numerous "others," and in the stubborn unwavering belief in the human capacity to overcome adversity.

Firmly embedded in the Maryknoll spiritual imaginary is a core belief in the dignity of the human person created in the image and likeness of the Creator God, who has given all people infinite potential to be architects of their own destinies. Maryknoll Father James Keller, founder of the Christophers, and Al Nevins among others, articulated that vision better than most through the media of the printed word, radio, and television in the post–World War II era. Today the stories of Maryknollers in the internment camps and certainly those who inhabit many other narratives in the midst of world-changing events need to be told and retold as they speak volumes of the best of the Maryknoll spirit and what I believe will be our living and lasting legacy and contribution to the American and world Church.

Theologian David Tracy comes very close to capturing the essence of such experiences in his treatise on what constitutes a classic text in his magisterial work, *The Analogical Imagination*. Tracy uses the phrase the "journey of intensification into particularity." It is not stretching the notion too much to say that this kind of witness quali-fies as a classic text, one that in its very particular density of mean-ing speaks a compelling universal language accessible to people in diverse contexts. The endless nights in the internment camps that Doi describes as the "night of a thousand cranes," in reference to the Japa-nese art form of origami, epitomizes the multivalent epiphany encoun-ter of the "other" experienced by every generation of Maryknollers. It is but another variation on the theme of James Edward Walsh's poetic ode to the Chinese farmer boy in the rice fields in South China. Such images have nurtured us as we journey at the convergence of different crossroads. It is what was first reflected in *The Field Afar*, later *Maryknoll Magazine*, *Revista*, Orbis Books, and the personal writings and testimonies of countless missioners.

When Stephen Bevans and Roger Schroeder speak of the challenge of mission today as marked by the need for a "prophetic dialogue," are they not referring to these kinds of narratives? All of us have been singularly gifted with the destiny of experiencing Walsh's encounter with the farmer boy not once but many times over in our different but complementary journeys. The bigger challenge has always been to find a vocabulary to translate these stories to the Christian communities around the world that have so generously sent us out to mission in their name. In this we have been gifted with an extraordinary, expansive, and boundary-breaking Catholic and sacramental imagination.

Grounded in a Contemplative Worldview Leading to Action

Another key to understanding these journey or pilgrimage experiences lies in the contemplative dimension so integral to the lives of our three visionary founders; indeed, the founders preferred to be known as the "organizers" since in their minds and hearts Maryknoll was a foundation of women and men from throughout the emerging U.S. Church at the turn of the twentieth century. They saw themselves called to organize the dream and turn it into a reality. They, often more so than we, envisioned Maryknoll as a widely inclusive mission movement made up of many interdependent and interconnected gifts all placed at the service of the whole body. From those early years at the first headquarters in Hawthorne, New York, they welcomed and made room for everyone, a tradition we strive to live out today by inviting and enabling others to join in proclaiming Christ's saving, liberating, and reconciling mission. Symbolic of this open inclusive spirit is the striking and near iconic photo of Mollie Rogers with her cape unfurled in a welcoming gesture. She seems to beckon each of us to "come on in and join us; God has yet a great work for us to do."

Foundational and fundamental to the religious, social, and cultural imaginaries of these three "organizers" was a firm belief that mission from the United States needed to be grounded in the Church's contemplative tradition as well as in the robust American spirit if it was to succeed. All three—Walsh, Rogers, and Price—cultivated strong partnerships with Carmelite communities in Baltimore and Boston, relationships that they nurtured and encouraged and that have been carried on by each subsequent generation. I trace the roots of my own gifted partnership with the Reno, Nevada, Carmelite community to that precious spiritual heritage, as do many of my sister and brother missioners affiliated with other contemplative communities. The popular activist image so often associated with Maryknoll tells only half the story. Encounters with farmer boys, Sudanese freedom fighters, or people in internment camps cannot be fully understood as anything less than an in-depth experience of the contemplative spirit.

Our self-understanding as missioners stands or falls on the integration of action and contemplation into our identity, and more so now at this critical juncture. Some twenty years ago a controversial study on the spirituality of Maryknoll priests and Brothers concluded, wrongly I believe, that many of us had become too "functional" and had lost a sense of the sacred. The evidence on the ground, in my experience, flies in the face of that assertion, but keeping a balance has been an ever present challenge. We neglect the contemplative side of our missionary vocation at our own peril. No less an authority than Karl Rahner pointed out that Christians of the future have to be mystics in order to fulfill their baptismal promise. By the same token it could be said that missioners of the future will need to be mystics in order to carry out one's discipleship in new and creative ways across borders and in the nooks and crannies of the global landscape. Such is the inspiration behind this prayer composed by John J. Walsh, not related to James Anthony Walsh or James Edward but a kindred spirit.

> May we be prophets
> Proclaiming the Reign of God in all things.
> May we be mystics
> Experiencing a real sense of at-one-ness with God,
> With all of humanity
> And all of creation.
> Mission is to go to a no-place, serve God's no-bodies
> and in the eyes of the world accomplish no-thing.

In this, may we realize we are at the center of
What time, meaning, and history are all about.
Oh God, give us the courage to
Dream new dreams,
Think new thoughts,
And go forward into the future with the Spirit.
Oh God, fill us with the joy of the Gospel,
And may we pass it on to others,
Pressed down,
Flowing over,
Full measure, above and beyond.

Frontier Trouble Shooters, Rabble Rousers, and Disturbers of the Peace

One of the premier Maryknoll mission thinkers of the twentieth century was John Considine, a major player and motivator in our early years, the World War II era, and beyond in his founding of the U.S. Bishops' Conference Latin American Secretariat. Considine coined the image of the Maryknoller as a "trouble shooter," the quintessential, pragmatic, and self-reliant fix-it handyman out in the boondocks. Taken to the extreme, this image may explain the dangerous tendency to become too functional or overly activist.

Others have labeled us, rightly or wrongly, "trouble makers" or "rabble rousers" or, in some cases, worse, most likely due to our affinity with the Jeremiah prototype so deeply embodied in the American religious psyche. Maryknollers have always fit the profile of American Jeremiahs and hopefully always will. There is no doubt that a case can be made that the strong allegiance to the reign of God in Maryknoll's mission theology (Matt. 6:33) bears a close identification with the Social Gospel movement in American religiosity of the nineteenth century as spelled out in the writings of the highly esteemed Protestant theologian H. Richard Niebuhr in his classic *The Kingdom of God in America*.

While strongly rooted in the "Americanist" current of American Catholicism at the time of Maryknoll's foundation in 1911, Maryknollers by and large have crafted another identity, one akin to that of "planetary citizens" who are able to finesse their American identity with the canny ability to relativize any semblance of American "exceptionalism," even in the midst of Walter Lippmann's so-called "American Century." If the proverbial shining "city on a hill" has a rightful claim on our American spiritual heritage, it has never become an absolute measure of the depth of our mission witness. At least consciously, Maryknoll never was a willing partner in the U.S. imperial expansionary project of the last century. Our willingness to bring the voices and human faces of the people we dwell among to the halls of Congress and the United Nations through our Office of Global Concerns is highly regarded in our nation's capital.

The frontier spirit of the robust Teddy Roosevelt era a hundred years ago certainly has left its unmistakably unique stamp on the Maryknoll character and imagination. At a distance one could say that geographic considerations determined our spiritual destiny. When we closely examine a distinguishable pattern in the choice of mission territories, they are most always on the periphery of the countries where we started: from Canton in south China, to the Amazon regions of northern Bolivia, to the Lake Victoria borderlands between Kenya and Tanzania in East Africa, to northeast Brazil, where the sun first rises in the Americas every morning. Peripheral, insignificant places on the map, and submerged towns and squatter settlements found in places like the vastly beautiful but harsh terrain of the altiplano of Peru, the far reaches of North Korea, the highlands of Guatemala, and hundreds of other out-of-the-way places exert a pull on our personal and collective imaginations. They are our spiritual lodestars that have shaped a distinct identity and global perspective as we have learned the fine art of straddling the global and the local.

Never did we rush to establish missions near the comfort zones and centers of political and economic power or cultural influence in all the countries in which we have served. Ours was, and continues to be, the proverbial "errand into the wilderness," although the frontiers of mission have shifted radically and are no longer defined by territorial or geographical language and criteria. Today new borderlands and frontiers, both real and symbolic, indicate a different kind of internment camp of times past and direct us to unheard of regions of emerging peoples on the move, unexplored horizons, and territories of a fragmented world where the body of Christ is most broken. These yet to be fully defined territories still beckon us outward to become responsible planetary citizens with an inclusive and expansive world-view. We still follow the same star to new Bethlehems as did the Magi two thousand years ago, and we still return to our home countries by different alternate routes.

The epiphanies we experience on the journey today and in the future will be in continuity with the epiphanies early missioners experienced in internment camps, hidden villages that dot the countryside, and the teeming slums of megacities. They will engage us in encounters in the new *areopagus* of immigrants, the horrors of human trafficking, accompanying those afflicted with AIDS, aiding displaced refugees, and also engage us in fruitful dialogue with those in academic centers and those young people locked into social networks. Who could have imagined that Maryknoll's original mission among the Chinese would later evolve into one of building bridges by facilitating the formation and educational renewal of future Church leaders for Catholic Christians in China?

Anthropologist Victor Turner's popular notion of *liminality* presents yet another interpretive key to our self-understanding as missioners. Threshold experiences of crossing frontiers, real or symbolic, of living in a constant suspended state of betwixt and between, position well the missioner for life-changing encounters. What could be more liminal than a mission lived out in an internment camp in the middle of one's own native land? The liminal state that relativizes one's presumed superiority in the face of the "other" and the one who unmasks our tendencies to shape them in our own image and likeness have been unmistakable features of the Maryknoll journey since the outset in 1911.

Today, it seems that the idea of American "exceptionalism" and the questionable theory of a "clash of civilizations," coupled with the revived myths of selfishness perpetrated by the emboldened followers of Ayn Rand, have reemerged. They run counter to our promotion of more intercultural dialogue and the acceptance of the "others" of the world, including those less fortunate. An embrace of intercultural dialogue worldwide has marked us as radically countercultural in our own land. Thus we need to turn to and reclaim those pivotal moments in our journey where our American identity and ties to the homeland have taken a secondary place in working for greater global understanding through intercultural dialogue and planetary solidarity. In other words, we strive to give witness to a globalization of solidarity from below where human capital translates into networks of social capital in the search of the common good.

Story Brokers, or Going for Broke:
An Accounting and an Audit

At the same time, we still have a huge outstanding debt to pay back to those Christian communities who have sent us out to embrace the challenge of new frontiers. It remains a duty we must not shirk in the new millennium as borders blend and shrink. Missioners of the future will not be so much Considine's "trouble shooters," social activists or trouble makers, disturbers of the peace or even less some kind of functionalist multitasker cyberwizards. Rather missioners can serve as story brokers, tellers of tall tales, whose stock in trade is to continue to share the stories and dreams of those we have been privileged to see and hear and to dwell among. Either we become those mystical, prophetic story brokers or we default. If we default to a comfortable journey, our communities will circle their wagons and close in on themselves. Our journey must be an "intensification into particularity," using Tracy's phrase, but the "particular place" may be a place where we first started out. T. S. Eliot once noted that the end of a journey arrives at the place it began although it is seen as for the first time. Today we see Maryknoll's places of origin, such as China, with a new and loving eye through the prism of those other places and lands we have embraced and have been embraced by.

It is high time we renew our relationship with people all across the growing multicultural, ecumenical, and religiously plural (and sometimes awfully messy) mosaic landscape in the United States. In short, we must invite them to become stakeholders in God's mission with us in new kinds of partnerships. We are not the sole owners of God's mission, and we are not the only pioneers on the front lines and in the trenches. We have learned the hard way that we can no longer be independent Marlboro men and women, Westchester cowboys, or the Marine Corps of the Church, exceptional specialists who come home every so often to pick up some extra change and then sneak back to the false security of secluded mission compounds seemingly untouched by the surrounding realities. We need to tell the people that we are all in this together, that we share collective responsibilities for the fate of the planet and humankind across all kinds of borders, boundaries, and barriers. As one of our missioners wisely quipped, "Missionary commitment begins at the arrivals area of Kennedy Airport!"

F. Scott Fitzgerald once said that in American life there are no second acts. The Maryknoll story and journey defy that dictum and challenge its conventional wisdom. Yes, we do dare to believe in second and third acts, that we can come home again with humility, overflowing with gratitude but loaded down with a different set of baggage and skills and ways of being in the world. This will enable us to celebrate the gifts we have received and the lessons we have learned. Most of all, it will help us renew ourselves in this abundant warehouse of new stories of the breaking in of God's reign. We have been blessed to see the world with new eyes, from different angles, even from upside down (in Spanish, *patas arriba*). New horizons and perspectives have beckoned us to the many ways that God's infinite graces are operative in renewing and transforming the Earth. In the embrace of our homelands—which now go beyond the United States as Maryknoll is increasingly made up of missioners from many lands—we will continue to reflect new faces and cultural experiences and increasing diversity along with a constellation of new ways and affiliations.

Indeed, this symposium has become, to borrow a phrase from Robert Schreiter, a "point of semiotic density," a new kind of missionary crossroads. In Latin America we call this encounter an *apacheta*, a place of renewal in every dimension of our common mission vocations in the midst of our vulnerability and limitations. As Maryknollers we actively seek your critiques and your insights in the hope that you will accompany us in renewing and building partnerships for our continuing journey in search of that elusive but ever so present reign of God.

Affability, Availability, and Adaptability Revisited

Early on an attempt was made to characterize the elements of a Maryknoll spirituality around the three "A"s of "affability, availability, and adaptability," to name the constitutive parts or pillars of the ideal prototype envisioned by our first missioners. The task for each generation is to dust off these qualities to see what they might mean in each new historical period. Then we must reinterpret them and ask ourselves if they are still relevant for the challenges of the current stage. Can we still build a missionary presence today on the foundation of these principles or pillars? This is an open and intriguing question for us—friends, foes, and partners alike—to raise during the celebrations and events of these centennials of 2011 and 2012.

One might say that Mollie Rogers has taken care of the affability issue once and for all, so it might not be necessary to revisit that area. By and large we have done nothing to squander this part of our heritage. It is safe to say that the "saving grace of a sense of humor" still permeates the Maryknoll spirit wherever one encounters it here and overseas. Someone once commented half in jest but with a certain degree of seriousness that the most that any one of us will ever accomplish is to provide cheap entertainment for the folks we have been sent to serve. But behind this veneer of laughter is a reservoir of a deep joy that enables everyone of us not to be mistaken for anything else but a missioner. The other two "As" of availability and adaptability, I believe, might involve a bit more reflection and a lot of hard work to see how they still might apply.

The availability issue means that we must still be able and willing to respond to new opportunities and challenges, even in a time of diminishing human resources. One of the challenges here, because of our aging and dwindling workforce, is to take on a posture that passes on our vast knowledge and experience and enables others to assume their missionary responsibilities. How we create new spaces for creative ministries and new ways of being in mission for other protagonists will be the measure of how we live up to this dimension of our spirituality. This might mean leaving the false security of places that we have become too accustomed to, those "comfort zones." We must not forget the message behind James Edward Walsh's well-known wisdom that the "missioner is to go to a place where he or she is needed but not wanted and to stay until he or she is wanted but no longer needed." The extent to which we become available for more enabling apostolates can and will contribute to the renewal of the missionary vocation. In these times, when the whole missionary enterprise comes under more scrutiny and critique from every sector of Church and society, or is even ignored or not taken all that seriously, our openness and availability to respond to new sociocultural situations are challenges of the highest order.

Availability to enable other mission partners and generate new mission activity goes hand in hand with the kinds of critical adaptability needed to innovate, retool, and refashion our mission response in the twenty-first century. We must assist in the Church's call for a "new evangelization." In reframing this question of adaptability I may be restating our commitment to lifelong learning so we can better become those prophetical and mystical actors and protagonists needed for the second and third acts. Even if our role is a minor supporting one, it is no less critical for the continuation of God's mission in the new *areopagus*. Adaptability means more than a few cosmetic changes. Rather, it requires more than a few fundamental paradigm shifts.

It is safe to say that the three principles of affability, adaptability, and availability were quite operative in the minds and hearts of those who journeyed with the Japanese-American people to the internment camps during World War II and in other moments in similar adverse circumstances throughout the past century. I dare say that in a newer context they are still operative but sometimes dormant, sometimes taken for granted, and always in need of renewal. That, my friends, is where we need to weave our stories into a credible narrative for the good of the whole. Because we cannot do that alone, we invite you to join us as people and partners have done so generously and creatively since the outset. Together, affable, adaptable, and available, we can live out the dream of a mission movement in service to God's reign.

2

Response to Stephen Judd:
Maryknoll Sisters in Mission

Janice McLaughlin, MM

In his powerful presentation, Steve Judd raised many important themes that helped to define and shape the first hundred years of our Maryknoll history as well as themes that will take us into the future. He told us, among other things, that missioners are meant to serve as "story brokers, tellers of tall tales, whose stock in trade is to continue to share the stories and dreams of those we have been privileged to see and hear and to dwell among."[1]

So let me begin with a story. This story took place just two months ago in the new nation of South Sudan, where I was to give peace-building workshops to various groups. Everywhere I went, the priests and Sisters I met shared stories about our Sisters who first went there in 1976 and who stayed through the long years of war. The Sisters were uprooted many times and displaced together with the local people. One of the priests shed tears of joy when he heard that our Sr. Ruth was still alive and working on the West Coast. "Both of my parents were killed during the war," he told me. "Sr. Ruth was like a mother to me. Every day after school I went to her office at the pastoral institute and she gave me work to do. She taught me so much and made me feel needed and loved. She is responsible for my vocation."

I can't think of a better definition of a missionary—one who makes others feel needed and loved, who connects them to others and to God. We Maryknoll Sisters call ourselves bridge builders, and our logo reads, "Making God's love visible." Our founder, Mother Mary Joseph, defined our spirit as "being a reflection of the love of God—nothing more nor less than that," she said, "a reflection of the love of God."[2]

In my brief response, I will share more stories and some examples of what I think this has meant in the past and what it might look like in the future. In describing three aspects of our lives as missioners—our identity, our ministry, and the challenges we face in the future—I

16

am focusing on two seemingly opposite movements within Steve's presentation—continuity and change, continuity with the past, and change as we look toward the future with hope.

Continuity: Call to Universal Mission

Almost a hundred years ago, on January 6, 1912, to be exact, three young women traveled from New York City by train to Hawthorne, New York, where they were met by Fr. James Anthony Walsh, who dubbed them "the three wise women."[3] Mary Louise Wholean, Sara Teresa Sullivan, and Mary Augustine Dwyer had come to assist the fledgling mission movement that would become Maryknoll. "We were strangers to each other and differed in age, training, and disposition," wrote Mary Louise, "but we had been brought together and were henceforth to be united by the common desire of serving the cause of the foreign missions."[4]

This desire to serve the cause of mission is the strongest link of continuity between the past and the present. Women from many lands continue to make the journey to Maryknoll in order to become missioners. In the words of our Constitutions they come "to participate in the mission presence and activity of the universal Church so that God's Reign of peace, justice, and love may be proclaimed and witnessed to throughout the world."[5]

This willingness to leave home and country and cross borders of every kind continues to distinguish us. "Today we are nearly five hundred women from twenty-two different nations working on four continents. Regardless of where we serve or what we do, we journey with the people, adopting a lifestyle in harmony with the local community and local needs."[6] Just last month, we assigned four of our newest members to mission: two young women from the Philippines will be going to Bolivia, and two others will be sent to Brazil, one from East Timor and one from Korea. I believe that the call to universal mission is the strongest link with our past and will continue to lead us into the future.

Change: International Membership

The international background of our newest members represents a change in the face of mission. Our multicultural identity offers a rich mosaic of a globalized planet where national borders are becoming increasingly irrelevant. The diversity of our members is a clear witness to the fact that we are "planetary citizens," as Steve noted, and that the Gospel is for all people of all times.

From our early days, Maryknoll Sisters embraced women of other cultures. The first international member to join the congregation was Sister Marianna Akashi, a Japanese woman who was received at Maryknoll on June 28, 1921, the eve of the Maryknoll Society's tenth anniversary and the same day that the assignments of the first six Maryknoll Sisters to China were made.[7] At the present time, few of our members who are under the age of sixty come from North America. Women from Tanzania are working in Brazil, Bolivia, and the United States; Koreans are working in Zimbabwe, Namibia, Guatemala, and Bolivia; women from the Philippines are in East Timor, China, Japan, Tanzania, and the United States, and so forth. This reality affects both the way we do mission and the way we are perceived.

I was fortunate to live with two of our new members from Korea in Harare, Zimbabwe. One of them is a professional dancer and the other has a black belt in tai kwon do. What do you think they do for their ministry? The dancer joined the National Ballet and started an outreach dance program with poor and disabled children in the African townships and squatter settlements. The black belt champion set up an after-school enrichment program in an impoverished area; it attracts as many as four hundred youth each week who participate in drama, arts and crafts, music and dance, poetry, and, of course, martial arts. This is the new face of mission.

Continuity: Collaboration within the Maryknoll Family

From the outset, the Maryknoll movement brought together various expressions of the mission vocation with priests, Brothers, and Sisters joining hands to spread the message of God's love and compassion. The laity came on board in 1975 after the Second Vatican Council, stressing the vocation of lay members in the Church. As we continue to seek new forms of partnership, the Maryknoll Affiliates was formed twenty years ago. This collaborative presence has been strengthened in recent years with joint projects and joint mission endeavors.

We also partnered with other groups from the start. Mother Alphonsa Lathrop, who founded the cancer hospital at Rosary Hill, gave the two thousand dollar gift that enabled Mary Josephine Rogers (Mollie) to leave home and join the women at Hawthorne. The Franciscan Missionaries of Mary were mentors and friends and gave us all the furnishings in our first kitchen. The Dominicans at Hawthorne kept us supplied with food. We were trained in religious life first by the Immaculate Heart Sisters from Scranton, Pennsylvania, and later by the Sinsinawa Dominicans. They all helped to shape us and to give us an appreciation of the many and diverse gifts in the Church.

Lay men and women also played a prominent role in the early days and continue to do so. The Teresian Diaries chronicle the support and friendship that we received from a variety of people. Julia Ward is often mentioned as one of our greatest benefactors. She designed the Maryknoll habit and took Mollie Rogers to Europe, where she visited Lourdes and Rome. It was during this influential trip that Mollie got the idea of having a contemplative community as an integral part of Maryknoll. The list of those who were partners and friends is long and deserves to be recalled as we celebrate the first hundred years of our history.

Change: Intercongregational Initiatives

I believe that we are now being called to go beyond our Maryknoll roots to join hands with others in intercongregational and international projects. Solidarity with South Sudan is one such model. It was established in 2008 in response to a call from the bishops of Sudan to support them in rebuilding their nation after a comprehensive peace accord was signed in 2005. This initiative has the support of more than 170 religious congregations from around the world. Presently twenty-five volunteers in South Sudan are training teachers, nurses, and pastoral workers. "The age of competition is over," declares Fr. Joseph Callistus, a Claretian priest from Sri Lanka, who is the project director in Juba. "The age of collaboration is NOW."[8]

"No one congregation could have met the needs here," he said, pointing to the amazing work that has been accomplished in just a few years by this collaborative initiative of men and women, priests, Brothers, and Sisters from nineteen congregations and fourteen nationalities. I was privileged to spend three weeks with them in July and August this year. As I facilitated workshops in conflict transformation for nurse trainees, seminarians, and broadcasters with Radio Bakhita, I witnessed firsthand the benefits of such international, intergenerational, and intercongregational outreach. I believe that this is truly a new paradigm of mission, which will become more and more common.

In the future I doubt if there will be Maryknoll projects or Dominican projects or Medical Mission projects, and so on. Rather there will be collaborative efforts to address urgent needs that call for a pooling of personnel, resources, and expertise. Imagine what a difference we could make if all missioners worldwide, Catholic and Protestant, were to tackle the issue of violence against women, for instance, or the problem of human trafficking. What if the response came from people of all faiths! Our interconnected world calls for such global creative and prophetic initiatives.

Continuity: Solidarity with the Suffering

Steve Judd began his presentation with the example of Maryknoll's response to Asian immigrants in the United States at the beginning of World War II and the internment of more than a hundred thousand American citizens of Japanese ancestry in camps located in isolated places in the American West. He points out that Maryknoll priests, Brothers, and Sisters joined them in the camps and ministered to them there. I spoke recently to several of our Sisters of Japanese origin who were interned in the camps with their families. Each said how much it meant to them that Maryknoll did not abandon them. Like the Sudanese priest I mentioned earlier, they said that this solidarity influenced them to join Maryknoll.[9]

To imagine how radical this identification and solidarity with Japanese political prisoners was at that time in history, one only need think of what it would mean if religious men and women today would visit the so-called terrorists imprisoned here in the United States and elsewhere around the world and would seek permission to stay at Guantanamo with them! In fact, I know that this is actually the case on the African continent, where the African Council of Religious Leaders is establishing dialogue with members of various groups in North, East, and West Africa who are labeled as terrorists, such as Al-Shabaab in Somalia.[10]

Over the years, this example of solidarity with those suffering injustice would become a hallmark of Maryknoll. These pilgrimage experiences have transformed us and enabled us to escape from the narrow boundaries of our North American identity to become citizens of the world with a special option for those who are poor and marginalized.

Change: Challenging the Root Causes of Injustice

The Second Vatican Council had a big impact on Maryknoll, as I am sure it did for most congregations. As we studied the Vatican documents, especially the *Church in the Modern World*, we came to realize that we needed not only to minister to the poor, homeless, and hungry, but also to ask the question, "Why?" Why are so many forced to live in utter squalor while a few in positions of power and privilege enjoy the wealth of a nation? This growing awareness of inequality led us to analyze its root causes and to begin to take action for justice.

Maryknoll Sisters established a Social Concerns desk at our Center in New York in the early 1970s, around the time the Synod discussed justice (1971). (A joint Office of Global Concerns with all three branches of Maryknoll was established in late 1997.) We began to question U.S. foreign policy around the world, especially in Latin America, where the CIA participated in action against popular governments in such countries as Guatemala, Bolivia, and Chile. In the 1970s and 1980s, our members joined in movements for change in Guatemala, Southern Rhodesia, Taiwan, and the Philippines. Some were arrested and deported. The rape and murder of the four church women in El Salvador in December 1980 brought home to us what it means to "suffer the same fate as the poor."[11]

Our action for justice took another leap forward when we included the "integrity of creation" in our justice ministries. We have decided that we must defend not only human life but also the life of the planet, as we recognize our oneness with all creation. Maryknoll Sisters around the world have made ecojustice a priority. Just as the struggles for justice in Latin America led to a new theology of liberation, the growing imperative to care for the health and well-being of the Earth is also leading to a new theology that is closely linked to a new cosmology.

Wangari Maathai, the first African woman to win a Nobel Peace Prize, died in 2012. A biologist and a leader of the environmental movement in Kenya, she started the Greenbelt Movement. She "made visible the links between trees and soil, war and peace, and the human body and spirit."[12] In an interview with Krista Tippett on National Public Radio in 2006, Maathai, a practicing Catholic, explained how her image of God was changing: "I tell myself that of course we're now in a completely new era when we're learning to find God not in a place, but rather in ourselves, in each other, in nature. . . . When I look at Mount Kenya—it is so magnificent, it is so overpowering, it is so important in sustaining life in my area—that sometimes I say yes, God is on this mountain."[13]

Continuity: Living without Borders

Steve uses the term "liminality" to express the reality of partnership with those to whom we minister. He speaks of "the threshold experience of crossing frontiers, living in a constant suspended state of betwixt and between" that "relativizes one's presumed superiority" and "unmasks our pretensions to shape them in our own image and likeness." I would like to introduce the concept of "borderlands" as another way to express this new reality. According to Gloria Anzaldúa, "Borderlands are physically present wherever two or more cultures edge each other, where people of different races occupy the same territory, where under, lower, middle, and upper classes touch, where the space between two individuals shrinks with intimacy." She goes on to say: "To survive the Borderlands you must live *sin fronteras* (without frontiers), be a crossroads."[14]

I believe that this ideal of living without frontiers, to continually be a crossroad, is the essence of our mission vocation. In a recent study of Sister Ita Ford, one of the four church women brutally murdered in El Salvador in 1980, historian Marian Mollin asserts: "While she entered the country as a U.S. foreign missioner—an outsider—El Salvadorans have clearly integrated her into how they memorialize their recent national history, where they portray her both as one of the multitude of victims from this period of widespread violence and bloodshed, and as a special and respected martyr."[15] Mollin continues to explore the difficulty of overcoming the barriers that divide those who come from outside with certain privileges and power from the local community among whom they live and whom they come to serve.[16]

Toward the end of her life Ita reflected that "being foreigners can be a two-edged sword," with advantages and disadvantages that need to be carefully weighed. Mollin concludes that it was the act of suffering that forged the closest and most genuine bond between Ita and the people she chose to serve, making her at last a part of their world.[17]

Change: Religious Life as a
Prophetic Life Form in the Church

This powerful statement leads me to my final point—our identity as women religious in this challenging time in the Catholic Church. For this closing remark, I can do no better than to quote theologian Sandra Schneiders in her latest book, which was written in response to the Apostolic Visitation of Religious Women in the United States.[18] In this groundbreaking work, Schneiders reflects on the changing nature of religious life, pointing out that until 1900 the only accepted form of religious life in the institutional church was monastic or cloistered. Although Leo XIII recognized "Congregations devoted to works of the apostolate" as another authentic form in the apostolic constitution *Conditae a Christo*, it wasn't until the Second Vatican Council that this became a reality.[19]

Schneiders describes religious life today as a "prophetic life form in the Church" and calls religious "the greatest source of hope for the contemporary Church."[20] She helps us to recognize that our life will continue to undergo change as it adapts to the needs of each age. We will never again be a large labor force maintaining Catholic institutions. Rather we will be like the lamp put on a stand that sheds its light into the darkest corners of society, like the salt that adds flavor to the ordinary actions of daily life, like the widow's mite that is small but significant because it is a total giving of self. We will be that reflection of God's love that I mentioned at the beginning as defining our missionary charism.

I end with an invitation to each of us gathered for this centennial symposium, an invitation full of trust in God and hope in the future that is as yet unknown. The invitation came from our founder, Mary Josephine (Mollie) Rogers, to seventeen-year-old Margaret Shea, the youngest of the pioneer women who would become the first Maryknoll Sisters. As Margaret (later Sister Gemma) debated what she should do with her life, Mollie smiled and simply said: "Let's just go together and see what God has in store for us."[21]

Notes

1. Steve Judd, "The Maryknoll Journey: Coming Home by a Different Route," address at the Society's Centennial Symposium, October 6, 2011, Chicago Theological Union.

2. Constitutions, no. I.7, Mother Mary Joseph, 1932.

3. Jeanne Marie Lyons, *Maryknoll's First Lady* (New York: Dodd, Mead, 1964), 64.

4. Mary Louise Wholean, *Teresian Diary*, January 1, 1912, box 69, folder 4, Maryknoll Mission Archives, quoted in "Mollie's Legacy of Love, First Three Women Volunteers," no. 4, Reflections compiled by Maryknoll Contemplative Community and the Sisters Centennial Retreats–Reflection Committee, April 2011, 3.

5. Constitutions, I. Nature and Purpose, no. 4, 3.

6. "Maryknoll Sisters, Celebrating a Century," Centennial Brochure.

7. Theresa Baldini, homily on the reception of Sisters Ann Mutina and Immaculata Tegete, Maryknoll, New York, August 7, 2011.

8. Interview by the author with Joseph Callistus, Juba, South Sudan, August 12, 2011.

9. Interviews with Sistes Ann Teresa Kamachi, Maryknoll, New York, August 24, 2011, and Sister Stephanie Nakagawa, Maryknoll, New York, August 25, 2011.

10. Newsletter, "African Council of Religious Leaders," Religions for Peace, 4 (May 2011): 3. (The *Gurti*, House of Elders, in Somalia is reaching out to cooperative members of Al-Shabaab for their engagement.

11. Archbishop Oscar Arnulfo Romero, quoted in Judith Noone, *The Same Fate as the Poor* (Maryknoll, N.Y.: Orbis Books, 1999).

12. Krista Tippett, "On Being" Newsletter, September 29, 2011.

13. Ibid., 3; interview with Wangari Maathai, 2006.

14. Gloria Anzaldúa, *Borderlands/La Frontera: The New Mestiza* (San Francisco: Aunt Lute Books 1987).

15. Marian Mollin, "With the People, but Not of the People: Gender and Cross-Cultural Contact in the Life and Work of Sister Ita Ford," paper written for the Berkshire Conference on the History of Women, June 2011, 1.

16. Ibid., 1–2.

17. Ibid., 11–12.

18. Sandra M. Schneiders, *Prophets in Their Own Country: Women Religious Bearing Witness to the Gospel in a Troubled Church* (Maryknoll, N.Y.: Orbis Books, 2011).

19. Ibid., 54–55.

20. Ibid., 78.

21. Sister Jeanne Marie Lyons, *Maryknoll's First Lady*, 81.

3

Response to Stephen Judd: Maryknoll Brothers in Mission

Wayne J. Fitzpatrick, MM

There are many common threads throughout Steve Judd's paper that shape the personality of the Maryknoll missioner and those attracted to the Maryknoll mission movement. The defining moments he referred to are unique to the Maryknoll mission experience—the accompaniment of those in need, a common shared experience of displacement of those served by Maryknollers, and displacement of the missioner due to the social and political climate of the missions served over the past hundred years. These examples are powerful and also hopeful for the ongoing journey in mission for Maryknoll.

From these defining moments the Maryknoll spirit began to develop and take shape in the lives of the missioners. I am reminded over and over again that the articulation and experience of the Maryknoll spirit and movement must be rooted in the storytelling of the journey—a passing on of the dream and legacy of these early visionaries that began with James Anthony Walsh, Thomas Frederick Price, Mary Josephine Rogers, and Thomas McCann. The early intimate relationship among these four creative and adventurous individuals, people of deep faith and trust, yielded generations of missioners and friends of Maryknoll with that same energy, spirit, and deep desire to keep the movement developing with the signs of the times. They never expected that this mission movement would be defined once and for all; they somehow knew that it would be shaped, defined, and changed with each new missioner and each generation of Maryknollers as well as by the many people who claim a part of Maryknoll's spirit and vision.

I have intentionally included Thomas McCann as one of the early significant characters and pioneers in the birth of this missionary endeavor called Maryknoll. It can be said that he challenged the founders to think outside the box and welcome him into the mission movement as a layperson.

Thomas McCann, from Brooklyn, New York, arrived in Hawthorne on May 9, 1912, to speak with James Anthony Walsh about joining the new missionary endeavor called Maryknoll. He had been encouraged to do so by Monsignor Joseph Freri, national director of the Society for the Propagation of the Faith, where Thomas McCann was working as a young man. Thomas entered Maryknoll on June 1, 1912, as one of the early pioneers and a key player in creating the story of dreams and hopes for the Maryknoll movement. As Thomas McCann pushed the envelope of the early dreamers, their positive response affirmed his desire to share and help shape the early Maryknoll years as a *lay man*—later to be called Brother Thomas. It is important to note that very few societies of apostolic life partnered with the charism of Brothers in their mission efforts.

That initial response and fire within of Thomas McCann has carried the missionary Brotherhood forward to this day. At the time of Thomas McCann's death, James Anthony Walsh wrote:

> Brother Thomas made important contributions to the Society by his hospitality and work in the promotional field. . . . The fact that he never was assigned overseas never dampered his enthusiasm for this new Missionary Society. . . . His devotion to Maryknoll and the missions was enthusiastic. He helped much in making Maryknoll known and loved.

I want to touch briefly on the contemplative dimension of Maryknoll, an important common thread in Fr. Steve Judd's presentation. Steve indicated that "foundational and fundamental to the religious, social, and cultural imaginaries of these three 'organizers' was a firm belief that mission from the United States needed to be grounded in the Church's contemplative tradition as well as in the robust American spirit if it was to succeed." Indeed, the contemplative dimension has always been at the core of the Christian vocation and in a special way the missionary vocation.

In 1932 Mother Mary Joseph gave several conferences to the pioneer group of the cloistered Maryknoll Sisters. She noted:

> This house [cloister] was established in order to strengthen our missioners through the prayers and sacrifices of those who would be here and we expect much from each and every Sister in her life of

prayer and in her life of sacrifice. If any of you thought that this was founded to help you with your cloistered life you certainly have the wrong idea. It was created for the benefit of Maryknoll—your Sisters and your Priests and Brothers—and naturally you pray for all mission endeavor and for those who ask for your prayers, but it was not made for you as individuals. That you were chosen meant that you asked to come and that you seem to have the characteristics necessary to live this life.

In 1984 the Maryknoll Society (in that same spirit of Mother Mary Joseph) reflected on the contemplative dimension as the delegates of the 1984 Chapter discussed a chapter motion that called on Society members to strengthen the contemplative dimension of the mission vocation:

> We recognize the contemplative dimension to have been among our Founder's charisms, and many Maryknollers have demonstrated its presence in their lives as contemplatives in action. . . . We wish to eliminate any lingering dichotomy between CONTEMPLATION and the ACTIVE LIFE. We wish to develop the contemplative dimension because the poor and the cultures with whom we carry on this dialogue are often more advanced in this than we are.

Flowing from the contemplative dimension is our story—our story of the dream and journey. Storytelling is essential for the life of the Maryknoll mission movement. Steve reflected on this important dimension of the missioner's life, noting that "missioners of the future will not be so much . . . [the] trouble shooters. . . . Rather missioners can serve as story brokers, tellers of tall tales, whose stock in trade is to continue to share the stories and dreams of those we have been privileged to see and hear and to dwell among."

The older we become, the more reflective and contemplative we seem to become. We must be challenged to continue to tell the story of the early organizers and the many men and women who taught me as a missionary Brother. The spirituality of the missioner is a spirituality of storytelling. Our task is to synthesize a lifelong experience of the missionary vocation and movement (that we affectionately call Maryknoll) given to us and share the story with future missioners and all people who come under the umbrella of the Maryknoll movement. This was the ongoing dream of Mary Josephine Rogers, James Anthony

Walsh, Thomas Frederick Price, Thomas McCann, Bishop James E. Walsh, Sister Gemma Shea, Brother Aloysius, and the march of hundreds of Maryknoll women and men over the generations and through their journey through the changing face of our world and Church. The ongoing dream of the mission journey continues in the men and women in formation, the Lay Missioners, the Maryknoll Affiliates, and all the benefactors and sponsors of Maryknoll.

The journey in mission continues. Journeys are usually visualized as movement, change, adventure, curiosity, and hope. Similarly, the mission journey is not passive but rather alive and active in the stories and contemplative experiences of the women and men who claim a piece of Maryknoll today and take that fire within into the future. Our future—the mission movement called Maryknoll—claimed by so many will be characterized not always about *what we do* but rather *who we are* as Maryknoll.

4

Response to Stephen Judd:
Maryknoll Lay Missioners in Mission

Merwyn De Mello, MMAF

St. Paul, in his first Letter to the Corinthians, writes that Christ is like a single body, which has many parts; it is still one body, even though it is made up of different parts (1 Cor. 12:12). The gifts of the Spirit are given to us in order to be exercised in harmonious collaboration for the good of the whole Church. Centennials as milestones are as much a time for celebration as a time for reflective pause.

In his presentation, Fr. Steve Judd spoke about the need "to tell the people that we, Maryknoll, are all in this together, sharing collective responsibilities for the fate of the planet and humankind across all borders and barriers." Indeed, Maryknoll is made up of people from many lands and will continue to reflect new faces and more and more diversity with all of the wonderful colors of the human spectrum.

The Challenge of Diversity and
Changing the Dominant Culture Dynamic

I am awed and deeply thankful to be part of the history of the entities around me—a hundred years of the Maryknoll Fathers and Brothers, nearly a hundred years of the Maryknoll Sisters, and thirty-six years of Maryknoll's Lay Missioners. Using a cosmic lens we can say that the universe has been in existence for millennia, so a sense of youthful newness then transcends our respective eras in mission service.

At this very moment at Bethany, our Maryknoll Lay Missioners center in New York, our annual Orientation Program is under way. Thirteen laypersons, one African American, two Filipino Americans, one Indian American, and nine Euro Americans are each bringing their unique professional and life experience as they prepare for overseas mission service. This group is joined by four Maryknoll Sisters, all of Asian origin, and in June this year, we celebrated the ordination of Maryknoll priest Fr. Rodrigo Ulloa-Chavarry, now serving in Nepal.

This is indeed a reflection of the wonderful color of the human spectrum that is the Maryknoll mosaic!

According to the statistics of the United States Conference of Catholic Bishops for 2005, since 1960 Latinos have contributed to 71 percent of the growth of the U.S. Catholic Church. Add to this the numbers of Native American, African American, Asian, Pacific, and African Catholics, and we are struck by the changing face of the U.S. Catholic Church. With our common vision for service in mission I like to identify us collectively as the Maryknoll Mission Movement, a movement that strives to be representative of this changing face of the U.S. Church and able thereby to serve more effectively as a bridge-builder both within and outside the United States. How much more effective is mission *ad gentes* when Maryknoll Lay Missioners, Sisters, Fathers, and Brothers are sent into mission from our own abundance of diversity? Will this not then call for a paradigm shift, a change in power dynamics? The future will usher in a reality that is no longer predominantly white American Marlboro-style men and women missioners. Instead there will be a diversity drawn from among those cultures and ethnicities where Maryknoll has served through its centennial decades.

Some questions to consider include how this diversity will change the face of Maryknoll and how we do mission, and what will it require of our own structures, our internal power dynamics.

The Emergence of a New World Order

In his presentation addressing challenges today to mission *ad gentes*, Robert Schreiter calls upon mission *ad gentes* to address the fragmentation of the world, one of the many concomitant evils of globalization. We continue to reap the devastating consequences of that fragmentation in a world order today dominated by a military-industrial complex that empowers corporate interests and the elite. This world order thrives at the expense of human development and dignity and, ultimately, all of God's wonderful creation.

This fragmented *gentes* cries out for change, and the "dominant culture" indeed must change. Let us look around us at Occupy Wall Street, the burgeoning social movement in our midst today. Even in the Middle East an Arab Spring has blossomed, signaling hope for change. With my peacebuilder lens I can see the spiritual power within these movements.

Where does mission *ad gentes* locate itself within that cry for change? A theological response to mission *ad gentes* calls for the development of trust and the promotion of hubs of peace with the capacity to transform conflict emerging from within social and religious realms.

As a transnational organization driven by the spiritual values of dialogue and reconciliation, the Maryknoll Mission Movement offers a value system to counter the objectivism promoted by the followers of the Ayn Rand school of thought, which maintains that the moral purpose of one's life is the pursuit of one's own happiness or rational self-interest. Further the only social system consistent with this morality is the full respect for individual rights embodied in laissez-faire capitalism. However, in order to challenge the dominant order any mission movement needs to firstly be reconciled within itself, so that when it represents itself as an agent of justice and truth-telling it does so with bona fide credentials.

The mission statement of the Maryknoll Lay Missioners calls for "the creation of a more just and compassionate world." From our location with the excluded and disenfranchised, can the Maryknoll Mission Movement articulate our shared vision for this new world order, acting as a mirror for how the U.S. Church moves ahead in mission? This requires an ability to read the signs of the times. We must refract the light of our experience through our timeless lens of Jesus' teachings and example in order to discern, dialogue about, and experiment with "ways forward."

Maryknoll missioners are poised to be on the cutting edge—in cosmic terms, where the expansion of the universe is a dynamic process into an uncharted future—of meeting this challenge of mission today.

Questions to which we must respond include: (1) Can the Maryknoll Mission Movement serve as a midwife ushering in the new world order? (2) Where do we start, from within ourselves or from the outside? (3) Can the Maryknoll Mission Movement seize the opportunity of its centennial and as in the past claim another pivotal moment in its history, an opportunity to give witness to global solidarity? (4) How do we give voice and space to our own Jeremiah prophets?

Collaborative Partnerships

In his recently published book *A New Vision for the Catholic Church: A View from Ireland* (Dublin: Columba Press, 2011), Gerry O'Hanlon asserts that the "current basic model of Church" cannot and should not survive, and he views the present crisis in the Church as "an opportunity to imagine something different, new, more faithful to Vatican II and to the New Testament." I believe O'Hanlon offers insights from which we can draw at this auspicious threshold in Maryknoll's history. While "survive" is a strong and somewhat fatalistic term, perhaps an appropriate choice for what is required might be "metamorphosis" or "transformation."

In proposing a visionary way out for the Irish Church mired in scandal, O'Hanlon recommends that Ireland request a third Vatican Council to broach issues such as reformation of the Roman curia. He suggests that issues such as "canon 129 [the role of laity in decision making], ecclesial teaching on sex and gender could be raised." How visionary and groundbreaking would it be if the Maryknoll Mission Movement planned a council or consultation with the creative liberty to initiate processes that would redefine mission *ad gentes* as a collaborative partnership?

During my service as a Lay Missioner in Zimbabwe, Maryknoll Lay Missioners and Maryknoll Sisters served effectively under a collaborative structure called the Zimbabwe Maryknoll Mission Presence, a model in which members had equal voice in decision making. In that challenging environment, the solidarity fostered by such a collaborative model served well our social and mission service.

What would be the framework for establishing a council that would redefine mission *ad gentes* as a collaborative partnership for the Maryknoll Mission Movement? What would be a model of governance that would value equality and solidarity?

Sharing of Resources

As we enter into our respective new mission eras, narratives of abundance and of scarcity are a defining problem confronting the Maryknoll Mission Movement. Our respective entities are where they are today as a result of the commitment, hard work, and vision of our venerable ancestors and visionaries: Mollie Rogers, James A. Walsh, Thomas F. Price, and John Considine. These visionaries were aided abundantly by the inexplicable love of a God who loved the world into generous being.

An article by Walter Brueggemann, "The Liturgy of Abundance: The Myth of Scarcity" (*Christian Century*, March 24–31, 1999), sheds light on our current narratives. Brueggemann uses the story of the feeding of the multitudes as recorded in the Gospel of Mark to advocate a new economy. In taking, blessing, breaking, and giving the bread Jesus conducts a Eucharist of plenty, demonstrating that the world is filled with abundance. This reframes the economy from one of scarcity to one of abundance. When resources are broken and shared, there is enough for all. Brueggemann notes: "Jesus is engaged in the sacramental, subversive reordering of public reality."

During our many years in mission we have shared from our abundance and have been blessed a thousand times over. Yet times have changed, and as I walk our holy Maryknoll grounds, a dialogue I often enter into is about scarcity within and the need to conserve lest "the cup runneth dry." This feeling comes out of a legitimate notion of fear in uncertain economic times. Do we govern our internal resources upon the dictate of a market ideology where the future is secured by collateral? In the miracles of the loaves and fish, Jesus transformed the economy of scarcity into the mystical generosity of abundance through sharing. Separately our institutions may feel stretched, but together we are blessed with our Creator's generosity.

In preparing for our Lay Mission Orientation Program I have tapped into the generous abundance of Maryknoll resources and have experienced the fruits of collaboration that benefit the seventeen men and women in orientation. It is our openness to God's spirit that will empower us to take the risks needed to benefit the growth of the Maryknoll Mission Movement. Let our faith sustain us, and let us believe that the Creator will empower us to share generously so that the fruits of the Maryknoll Mission Movement abound. Will it be possible for us to take the risks involved with shared resources? Can we join our practices, procedures, and structures in order to allow for that generosity to flow as a blessing to us all?

Reconciliation, Justice, and Peace:
The Role of Women and Laity in the Church

I cite a passage from James E. Walsh's opening talk at the Maryknoll Sisters Congregation's Third General Chapter in 1936:

> Your vocation . . . consists in being missioners the same as the priests [and brothers]. You do anything and everything connected with mission work, and you should consider yourselves apostles. You are a missionary congregation, and the emphasis with you would be in evangelical work, the same as in our own case. You are not merely a group of auxiliaries . . . doing what you are told. You brought something new—the Woman Apostolate.

Fr. Judd has cited examples of this "woman apostolate": the ministry of Lay Missioners Susan Nagele, Liz Mach, and the martyred Maryknoll Sisters of El Salvador, Carla Piette, Maura Clarke, and Ita Ford. These agents of peace, justice, and reconciliation endured unconditional self-sacrifice in faithfulness to the Gospel mandate. Walsh's affirmation of the equally important vocation of the Maryknoll Sisters could be read in the consideration of our context today. Our vocation as laity, although different, is equally important for mission today and will be crucial in the years to come. In order for the Church to secure its credibility as a family of God, it needs to experience the domestic practice of reconciliation, justice, and peace in the mission of laity and the role of women. The relevant process will be determined by the context, be it the mission of the laity, the role of women, or the meaning of the Gospel, as we promote diversity and equality within our own structures.

In an essay addressing the theme of the Second African Synod held in Kenya in March 2010, Teresa Okure, a professor of New Testament and gender hermeneutics at the Catholic Institute of West Africa in Nigeria, writes that the primary place for practicing reconciliation, justice, and peace is within the Church. As a peace-building practitioner I recognize that reconciliation, justice, and peace are often illusive and elusive and can be achieved and sustained only at both the macro and the micro levels. Can we be bona fide agents of justice and peace if we are not first reconciled within and among ourselves?

Some questions I would ask include (1) Does Maryknoll recognize its agency role within the larger theme of justice, peace, and reconciliation? (2) What is demanded of the Maryknoll Mission Movement in order to bring about peace, justice, and reconciliation within our own ranks and structures? (3) How is this issue of reconciliation from within addressed, especially in relation to structures, using its God-given resources? (4) How do we provide continuity with our early visionaries in proclaiming that women are not merely a group of auxiliaries in our Church?

Conclusion

The Maryknoll Society of Fathers and Brothers, and indeed the Maryknoll Mission Movement, has traveled long and far over the last decades. It is ready for the next hundred years, filled with a maturity of spirit and a willingness to learn from experience. Drawing upon our collective wisdom and experience, we need to take hold of our destiny and be willing to take on risks in order to bring forth the reign of God. Let us take courage! "Get on our feet! And march forward in the Light of God!"

5

The Future of Mission *ad Gentes* in a Global Context

Robert J. Schreiter, CPPS

It is indeed an honor and privilege to be part of this theological symposium that celebrates the hundredth anniversary of the founding of the Catholic Foreign Mission Society of America, known to the world as Maryknoll. Over the past thirty years or so, I have had the opportunity to work with Maryknollers in a variety of ways and so have come to appreciate the many ways in which they have served the Church in their missionary endeavors. This symposium is dedicated both to examining that work from a theological point of view as well as to looking ahead so as to discern in some small measure possible future directions in their mission. More specifically, I have been asked in this presentation to look at the central feature of Maryknoll's charism, of serving the Gospel and the Church as an *ad gentes* missionary society, that is, going out "to the nations" in the service of God's mission.

This particular kind of service has been subjected to a great deal of scrutiny over the past twenty years, as vocations to such missionary societies have dwindled in their home countries, and as the world itself is being reshaped.[1] The Second Vatican Council's call for the entire Church to be missionary has somewhat blurred the vision of *ad gentes* mission as a specific and even unique vocation. This occasion of celebrating the United States' foreign missionary society thus offers the opportunity to look again at this kind of mission, specifically within the context of this country as a mission-sending site for bringing the Gospel to other parts of the world.

I have been asked to take a critical look, first of all, at the past of mission *ad gentes* and try to assess its strengths and weaknesses, its successes and failures. Then, secondly, I have been asked to direct our gaze toward the future of this form of mission and imagine the forms it might be taking, given the shifting contexts and the resources that might be brought to bear upon it.

To look at the past and try to gaze into the future requires more than recounting the events that mark a history and attempting to predict what might be occurring in the time immediately ahead. One must give all of these discrete facts and accounts some kind of frame, both to create a more coherent story, as well as to alert listeners to the suppositions that support that story. That is where I will begin, by trying to create a bigger picture in which mission *ad gentes* has been taking place. This bigger picture extends not only into the past, but stretches into the immediate future. It is easier to look back a hundred years than it is to peer into a story yet to occur.

This presentation, then, is in three parts. The first part provides a framework for the story of Maryknoll and suggestions about where a missionary society *ad gentes* might go in the decades ahead. That frame will be the larger history of mission in the Church. The second part will be a closer reading of *ad gentes* mission as it developed in the past two hundred years, trying to chart its successes and failures. A shorter and final third part will hazard some guesses about the future of such a form of mission in the first part of this twenty-first century. All of this is intended to celebrate Maryknoll's achievement as well as to cast a critical eye toward those factors that are likely to have a role in shaping it in the years ahead.

Mission *ad Gentes* in the Larger History of Mission in the Church

In this first section I would like to trace in broad strokes the larger history of mission in the Church and try to situate within it the specific form of mission *ad gentes* that arose at the end of the eighteenth century. By doing so, I hope to give some perspective not only upon the immediate past, but also upon our current situation in mission today.

Although today when we think of mission "to the nations" we immediately think of Christ's charge to the apostles at the end of Matthew's Gospel—"Go out and make disciples of all nations, baptizing them in the name of the Father and of the Son and of the Holy Spirit" (Matt. 28:19-20). Any student of missionary history knows that the Church's engagement in the mission *ad gentes* has been an uneven one, with long periods when there was little or no concerted and organized missionary activity. To be sure, there were always individuals who distinguished themselves by their missionary zeal; there were others, too, specifically commissioned by ecclesiastical authorities to undertake mission. But the kind of missionary effort that the Church engaged in during the nineteenth and twentieth centuries was something quite special.

We need to remind ourselves, too, that efforts at evangelization did not occur in a vacuum. We can trace the missionary activity of Paul and others in the first century along the roadways built throughout the Roman Empire. Later it would be trade routes that would serve as the arteries of mission, as Syrian traders made their way to China and to the Malabar coast of India. Mission has almost always had a discernible material infrastructure that should not be overlooked as we try to understand just how the Word of God made its way to distant peoples. This infrastructure is of course not unique to Christianity; it is much in evidence with the spread of Islam, especially east and north of Arabia, and of Buddhism along the Silk Road. Christianity, Buddhism, and Islam were brought into territories by invading armies as well.

Mission cannot be reduced to its material infrastructure, of course, but that infrastructure cannot be overlooked. Another factor to take into consideration was the biblical motivations for mission. We often presume today that the clarion call to mission issued by Christ at the end of Matthew's Gospel has always served as the summons to mission. As mission historians have pointed out, however, through much of the Church's history the biblical injunction to mission was not Matthew 28:19–20, but Luke 14:23. This is a passage within the parable of the great wedding feast, where the master bids his servants to make those who have been invited come in to the feast. In other words, evangelization was not about going out to the distant nations, but making people come in to the Church.[2] For the Latin Church, Europe and the Church were largely seen as one. Well into the fifteenth century, the name for the continent we call "Europe" was simply "Christianitas." Matthew 28:19–20 begins to take pride of place only in the late sixteenth century. Indeed, the efforts at conversion come to be called "mission" only in the fifteenth century. Up to that time *missio* had referred to the "sending" (for that is what the word means in Latin) of the Son and the Holy Spirit by the Father into the world. It was first among the Portuguese adventurers that the groups sent out by the king were first called "missions"—a term applied to military, trade, and religious groups alike.[3]

So it is on the last half millennium—from roughly 1450 to the present—that I wish to focus on here. For it is during this period that the Catholic Church began to make more coordinated and concerted efforts at "going out to the nations"—mission *ad gentes* as we have come to know it today. For Protestants, the story begins later, at the end of the eighteenth century, for all practical purposes. (Luther, for example, did not see much point in going out beyond Europe; his focus was upon the reform of the Church within Europe.) Apart from forays into the northwest corner of the North American continent, the Orthodox Churches do not come to engage in mission as "going out" until the twentieth century.

So what was it about the past five hundred years that prompted the rise of mission *ad gentes*? I would like to proffer here a factor in the environment of mission that helped make it possible—a feature that continues down to the present time. That factor is globalization.

Globalization as a Factor in ad Gentes Mission

When we hear the word "globalization," we most likely think immediately of the last twenty years in which communications technology has revolutionized our sense of time and space, and the spread of neo-liberal capitalism as the sole economic form shaping our world today. That is of course true. But as students of globalization have looked at how globalization develops, they have come to posit that there have been earlier gambits of globalization as well. In the broadest conception of globalization, any qualitative leap in the possibility of commercial trade or other forms of exchange that opens up a social group to the wider world can be called a step toward globalization. On such a reading, globalization might be said to have begun in the Bronze Age in the Middle East and in China. More common, however, has been a focus on the West, and the developments since the fifteenth century when the development of more seaworthy sailing vessels and the invention of instruments for determining positions at sea made long-distance sea travel possible. To be sure, such an approach ignores parallel developments in sea travel in the Arabian Peninsula and in China, which occurred earlier than it did in the Mediterranean world. But it is more useful here, in telling the story of Christian mission in the Latin Church, to concentrate on the West.

With this admittedly Western-centered view, globalization can be said to have occurred in three waves. The first wave was marked by the Portuguese and Spanish explorations of the rest of the world, followed in due course by the British, the Dutch, the French, and then others. This depended upon developments in technology for seafaring travel and was at its peak from the late fifteenth into the late seventeenth century. It is during this time that the great mission outward from Europe took place, with heroic figures such as St. Francis Xavier becoming the iconic missionary. Mission *ad gentes* accompanied the traders, and the agents of mission were the mendicant orders and new societies such as the Jesuits. In 1622 Pope Urban VIII established the Congregation for the Propagation of the Faith in Rome to coordinate international missionary activity. In 1663 the Missions Étrangères de Paris was founded, a group of diocesan priests who become the first missionary society devoted exclusively to the apostolate of foreign missions.

Much has been written about the interconnections between Christian mission in this period and the political and economic agendas of the kingdoms that made the journey to distant lands. My purpose here is not to retell the story so as to repudiate or justify those connections. All I want to say is that this first round of globalization made both empire and world mission as we have come to know it possible. It made travel to places distant from Europe possible. But it also placed potential limits on mission when those travel routes waned. Rather than filling out the details of that story, at this point I would like to turn to the second wave of globalization, which begins at the turn of the nineteenth century and continued up to the outbreak of the First World War in 1914. The Canadian philosopher Charles Taylor has described this period (he extends it up to the year 1960) as "the Age of Mobilization."[4] It is during this time that we see the rise of the missionary societies *ad gentes*, of which Maryknoll is a prominent example.

Missionary Societies ad Gentes in the Age of Mobilization

The nineteenth century[5] saw dramatic changes that altered the face of Europe in ways more radical than any we have seen since. The effects of the French Revolution created political instability and change in the governments of Europe, which ended in the collapse of three great imperial powers—Germany, Austria, and Russia—in the First World War. The nationalist fervor that accompanied the rise of liberal democracies in this period set off the "Age of Mobilization," wherein movements emerged in societies to organize together populations to promote certain interests and causes. It is in this time that political parties start to take shape, as well as trade unions, and even—paradoxically—anarchist movements (the equivalent of post-9/11 terrorist organizations). The formation of new social groups and movements dedicated to specific purposes is a distinguishing characteristic of this time.

The Catholic Church experienced these political and social upheavals as a threat to its long-standing position in European societies. If the sixteenth-century Reformers had challenged the Church on ecclesiastical grounds, the French Revolution and the political liberals now challenged its political standing. In the currents of the age, the Church found itself mobilizing on many fronts as well, responding to political, economic, and social change. Hosts of new religious orders of men and women were founded to address social issues on local and immediate levels as well as issues with broader horizons. Associations for groups in the working class were developed to combat similar socialist organizations. In 1822, the Society for the Propagation of the Faith was founded in France to mobilize laity in support of foreign mission.

Alongside this political, economic, and social upheaval came a new wave of globalization, marked by advances in technologies of travel and communication. The invention of the steam engine at the dawn of the nineteenth century would revolutionize both sea and land travel. The Atlantic could now be crossed in a week instead of a month. The reduced cost of such travel made mass emigration from Europe's poverty possible. The development of the telegraph in midcentury and the telephone three decades later compressed space dramatically for the first time, as communication that had taken months before could now be achieved in seconds.

Protestant missionary societies begin to emerge in Britain at the end of the eighteenth century to follow the routes of British commerce around the world, especially to India and later to Africa.

In the crucible of change on the European continent, one finds the formation of new Catholic religious orders riding the wave, as it were, of this second round of globalization, to create societies devoted exclusively to overseas mission.[6] What is interesting about these new developments is precisely the mobilization of young missionaries— both men and women—to go overseas for the sake of spreading the Gospel.[7] Such travel was now possible because of the improvement of sea travel. It was often portrayed as heroic, echoing the reports of trav- elers to these distant and "unexplored" (at least by Europeans) lands. And this mobilization took place most often within a national—and sometimes nationalist—context. These new missionary societies were stamped with a distinctive national character, even as some of these regions of Europe were emerging as nations for the first time—French, German, Belgian, Dutch—and later Irish and Italian societies. Part of the national(ist) agenda of these nations in Europe coincided with the rise of these national mission societies. But perhaps more importantly, cultural characteristics of the regions from which these national societ- ies hailed would come to shape how they carried out mission.[8]

Maryknoll emerges in the first decade of the twentieth century as such a national society—first of priests and Brothers, and then of Sis- ters. Similar to many of those similar societies in Europe, the Catholic Foreign Mission Society of America was the dream of two diocesan priests: Fr. Thomas Price and Fr. James A. Walsh. As has been noted by others,[9] the U.S. Catholic Church had barely emerged from itself being considered by Rome to be a "mission territory" when Frs. Price and Walsh began to realize their dream. Yet in the ensuing decade the attitudes of "mobilization" so common in the rise of the mission soci- eties *ad gentes* in Europe quickly found a home in both the Maryknoll Society of Fathers and Brothers, and the Congregation of Maryknoll Sisters of St. Dominic. Just as one can detect distinctively "German" characteristics in, say, the Society of the Divine Word (also known as the "Steyler Missionare") or Flemish nationalist characteristics in the Missionhurst Missionaries (known in Belgium and elsewhere as the "Scheut" Fathers), so too, as James Keane has pointed out in a recent article, the Maryknoll Society is distinctively American in its self-conception as a mission society and recognizably American in some of its missionary methods. If not perhaps directly in intent, then certainly how *The Field Afar* (later to be renamed *Maryknoll Magazine*) was received reflected an American point of view. Did how these American missionaries conceived of their distant and difficult mission not mirror in some way Frederick Jackson Turner's "frontier thesis"—articulated just fifteen years before the first appearance of *The Field Afar*—of pushing back the western frontier as emblematic of the American spirit? Even today, at least one Maryknoll missioner has described his Society as the "Church's marines"—in the sense of willing to go into difficult places to do what needs to be done on behalf of the Church.[10]

I note these things only to point how much the Maryknoll Society followed the patterns of the national mission societies *ad gentes* that emerged in the second wave of globalization. As was the case in many other mission societies, China especially beckoned as the premier "Field Afar." Pointing out these parallels does not diminish Maryknoll's distinctiveness; rather, it helps situate Maryknoll's story in a larger narrative of a unique social form within Catholicism that took shape within the second wave of globalization and came into crisis and challenge as that same wave ended. For with the collapse of empires in World War I came also a heightening of national boundaries against trade that was evidenced in the international financial crisis of the 1930s, the political crisis that brought Europe back to war in the following decade and led to the geopolitical division of West versus East that was to continue until 1989.

In that time, especially that of decolonialization from the 1940s through the 1970s, the concept of mission that had so flourished during the second wave of globalization also came into crisis. Was missionary work so intertwined with colonialism that the presence of foreign missionaries in the newly emancipated countries could only be read as a colonial remnant of a past that threatened creating a different kind of future? The 1970s became a time of great questioning of mission *ad gentes*, which gradually eased in the early 1980s as new perspectives were found on the presence of foreign missionaries in developing countries.[11] But before continuing that story, it would be worthwhile to take stock of this remarkable period of the nineteenth and twentieth centuries, when the mission societies *ad gentes* made their appearance and left such an indelible mark on mission and mission consciousness in the Catholic Church.

Mission *ad Gentes:* A Balance Sheet

Where has the work of the missionary societies *ad gentes* brought the Church's mission at this point in the twenty-first century? A brief summing up of the plusses and minuses is in order before proceeding further to look at the future. To be sure, not all that has happened (or not happened) in the Church's mission can be attributed to the mission societies *ad gentes.* But both the advances and the setbacks are unthinkable without reference to them.

On the positive side, the dramatic growth of Christianity in Africa has been especially due to the work of missionaries. In 1900, there were but ten million Christians. Today there are over 350 million Christians there, and the number continues to grow. Nowhere have the results of mission activity been so salient as they have been in Africa.

On a broader scale, the widespread awareness of and commitment to mission that is now found throughout the Church is markedly different from what it was at the beginning of the nineteenth century. The Declaration on the Missionary Activity of the Church (*Ad Gentes*) at the Second Vatican Council is witness to this: reflection on the Church was unthinkable at that time without a reflection on the missionary activity of the Church. The Trinitarian theology of the *missio Dei*—of the work of the Trinitarian God in the world—could only have matured in a pervasive understanding of the Church's mission that went far beyond that of "professional" missionaries. That the Church itself was to be resituated within this theology of mission points to the power and pervasiveness of this development.

The universal call to holiness of all baptized Christians at the Council raised the laity from the second- (or third-) class position in the Church to a level of greater equality. This in turn was to provide a site and an outlet for the ministry of the laity in mission. The breadth and pervasive character of the lay missionary movement we see today was made possible by the twin factors of a new status for laity within the Church and an emphasis on the essentially missionary character of the Church. That latter factor came about because of the intensity of the missionary movement a century and a half prior to the Council.

The agents of mission today are not only more distinctively lay. They hail for the most part from countries that themselves were considered mission territory through much of the twentieth century. The largest mission-sending country in the world today (measured as percentage of its members who are engaging in foreign missionary work) is South Korea. Indeed the majority of today's foreign missioners do not come from Europe and North America, but from Asia and Africa.

Within these features of the worldwide Church that have resulted from the missionary movement, Maryknoll takes pride of place for its actualization in the United States. The effective use of the media, especially *Maryknoll Magazine*, created a strong commitment to mission among U.S. Catholics. The work of both Maryknoll men and women is etched on the American Catholic imagination. The emergence of Maryknoll Lay Missioners as the third pillar of U.S. mission has given concrete form to lay engagement in mission over the past three decades. Whatever success mission has achieved in these past two hundred years—and those successes have been considerable—Maryknoll has certainly been central within it.

But are there setbacks to be noted as well? These are of a more variegated lot. They cannot all be called "failures" by any means. They represent, for the most part, the unintended consequences of some of the successes just mentioned. And some are just puzzlements arising from the data.

The first such item to be noted is one of these puzzlements. In 1900, Christians constituted 34 percent of the world's population. In the year 2000, after a century of intense evangelization, Christians constituted a little over 33 percent of the population. Christians ran very hard, as it were, to stand in place. What this means remains a matter of debate. The fastest growing religion today (through both conversions and population growth) is Islam. The House of Islam now has more than a billion members, making it slightly larger than the Roman Catholic Church. The resurgence in religious practice and commitment to religious traditions that has been a feature of the past two decades makes a clearer reading of the state (or the fate?) of Christianity impossible at this time. Does this "steady state" of Christianity say something about Christianity's position and role amid the other great religious traditions that is different from the traditional message that Jesus Christ is the definitive savior of all humankind? This is the most neuralgic theological point that the Church faces today, since it touches upon the very identity and destiny of Christian faith.

Let me add to this one unintended consequence of mission success. By raising mission awareness to such a level that the Church now can see itself as essentially missionary, the role of lifelong foreign missioners has become blurred. It becomes more and more difficult to make a case for the singularity of the role of mission societies *ad gentes*. As we shall see in a moment, changes in the world itself have only added to that difficulty. This gives rise to the impression that, because of their relative success, mission societies *ad gentes* have worked themselves out of a job. The attempts to redefine mission activity, and the role of these mission societies within it, have become a regular preoccupation of the past decade and a half.

A second unintended consequence of the success of mission activity is the fact that the so-called mission territories or mission churches now send out missionaries. Thus the *ad gentes* character of these nineteenth- and twentieth-century mission societies has become more unclear. The descendants of erstwhile converts in the territories clamor to join the very mission societies that came to convert them. In many mission societies, these persons have become the majority of the younger members recruited by these societies. The mission churches established no longer send out their own missionaries. The question for the mission societies then becomes: Who are the "peoples" now to whom they are to be sent? And just what is the nature of their witness intended to be?

Here there has been internal struggle within the mission societies themselves, and between mission societies and the Congregation for the Evangelization of Peoples. Pope John Paul II's encyclical *Redemptoris Missio* in 1991 reasserted proclamation as the premier form of evangelization, in the face of the growing practice of mission as dialogue, inculturation, and social justice. So the big question becomes: Were the mission societies founded specifically for foreign mission—often representing a national effort to do so—a form of mission that has out-lived its usefulness, precisely because it has fulfilled its purpose? Or will mission societies morph into new or extended forms of mission that completely obscure or eliminate their founding idea of mission *ad gentes* itself?

Mission *ad Gentes:* The Road Ahead

This uncomfortable question brings me to the third part of this presentation, the future of mission *ad gentes*. I have already sketched developments in the second half of the twentieth century: the rediscovery of the centrality of mission to the Church's very existence, the enhanced role of the laity in the mission of the Church, and the increasing ambiguity in the role of the mission society *ad gentes* in light of these changes. Now I want to begin with a sketch of how the third wave of globalization is changing the world in which mission takes place. Then I will look at some of the responses that have been coming from mission societies. Finally I will conclude with some thoughts about the decades ahead.

The Third Wave of Globalization

By most accounts, we are at least two decades into a third wave of globalization. Like previous waves of globalization, the current one grew out of advances in technologies for travel and communication. The developments in air travel in the last third of the twentieth century have made long-distance travel more accessible to large numbers of people. This is evidenced in the migration of people that is part and parcel of today's world, where one out of every thirty-five persons on the planet is in migration. In terms of communication technologies, the personal computer, the Internet, and the spread of cellular telephony have changed the capacity for communication. As recently as twenty years ago, more than two-thirds of the world's population had never made a telephone call, and the great majority of the world seemed excluded from the new networks of communication. The cell telephone has dramatically changed all that, so that the number of people without access to telephones continues to drop dramatically.

I will not dwell here on the dimensions of this third wave of globalization and both the positive and negative features that it has generated since these are widely discussed and are relatively well known. I want only to draw attention to three consequences of this current round of globalization that have direct consequences for how we understand mission *ad gentes*.

First of all, this wave of globalization has dramatically compressed time and space. With the Internet and the current generation of telephones, one can communicate nearly instantly with many parts of the world. The media bring us events from the other side of the world as they are happening. Long-distance travel by air can be completed in hours or a few days rather than weeks or months (short-term travel on the ground, however, can continue to take a good deal of time). This compression of time raises the question today: Just what does "the field afar" now mean? We may take cognizance of psychological and social distance as significant factors, but physical distance from a mission-sending center to a mission-receiving periphery is not the same as it was. The *gentes* of faraway are now often around us in our cities and even now in rural areas. Can the psychological and social "faraway" constitute a strong enough metaphor to carry the weight of a mission *ad gentes* identity for missioners today?

The compression of time and space has a related effect, known in globalization as "deterritorialization." Elements of culture now float free of their original locations. The nation-state plays less of a role in defining social identities. One sees this in religious life in general today, and in mission societies in particular. The majority of the younger membership of societies established in Europe or North America likely does not come from those two continents, but from where its members have been missioned. German is no longer an official language of the Society of the Divine Word. With one out of every six of its some seven thousand members coming from Indonesia, however, Bahasa Indonesia is. The superior general and General Council of the Society of St. Columban have decamped from Dublin and are now located in Hong Kong. Territory and national culture are thus increasingly not boundary markers for mission—and mission society—identity.

Second, this compression of time and space has changed a quantitative aspect of mission commitment. This is a spillover from the compression of time in the wider society. With the ideal of lifelong employment with a single firm or organization now a thing of the past in neoliberal economies, and with people in the wealthier segments of society living considerably longer than in the past, a commitment to something like lifelong mission *ad gentes* becomes more and more inconceivable. This hesitation to make such a commitment or incapacity even to conceive of such a commitment should not be written off as a failure in virtue or moral capacity. It simply represents a new social situation that material circumstances in our world did not previously permit. Thus, with the shrinking of "faraway" space has come a similar shrinking of "lifelong" commitment. Ways are still being found to create equivalents.

Within the burgeoning area of shorter-term mission commitment, a parallel pattern has emerged among lay mission groups, including Maryknoll's Lay Missioners. Renewable three-year commitments have created a new form of "lifelong" commitments that have continued in many cases of upward of thirty years. The quality of mission work that people in these more defined periods of commitment do, I dare say, can equal those of the erstwhile "lifers" of the past. But once again, while the qualitative and quantitative results are similar, one must also ask what impact this has on the erstwhile *ad gentes* missionary imagination.

A third consequence of current globalization is what has been called "hybridization." The compression of time and space, the coming loose of cultural markers from particular territories, and the movement of peoples create "hybrid" situations, wherein nothing remains in a "pure form." The experience of mixing in a multicultural reality moves us away from clear identities that may have been possible in the past—although sometimes that past is really an "imagined" one.[12] In effect, in many parts of the world this may be found in the quest for "purity" in religious and political forms—not only in the wealthy world, but also in poor parts of the world where people feel they have been betrayed by secular promises of prosperity. As a result all of us become, consciously or unconsciously, more "hybrid" in our culture. We borrow and adapt, we cross boundaries that would have not been crossed in the past—either because they were too "distant" or because they represented something completely unknown. In the nineteenth century and through the first two-thirds of the twentieth century, such hybridity was seen to weaken the pure form. So interracial marriage was called "miscegenation," something that would weaken the "superior" form of race. As I noted above, such thinking is still very much alive.

In the case of mission *ad gentes*, who is this "other" to whom we are now sent? They are no longer physically distant. They are also not so utterly "other" from ourselves. Again, this touches upon the imagination of the mission *ad gentes* as boundaries of otherness are blurred or erased.

Models for a Renewed Mission *ad Gentes*

So where does this leave those mission *ad gentes* societies formed under specific historical circumstances in the nineteenth and early twentieth centuries? They were successful, partly because they were the right forms at the right time—they engaged the historical moment. They were successful because they were able to catch the imagination of the young, who were ready to undertake heroic work and make great sacrifices, even possible death. They were successful because of the faith commitment and the hard and difficult work they required.

Those elements of imagination, faith, and hard work are still essential for mission work today. But the form they find today has been under question by missioners themselves for quite some time. And that questioning is not directed at what was created in the past. It arises out of living in a changed sense of circumstances. They fit the social conditions of the second wave of globalization extraordinarily well. Our search now is to find a fit for the commitment to evangelization under changed circumstances.

By way of concluding this presentation and opening up a little more room for our common exploration, I want to note four models of mission that might carry forward the imagination and commitment of this generation of missioners entrusted with the mission *ad gentes* into the decades ahead. Three of them will be already familiar to most of you. I want to note their possibilities and problems for mission today. The fourth is my own proposal, which, however, will no doubt be recognizable to you as well.

Each of these four models is intended to spark the imagination, as did the model for mission put forth by Fathers Price and Walsh a century ago, and by Mother Mary Joseph around the same time. What might be the mission *ad gentes* of our time, and more importantly, for the decades immediately ahead of us?

Mission ad Extra

One model that has been proposed is mission *ad extra:* mission outward from ourselves. This was always an essential element of the mission *ad gentes*—the "going out" from our familiar place and culture to a new place to bring the Gospel. That going out continues to carry a great deal of value, even in a compressed and often deterritorialized world. Many if not most missioners are able to recount how the struggle to learn new languages and cultures has changed them irrevocably and shaped their spiritualities. Going out is something fundamental to the missionary experience. It is a participation in the going out, the *mission*, of the Son and the Holy Spirit into the world. People who receive this "going out" can make their own experience of faith more "catholic" in the sense of awareness of the larger world of the community of faith.

At the same time, such a definition of mission will have its limits. It will require a purification of the imagination of the missioner from the "out there" as exotic.[13] It must cultivate a self-emptying rather than a colonial understanding of going out. And the "out there" can become harder to sustain in a highly pluralistic world.

Mission ad Altera

Others have suggested a second image of mission as mission *ad altera*, that is, to "others" or "other things."[14] Here the lingering territorial dimensions of the mission imagination in our contemporary situation may be overcome in order to seek out those who are "other," or who are made "other," who should be the goal of a mission *ad gentes* today. Such mission to the other might not require long-distance travel. It might be directed to the other in our midst: the immigrant, the homeless, the one who has never considered the Christian faith. This model of mission can raise some fundamental questions about the mentality and spirituality of mission *ad gentes*. The "frontier hypothesis" so central to the U.S. imagination, for example, disappears.

On the other hand, can "mission" be sustained in an *ad gentes* tradition without some sense of physical distance? To be sure, missioners have gone to distant places and have sought out the most "other" in those places. The question of physical distance continues to tug at this missionary imagination.

Mission in Altum

Pope John Paul II concluded the Jubilee Year of 2000 with *Tertio Millennio Ineunte*, his vision for the Church for the twenty-first century. He proposed an image for the imagination: "*Duc in altum*"—"Set out into the deep." In one way, this kind of mission was embodied in the Maryknoll Sisters' sense of mission as going to a place and working there unobtrusively for a long period of time. What John Paul II seems to have had in mind was the Church taking risks in its missionary commitment to seek out the new possibilities. Earlier, in *Redemptoris Missio* he spoke of the new *aeropagoi*, the new social spaces where evangelization might take place. In many ways, an essential part of who we are as embodied beings cannot now be overlooked. Where are those spaces—of many different dimensions and kinds—where we find the *missio Dei*, the mission of the Triune God—taking place? This calls for great work of imagination.

For a mission society, however, some immediate limits come to mind. Can one form an ongoing mission society around an ever-moving, ever-changing site—be it "in the deep" or in the "new *aeropagoi*"? Can the work of the imagination meet the exigencies of an embodied, social life? The mission societies *ad gentes* of the past—and here Maryknoll stands out in so many retrospective accounts that are appearing on the occasion of its centenary—were sites where a high dose of American individualism could be harnessed to a common mission. Such a vision will be necessary, I believe, in a social context where individualism is at a higher rate than it was a century ago.

Mission ad Vulnera

My fourth and final model of mission might be called mission *ad vulnera*—mission to the wounds. This kind of mission would focus itself on locating the breaches and the wounds in the contemporary world. It is a commonplace that globalization has opened up new breaches between rich and poor. It has created new middle classes even as it erodes them in other parts of the world. Globalization also excludes whole populations or leaves them behind.

The concept of mission to the wounds is hardly an original one. Many religious institutes were established to care for the most vulnerable or those populations that were radically underserved. This was especially the case with the apostolic congregations of women founded in the modern period. This kind of mission does not so much map out new territory as traverse it with a certain kind of imagination. The breaches we experience in the world—in climate change, in armed conflict, in poverty, in injustice of so many different kinds—are wounds that need to be healed. Advocacy for the Earth, reconciliation after conflict, and work for justice are all acts of healing the world, bringing about the reign of God, when God "will be all in all" (1 Cor. 5:28). Considering wounds—the wounds of our world and the wounds of Christ, evident even in his resurrected and glorified body—might provide the stimulus to imagination needed to help reshape mission in the twenty-first century. The missioner is less the hero or the martyr and perhaps more the bridge-builder, the one who can imagine a different kind of world where now division and suffering are found.

Conclusion

This centenary celebration of the Catholic Foreign Mission Society of America, and what it has wrought, is a time of thanksgiving for what it has given to the world and to the United States. It occurs at a time when the world is changing in yet another way and has been challenging the social and theological forms of mission that gave rise to Maryknoll. It now calls for a reexamination of the mission society *ad gentes* that has served God's mission in the world so well over some two centuries. This presentation has tried to look at that bigger picture of mission *ad gentes* and what it has meant for the Church and the world, as well as to suggest a way of extending that vision into the decades ahead.

Some of the conditions that have supported mission *ad gentes* in the past are no longer as evident as they once were. New conditions now impinge upon our work. What is needed is a willingness to examine honestly and faithfully where we now find ourselves and to seek out where God is calling us. It is an act of faith and an act of the imagination. If these come together, our response to God's call to mission will continue to enrich our world, a faithful, imaginative, and at times even prophetic response to the hope that lies within us.

54 *Robert J. Schreiter*

Notes

1. I have addressed this earlier in "Défis actuels à la mission ad gentes," *SEDOS Bulletin* (October 2001): 270-75. Also at http://sedosmission.org/old/eng/schreiter_1.htm.

2. On this, see David Bosch, *Transforming Mission: Paradigm Shifts in Theology of Mission* (Maryknoll, N.Y.: Orbis Books, 1991).

3. Paul Kollman, "At the Origins of Mission and Missiology: A Study of Religious Language," *Journal of the American Academy of Religion* 79 (2011): 425-58.

4. Charles Taylor, *A Secular Age* (Cambridge, Mass.: Harvard University Press, 2007).

5. British historian Eric Hobsbawm characterized the nineteenth century in Europe as the "long century"—from 1789 to 1914.

6. It is interesting to see how "mission" as a concept is being understood at this time. It refers not only (or even exclusively) to overseas mission, but also to the revitalization of local Churches within specific regions. Hence the "Congregation of the Mission" of Vincent De Paul, or my own congregation, the Missionaries of the Precious Blood, dedicated to the renewal of the Church in the Papal States.

7. It should be noted that the nineteenth century also witnessed a growth in population that made more young people available for such enterprises. Catholic families in particular were often very large, allowing parents to give one or more children "to the Church."

8. While this exists in the lore of these societies (especially among members not native to those countries) I am not aware that it has been thoroughly investigated. I have made some proposals regarding this in "El desplazamiento al hemisfero sur: Implicaciones para los institutos misioneros," *Spiritus* (June 2002): 7-15.

9. For a brief history of the early years, see James T. Keane, "Outward Bound: How Maryknoll Defined a Century of Mission Work," *America* (June 20-27, 2011), 10-14.

10. A quotation of Fr. Joseph Healey, MM, in a Catholic News Service release on the Maryknoll centenary (September 29, 2011).

11. Here the 1981 SEDOS Seminar on the Future of Mission played a key role. See the proceedings of that meeting, *Mission and Dialogue*, ed. Joseph Lang, MM, and Mary Motte, FMM (Maryknoll, N.Y.: Orbis Books, 1982).

12. At the same time, in wealthy societies individual and social groups may choose to create enclaves of sameness to protect themselves from this hybridity. One sees this at play in the United States in, for example, where people turn for their sources of news.

13. This would need closer examination. One wonders, for example, if the preoccupation with China among mission *ad gentes* groups in the late nineteenth and early twentieth century was caught up with such exoticism or Orientalism.

14. William Burrows, long-time managing editor of Maryknoll's Orbis Books, was, I believe, the first to suggest this approach.

6

Response to Robert Schreiter

Antoinette (Nonie) Gutzler, MM

I want to thank Fr. Robert Schreiter for his excellent paper, which highlights so well the challenges of the global context in which we engage the missionary task today. I also want to second his words that it is an honor and a privilege to be a part of this theological symposium. It is now my privilege to give a brief response to his paper, which has traced some aspects of the history of mission *ad gentes* in the Church and has presented challenges brought by our globalized world, challenges that will shape the contours of the missionary endeavor well into this century. My response is crafted through the lens of my missionary experience in Maryknoll, the context of my local church in Asia, and writings of the Federation of Asian Bishops' Conferences (FABC).

I would like to frame my response in three key phrases: a "qualitative leap," a "crucible of change," and "agents of mission." I define them as the "turning points" of mission in our globalized world and will discuss the theological and missiological journeys those phrases demand of the missioner. I suggest that what Bob Schreiter has offered to us is a key moment of "faith seeking understanding," a moment that is exciting for some and disturbing for others as it poses some "neuralgic" questions for the Church and the missionary enterprise.

The Qualitative Leap

The first phrase before us is "qualitative leap." Bob noted this in relation to globalization: "Any qualitative leap in the possibility of commercial trade or other forms of exchange that opens up a social group to the wider world can be called a step toward globalization." I suggest that the "exchange" that is opening the Church to a wider world comes from a "new age of religious and spiritual awareness" that impacts mission *ad gentes* today. It is an exchange that recognizes the Spirit's presence outside the bounds of the visible Church, as noted by John Paul II in *Redemptoris Missio*. He wrote: "The Spirit's presence and activity affect not only individuals but also society and history, peoples, cultures, and religions. Indeed, the Spirit is at the origin of the noble ideals and undertakings which benefit humanity on its journey through history" (RM 28).

Indeed, the experience of many missioners testifies to this presence of the Spirit and the realization that God has preceded us to the new lands where we went to preach the Gospel. Now this recognition is nothing new. The early Church Fathers called this reality the "seeds of the Word"—a preparation for the coming of Christ. But today, our theological journey takes us on a more reflective route, which has profound implications for the missionary task. A theological question regarding mission *ad gentes* is: Are these seeds *only* "preparatory" markings? Or are they signs of a genuine religious pluralism that our Church must take seriously? In other words, do they contain a revelation of God to us, a revelation that we Christians need to hear, to ponder, and to receive in order to further our journey into the Holy Mystery of God? The Asian bishops write that these seeds are the "treasury of the religious experiences of our ancestors, from which our contemporaries do not cease to draw light and strength. They have been (and continue to be) the authentic expression of the noblest longings of their hearts, and the home of their contemplation and prayer" (FABC 1, art. 14). As "faith continues to seek understanding" we ask if these words from the local church in Asia find echo in other local Churches throughout the world. And, if so, we ask what challenges and gifts do they bring to the universal Church and what models of mission do they call for.

Fr. Schreiter presented four models of mission, and as I read them I noted the prepositions *ad extra, ad altera, in altum* (in the deep), and *ad vulnera*. I would like to add a fifth model, one that is not "to" but "with whom." It is a model of mission not named as such by the Asian bishops, but it seems to express their missiology. The model is "*missio inter gentes*," mission *among* the nations. I present this as a model called for by our global context. It offers a space of solidarity, companionship, and partnership. And it is both proclamation and dialogue.

The Crucible of Change

I suggest that we are now in what I call a "Canaanite woman" moment of conversion in our understanding of mission. A "qualitative leap" is taking place, and it is happening within a "crucible of change." For just as Jesus was so certain that his mission was only for the Israelites, so we, too, have been certain that mission was *ad gentes* (to the nations, to preach, to teach, to baptize), confident in our certainty that we had the fullness of what must be preached and taught. But now we must engage the neuralgic questions that come to us through the "Canaanite women" of our mission encounters. If we follow Jesus in his preaching of the reign of God, then perhaps in this new moment of mission we hear the call to leave the safe borders that framed our preaching and teaching in the past. In other words, we are called to a moment of *kenosis*.

Now, to employ an insight of Margaret Farley, this *kenosis* finds its birth and strength in what she has named as the "grace of self-doubt."[1] This is not a grace that calls into question God's presence in our lives or that we have the call and responsibility to proclaim and share the Good News. Instead it is a call to examine and "empty" ourselves of a kind of "certainty" that does not allow new questions and insights about mission and our God-experiences to enter our discernment about mission *ad gentes*. We need this grace for we are in a new moment of "faith seeking understanding." It is a moment of humble listening to the stirrings of the Holy Spirit, and it is a call to leave a way of being in mission, to leave behind a way of thinking about God that may have grown comfortable. It is also an abandoning of borders, not only geographical borders but also spiritual borders so we can journey to the "other side," as Jesus did in his encounter with the Canaanite woman. I suggest that this can happen only within a "crucible of change" that is permeated with the "grace of self-doubt." In the words of Aloysius Pieris, this brings us to a "desert" moment of renewal where "our eyes glow with hope in the Future (of mission) which is not as clear as the past we have abandoned."

Some questions before us: Do we wish to and do we have the courage to make this journey? If so, how then do we make this movement from the past of mission into the future? This leads to another key phrase and turning point, the "agents of mission."

The Agents of Mission

Mission *inter gentes* brings before us a rich exploration of the giftedness that the women and men agents of mission bring to *missio Dei*.

There is the giftedness that comes from those who have already been engaged in mission *ad gentes*, most of whom, in the past, have been from the West. Another giftedness is brought by the "agents of mission" who come from a postcolonial and postmodern world.

I would like to say that those who have participated in *ad gentes* missionary activity in the past have done so with much passion, commitment, and openness to the horizon of the mystery of God that they have encountered in the spiritualities, songs, stories, dances, and symbols of various cultures, and that have thus been instrumental in carving a path into a mission *inter gentes* encounter.

This encounter takes place in a postcolonial world, one that is very different from the colonial world in which Maryknoll and other mission institutes began their missionary journeys. This brings unprecedented questions and challenges to our missionary endeavor, questions that could not have been thought of a century ago.

For example, in the awareness that Western culture was brought along with the Gospel, we now ask how that Gospel becomes truly inculturated in its own soil and is not simply a "potted plant" imported from the West? How do we address the reality that many may still regard Jesus and the Gospel as a "foreign" export of the West and therefore neither wanted nor desired? How do we react to the reality that others find organized religion devoid of meaning while they still crave a spirituality to guide their lives?

These challenges alert us to a new moment of grace as many of our new agents of mission are from this postcolonial world. They are and will be the new leadership for mission in this century and beyond. Their perspective and experiences of God as the Holy One from the depth of their cultures bring new insights into those aspects of the Gospel that touch the heart of the *gentes*.

Thus, it is important to reflect on *what kind of agents of mission* we wish to become and how mission is to be carried forth by this next generation of both long-term and short-term missioners. For example, do we "helicopter in" to do a specific task that we have been trained to do, something like the "doctors without borders"? This is an important question because while globalization has given us a new world order and an Internet world that enables an "Arab Spring" and other movements, we are faced with a choice. Do we as missioners access our world only in online virtual communities, or will we commit to face-to-face, person-to-person encounters that grow more deeply over time rather than through Facebook or Twitter?

In the fragmented, disoriented world that is part of our global context, missioners are those who enter the waters of our global reality, the waters of migration, climate change, trafficking, and conflict, among others, and immerse themselves in the languages, cultures, poverty, and religiosity of that context. Then the missioners must be willing to be transformed by those they meet and the situations they encounter.

As we engage our historical moment, all of the above has profound implications for mission *ad/inter gentes*. This centennial is a graced moment for the missionary voice to be heard.

What Maryknoll Has Learned

One question before us at this symposium is what Maryknoll has to say to the universal Church after a hundred years of engaging in the missionary enterprise with imagination, faith, and hard work. I do believe that Maryknoll is bringing the Church to a new moment of "faith seeking understanding," and I suggest the following.

First, the mission experience of Maryknollers affirms the theological significance of religious diversity and the importance of knowing our Scriptures so well that we see the markings of God in the Scriptures of other religious traditions. Therefore it is crucial to be about the work of "creating, sustaining, and transforming [the] disciples [of Jesus] who [then] take up the task of reweaving the tradition for each generation."[2] This indicates the importance of theological institutions, such as the Chicago Theological Union, which give their very best to "create, sustain, and transform" disciples into the "dangerous memory of Jesus Christ" and, in a multicultural setting, create the "condition of possibility" for a true mission *inter gentes*.

The way that "mission" is now woven into the fabric of Christian proclamation in this twenty-first century will look different than it did in the past, just as Paul's proclamation to the Gentiles looked different than what was proclaimed on Jewish soil. Indeed, the Christian proclamation will look even more different in the twenty-second century! This is a "turning point" into the global context that Bob has highlighted. It is the "turning" of Mary of Magdala in the garden with Jesus, not "back" to what was (a nostalgia for the early days of Maryknoll and mission), but a "turning toward" the future of *missio Dei* and the realities we must face in this new moment.

Second, the experience of Maryknollers over these past hundred years calls the Church to love the questions about God and mission more than the "answers." For example, how does one hold proclamation and dialogue in creative tension? How does the proclamation of Jesus the Christ as universal savior expand our experience and understanding of "Christ" who is the image of the invisible God and through whom and in whom all things were made?" A hundred years of Gospel proclamation has carved the love of God more deeply into the heart of the missioner and the ways that God has shown GodSelf within the different religious traditions of our world. We need to speak, to witness to our "mystical moments," just as James Edward Walsh did in his encounter with the "Farmer Boy" (a mystical experience of God's love), as did Mother Mary Joseph in her encounter with the heart of mission on a bridge in China. Maryknoll asks and challenges all in the Church to witness to the mystical moments that shape our understanding of the Holy One in this twenty-first century.

Last but not least, I think that Maryknoll clearly shows that the numbers in our mission institutes are not of primary importance. But in the context of our fragmented, globalized world, the following questions are of paramount importance: Are we happy missioners? Are we peace-filled people? Are we passionate in the pursuit of justice? Are we women and men in true partnership with all people of good will to further the Good News for all? It is the manifestation of these characteristics that come from Jesus that attracts people to the Gospel, a gospel that they may wish to follow or have as an important part of their lives even though they may not necessarily desire or seek baptism. The Asian bishops write that "God's grace may lead some to accept baptism and enter the church, but it cannot be presumed that this must always be the case. God's ways are mysterious and unfathomable, and no one can dictate the direction of God's grace" (Bishops' Institute for Interreligious Affairs, BIRA II, art. 12).

In other words, we must continue to do Christ-like deeds that witness to the reign of God. Perhaps in this new moment of "faith seeking understanding," the point is not to convert people to a religion but rather to live and act in such a way that people are moved to be transformed by the Gospel of Jesus. This type of *ad gentes* evangelization that occurs *inter gentes* does not have numbers that can be sent to a local bishop or to Rome as "proof" that one is living and preaching the Gospel, but it does have the power of leaven to transform the world.

As I was pondering an ending to this response, I came upon the card that my group chose for our profession in 1967 with a quote from Paul VI. If I may paraphrase a bit, it reads: "The missioner who would be of the church will be the bearer of a message that is strong and joyous, full of beauty and of poetry, full of vigor and of majesty." Those words of Paul VI still ring true and have the power to catch and excite the imagination and faith of young people for the challenges of mission today. For in the past years of Maryknoll the Gospel message *has* been borne strongly and joyously to the nations. Its beauty and poetry *have* been shared, and countless missioners *have* witnessed with vigor to the justice demands of the Gospel. Now we look to the future years of mission and the ways in which our global context calls us to be the bearers of this joyous message.

Notes

1. Margaret A. Farley, "Ethics, Ecclesiology and the Grace of Self-Doubt," *A Call to Fidelity: On the Moral Theology of Charles Curran*, ed. James J. Walter, Timothy E. O'Connell, and Thomas A. Shannon (Washington, D.C.: Georgetown University Press, 2002), 55ff.

2. Colleen Mary Mallon, *Traditioning Disciples: The Contribution of Cultural Anthropology to Ecclesial Identity*, American Society of Missiology Monograph, vol. 8 (Eugene, Ore.: Pickwick Publications, 2010), 3.

Part II

The Nature of
Global Mission

7

Mission in Dialogue
with the Peoples of Africa

Kenneth Thesing, MM

Africa is a huge and varied continent with fifty-four countries, some four thousand ethnic groups and languages, and a billion people. My reflections, based on my mission experience in Tanzania, Mozambique, Kenya, and Sudan, will focus primarily on East Africa.

Catholic missioners began modern evangelization work in Africa around the 1880s, with some earlier exceptions. By 1946, when Maryknoll began work in Tanganyika (Tanzania), there were just a few established missions, no indigenous priests or Sisters, and few trained catechists. Today this area hosts an almost entirely indigenous local church with a growing Catholic population. In 2011 Catholics averaged about 20 percent of the population in sub-Saharan Africa. Except for the northern African countries, where the population is almost entirely Muslim, the Catholic Church is established.

Maryknoll's Understanding of Mission in Africa

Maryknoll's paradigm of mission was clear: establish the local Church. Thus we established a seminary to form local candidates to the priesthood and worked to establish a local congregation of Sisters. Catechist schools were formed as Maryknollers also gave priority to the centrality of the catechumenate to train the first Christians.

One of the most significant developments has been the shift from parish development to involvement in specialized ministries. Today the emphasis of mission is accompanying and serving the local Church. By the 1970s, the Maryknoll Society began forming "mission units" in which small numbers of missioners went to another country or diocese for a specific task for a limited term. Even with its smaller numbers, Maryknoll took on new mission work in Ethiopia, Sudan, Zambia, Egypt, and Nigeria and more recently in Mozambique and Namibia.

In the early years almost all Maryknoll parishes began with a primary school and then a Church. This was a strategic decision as the local chiefs would give "communal land" for a parish if it included a school. It was also theologically sound as Maryknoll believed in holistic evangelization that invited the entire person to be with Christ. Thus, education, health care, water development, agricultural programs, and family training courses were part of the overall vision. In addition, in Musoma a new style of small formation programs began to spread, which later led to the small Christian communities movement, a popular pastoral model in East Africa.

Maryknoll also gave great importance to learning the local languages in order to effectively evangelize. Maryknoll established a Language Institute, and later a Society member founded the Maryknoll Institute for African Studies (MIAS) to increase missioners' understanding of local cultures. The Institute now stands beside the Catholic University of East Africa and Tangaza College, a theological consortium of religious communities with hundreds of seminarians and more than a thousand religious and lay students. As urbanization increased, Maryknoll moved more and more to the cities. An Institute for Fine Arts, a Montessori training center, the Amani (Kiswahili for peace) Counseling Center, a university chaplaincy program, centers for street kids, HIV/AIDS programs, developing media—all became part of the mix of evangelistic endeavors.

A conscious part of Maryknoll's mission outlook has been to work for justice, continually emphasizing work among the poor. This has been a firm pillar of integral evangelization along with preaching the Word, sacramental and liturgical life, interreligious dialogue, and prayer. Beginning in the 1960s "care of the land" was added, particularly in areas of severe land degradation; later tree planting and water catchment projects were added.

The Church in Africa

The African Church, like the African people, is filled with life and hope. Although life is often grim, it is also filled with celebration. The African Church is marked by that spirit: liturgies are celebrated with song and dancing, with drums and zither and other local instruments. Choirs and processions express the essential communitarian spirit of the people and the Church. While community is not lived perfectly in Africa, life is communal: it is shared and celebrated with song and dance, with conversation and food.

The Catholic Church has certainly become rooted throughout sub-Saharan Africa. The 130 million Catholics of 2001 are estimated to become 228 million by 2025. Africa has a local Church, with indigenous bishops, priests, men and women religious, many thousands of catechists, lay community leaders at parish and village levels, and increasing numbers of Church-based educational institutions from primary to university levels, with medical clinics, health centers and hospitals, and medical and business schools. Vocations to the priesthood, brotherhood, and sisterhood continue to increase, and Africans are increasingly members of diocesan and international religious communities. Many African seminarians and priests are also part of the world's presbyterate.

In 1973 the bishops of East Africa proclaimed that small Christian communities were to be the Church's pastoral model, and this emphasis continues to gain strength. In 1994 the First African Synod of Bishops proclaimed the "church as family," seeing both the human and Christian families as the basic building blocks of the Church.

In preparing for the Second African Synod (2009), the bishops of East Africa (AMECEA) acknowledged a Church that looked incredibly successful, with large numbers of conversions, growing numbers of institutions, thriving parishes, and many programs at diocesan and national levels. But the bishops also noted the increasing reality of political strife, continuing poverty, economic mismanagement, poor governance, and terrible corruption. The work is not over.

Challenges

The role of women in Africa is a significant issue. Missioners have worked hard to transform demeaning cultural practices and to develop alternative Christian programs and rituals. However, both government and Church struggle to implement their statements on enhancing the role of women. In July 2011 the East African bishops recognized this, pledging "to continue supporting efforts that seek to empower women to take their rightful place in society and in the Church." However, there is little discernible progress in how this might be realized in church structures.

Since the early 1980s HIV/AIDS has been a central concern. Civil and religious sectors in Africa have strived to help everyone understand the means of HIV/AIDS transmission, its treatment, and its prevention. With the highest concentration of the disease in the world, Africa struggles to deal with it with dignity and perseverance. The bishops of East Africa recognize that millions of people are living with HIV and millions more are dying of AIDS. They state: "We must never tire to remind our people that HIV/AIDS can be defeated."

The question of the poor in Africa and the question of justice are also unresolved. The 1971 Synod of Bishops document *Justice in the World* proclaimed that liberation, justice, and a preferential option for the poor form "a constitutive dimension of the preaching of the Gospel . . . of the Church's mission." However, poverty continues to be a pervasive problem.

In 2009 Pope Benedict XVI's encyclical *Caritas in Veritate* stated: "The way humanity treats the environment influences the way it treats itself and vice versa. The Church has a responsibility toward creation" (5). This is now a central part of Maryknoll's mission. Ecology, environmental protection and regeneration, and mission are inseparable.

And there are other challenges. As the numbers of priests and religious expand, the number of Catholics continues to grow faster, and a Church that is financially self-reliant is still a distant goal. Tribalism, ethnic conflict, and corruption remain continuing challenges. The message of "Reconciliation, Justice, and Peace" is not yet concretely realized.

Africa also confronts one of the major social and cultural issues today: the interface between political and religious Islam on the one hand and African culture and religion on the other. Incidents in Egypt, Nigeria, and Sudan indicate that much more work needs to be done by both Christian and Muslim leaders to practice living together in tolerance, justice, and peace. If not, there will be more violence and war.

What Lies Ahead

The worldwide Church is rapidly shifting its numbers from the North to the global South. Africa will continue to be a major part of that shift.

With the rapid increase in the number of Catholic universities and theological schools, Africa will soon have a stronger theological voice. Africa will also have an increasing number of bishops, archbishops, cardinals, presidents, and functionaries in the many offices of the Roman Curia. More and more, Africans will be the "face" of missioners throughout the world.

The population of Africa is predicted to reach two billion before 2050 and possibly three billion by the end of this century, approximately one-third of the projected world population. Africa is young and restless; its energy, both positive and negative, will be projected increasingly into the world. Several of the countries with the fastest growing economies are now in Africa, and the African continent is growing faster economically than the United States or Europe. Christianity and the Catholic Church in Africa are coming to prominence as frontline players on the world stage. It is our hope that this will lead to productive dialogue and a search for mutual knowledge so that more become "the salt of the earth" and "the light of the world" (Matt. 5:13–14).

8

Mission in Asia: Maryknoll's "First Love"

James H. Kroeger, MM

In their letter to Rome for permission to establish Maryknoll, the two priest founders expressed a preference for mission in Asia, specifically in China. Pope Pius X granted the request on June 29, 1911, and the first missioners left for China in 1918. From its China beginnings, Maryknoll has expanded into many other Asian countries: Korea (1923), Philippines (1926), Japan (1933), Taiwan (1951), Indonesia (1973), Bangladesh (1975), Nepal (1977), Thailand (1982), Cambodia (1989), and Vietnam (1992). In God's providence, Society members still serve within the local Church of *all* these countries.

Asia's Rich Diversity

During the 1998 Asian Synod, Cardinal Kim of Korea noted that Asia contains not only "various nations, but, one might say, many worlds." In fact, there are "many Asias." The Far East is a conglomerate of continents and giant archipelagos. It is a rich mosaic of cultures and subcultures with a wealth of spiritual heritages. Indeed, the "many Asias" have many gifts to offer the Church and mission.

The Context: Startling Statistics

Asia, the world's largest and most populated continent, constitutes one-third of the land area of the Earth. Of the world's twenty most populous nations (2010), nine are in Asia. If one shrank the world's population to a village of a hundred people (with all human ratios remaining the same), there would be sixty-one Asians, thirteen Africans, twelve Europeans, nine from South America and the Caribbean, and five from North America.

Religious Realities

Asia is the homeland of three eminent world religions: Hinduism, Buddhism, and Islam; 85 percent of the world's non-Christians live in Asia. Worldwide, Islam has approximately 1.4 billion adherents and numbers some 700 million-plus followers in Asia alone. There are approximately 115 million-plus Catholics in Asia, and they represent only 2.9 percent of the more than 4 billion Asians. Over 50 percent of Asian Catholics are found in one country alone (Philippines). Catholics in most other Asian nations are a small—even tiny—minority and frequently represent less than one percent of the population. Yet, no Asian local Church is so small or so poor that it does not have gifts to give, and, likewise, no Asian local Church is so large and powerful that is does not have something to receive.

Cultural Realities

The cultural gifts that Asia possesses are closely related to and often intertwined with its religious traditions. Together they have helped shape the histories and values of Asia's peoples. Certain Asian values may be described as "gifts of the spirit" that can enrich humanity—and the Church. Everyone can learn from Asia's religious-cultural experience, for example:

- from Muslims the Church can learn about prayer, fasting, and alms-giving;

- from Hindus the Church can learn about meditation and contemplation;

- from Buddhists the Church can learn about detachment from material goods and respect for life;

- from Confucianism the Church can learn about filial piety and respect for elders;

- from Taoism the Church can learn about simplicity and humility;

- from animists the Church can learn about reverence and respect for nature and gratitude for harvests.

- from Asia's religions, the Church can learn to be more open, receptive, sensitive, tolerant, and forgiving in the midst of religious and cultural plurality.

Social, Economic, and Political Factors

When one explores the realities of social, economic, and political matters, a stark reality emerges: the situations in Asia are extremely diverse and they defy any simple classification. For example, "some countries are highly developed, others are developing through effective economic policies, and others still find themselves in abject poverty, indeed among the poorest nations on earth" (*Ecclesia in Asia* 7). Ideologies, materialism, and secularism can hinder the development process at the same time as they tend to undermine Asia's traditional, social, religious, and cultural values. Although the Church in Asia is truly a small minority, it listens attentively to the reassuring words of Jesus: "Fear not, little flock" (Luke 12:32).

Worldwide Ramifications

In our globalized world, Asian influences have spread across the face of the Earth. Asia is no longer "out there," faraway and overseas, and the Church must not miss this opportunity to deeply encounter the Asian Diaspora. Allow a simple illustration. In 2000, the U.S. Catholic Bishops issued a beautiful pastoral letter: *Welcoming the Stranger among Us: Unity in Diversity*. In 2001, this document was complemented by a pastoral statement: *Asian and Pacific Presence: Harmony in Faith*. The conclusion of the 2001 statement contains these enlightening words:

> By being authentically Christian and truly Asian in the footsteps of Christ, they have brought us a more profound understanding of what it means to be truly Catholic. They have taught the Church in the United States the meaning of harmony; the necessity of dialogue with their cultures, with other religions, and with the poor; a renewed sense of family loyalty; the unity between diverse cultures and diverse Catholic communities; and the closeness of all God's creation.

Pathways into Mission

In the past hundred years Maryknollers have tried to situate their mission response within the local context. In recent decades this has been enhanced by the Second Vatican Council and the continental assembly of Asia's local Churches known as the Federation of Asian Bishops' Conferences (FABC). Twenty-eight countries are represented in the FABC, which grew out of a historic gathering of 180 Asian Catholic bishops during Pope Paul VI's 1970 visit to Manila. Because of the great diversity in Asia, I will focus on the wider Asian mission scene rather than individual countries by outlining eight individual themes or mission pathways.

Introduction to the FABC

The FABC has indeed fostered an "Asian Pentecost"! One can validly assert that the FABC is truly "Asia's continuing Vatican II." The FABC is a transnational episcopal organization, composed of a modest central structure with nine FABC offices, purposely scattered among various Asian nations. They are focused on evangelization, social communication, laity and family, human development, education and faith formation, ecumenism and interreligious dialogue, theological concerns, clergy, and consecrated life. Each of these offices sponsors a wide variety of activities that promote the growth of Asia's vibrant local Churches.

Operative FABC Paradigm of Being Church

The FABC paradigm of Church and missionary evangelization asserts that (1) the local Church is always the acting "subject"; (2) the "approach" of engagement is always dialogue; and (3) the "dialogue partners" are Asia's people, especially the poor, Asia's myriad cultures, and Asia's rich religious traditions. This "triple dialogue" paradigm that emerged during the First FABC Plenary Assembly in 1974 (a dialogue with Asia's peoples, cultures, and religions) has been consistently reaffirmed for its validity and application. It focuses on local Church, dialogue, and the realities of the Asian peoples. This operative paradigm of Church and mission is the interpretive key to understanding and appreciating the evangelization process in Asia today.

Centrality of the Local Church

The centrality of the local Church in the entire missionary project is vigorously asserted within this Asian ecclesiology: "The renewal of our sense of mission will mean . . . that the acting subject of mission is the *local Church* living and acting in communion with the universal Church" (FABC V, 3.3.1). The heartbeat of Asia's Catholics pulsates in and through the local Churches.

Vision of a Renewed Church

The Asian Churches have renewed themselves for both *ad intra* and *ad extra* service. There have been eight clearly observable movements in this renewal process (such as, for example, youth, interiority, people empowerment, and evangelization) (FABC VII, 2000). These movements have become defining marks and essential characteristics of the Church in Asia. They clarify both the identity and mission of genuine faith communities.

Missionary Local Churches

The model of mission is one of "exchange." Simply put, this means that mission is viewed as the "exchange of gifts between sister local Churches throughout Asia and the world."

Specific Mission Challenges

There are five sectors of people to whom the Church wishes to direct its mission of love and service. These sectors identified by the FABC are youth, women, family, indigenous peoples, and migrants and refugees.

Mission Motivation

Five core motives can respond to the question "Why evangelize?" (1) gratitude to God; (2) mission is a mandate; (3) "we evangelize because we believe"; (4) "we are incorporated by baptism into the Church"; and (5) "Gospel is *leaven* for liberation and transformation" (FABC V, 3.1–3.3.3).

FABC Vision: Potential Benefits

Both the Asian and U.S. bishops have spoken specifically about the genuine helpfulness of the "triple dialogue" approach of the FABC— valid in both Asian and U.S. contexts.

Conclusion

This presentation has highlighted some significant Asian developments in mission vision, theology, and practice since the Second

Vatican Council, and it has described the "Good News from Asia" about mission. It has also shown how Asia's local Churches have tried to follow the Gospel injunction: "What you have received as a gift, give as a gift" (Matt. 10:8). For Asia's local Churches (and the missionaries who serve in them), *to live is to evangelize!* We all have much to learn from the "Asian way."

9

Mission among the Peoples of Latin America: *Pachacuti:* The World Turned Upside Down

Raymond J. Finch, MM

In discussing the situation in Latin America, we have utilized the Andean concept of *pachacuti*, which literally means turning the world upside down, to understand mission in Latin America. From the very beginning, Christian mission among the peoples of Latin America has been and continues to be a *pachacuti* as the world was and continues to be turned upside down philosophically, politically, religiously, economically, and socially. It is not a matter of one group changing the status quo. In a *pachacuti* everyone loses their balance.

In Latin America the *pachacuti* was total. There was no possibility of separating the social, political, cultural, and economic aspects of the conquest, the evangelization of the Americas. As Catholicism was imposed, traditional Andean rites and symbols were forbidden, destroyed, and driven underground. The peoples of the Americas were quickly reduced to poverty and servitude as a new social order was quickly established. The Europeans were at the pinnacle, the children of Europeans born in America on the next lower rung, the elite of the Inca, Mayan, and Aztec empires on the next rungs down, those of mixed race on the next level, with the Indigenous and African slaves on the lowest level. The encounter of two worlds turned both upside down. Spain and Portugal embarked on a path of conquest, economic exploitation, and cultural and religious imperialism. The peoples of the Americas, once rich, boasting three empires and many more peoples and cultures, were reduced to subservience and became second-class citizens in their own land.

The Conquest

Evangelization of the peoples of America began as a joint venture of the state and the Catholic Church. Throughout most of the conquest and life of the colony the Church ethically and morally justified the subjugation, enslavement, and pillaging of the wealth of the Americas. At the same time it is important to remember that there were prophetic voices that spoke out against the means used to colonize, evangelize, and oppress. Two examples were Antonio Montesinos and Bartolomé de Las Casas. However, even they never questioned the superiority of European culture, Christianity, and Catholicism; only the manner in which they were imposed was questioned by the prophets of that day.

The evangelization and catechetical process was uneven at best. There was a mixing of Christian symbols with Andean, Mayan, or Aztec content and meaning. Frequently the Virgin Mary was identified as Pachamama in the Andean world or *Tonatzin, Nuestra Venerada Madre* in the Aztec context. The respect and homage paid to the Achachilas, the spirits of the ancestors, was at least nominally transferred to the cross and to the different saints enshrined on the crests of most hills. In rural areas, where the colonial powers had less control, Andean and Mayan religious ritual practices lived on, at times disguised as Christian feasts, saints, or symbols.

During the extended colonial period Spanish rule was uncontested except for very brief and sporadic Indigenous uprisings. The state supported the Church economically and protected its privileges, while the Church justified the rule of the crown and the system in general. The power and influence of the Church grew until it was present in all parts of the colonial Americas. One important exception was the Jesuit reductions, which put the Church and state at odds politically and economically. This fascinating experiment in evangelization and development could possibly be criticized for a certain level of paternalism but in fact it was extremely successful. It was perhaps its success that eventually brought about the rethinking of the Church-state alliance.

The new republics were a continuation of the class, racial, and cultural differences of the colony as the Spanish and Portuguese overlords were replaced by local elites. Economic relations, once controlled by Spain, were now manipulated by England, France, or the Low Countries. The legal separation that existed in the colonies between Indigenous and Spanish was abolished but the separation and asymmetrical social and economic structures continued. In terms of the Catholic Church, one important difference during the first years of the republics was a scarcity of leadership, priests, and economic resources. The colonies continued to depend on Spain for priests, bishops, and funds. In addition, Rome was slow to arrive at political agreements with the new republics.

During the colonial period there was a very limited presence of Protestants in a few cities, and these were usually commercial representatives of countries such as England. With the establishment of the republics the Protestant presence grew, at first to accommodate the growing diplomatic and commercial communities. When freedom of religious belief was introduced in many of the constitutions, the Catholic Church maintained its privileged position. It was in the early 1900s that different Protestant churches changed from strictly serving the expatriate population to establishing local congregations. And it was only in the second half of the twentieth century that different evangelical and historical Protestant churches began to make a concerted effort to establish congregations in the rapidly growing cities.

Although the Catholic Church retained its position of privilege and received both economic and other support from the new national governments, there was a slow but constant eroding of its power, influence, infrastructure, and presence, especially in rural areas. In general the Catholic Church maintained its position of dominance in the cities until they began to expand explosively in the 1970s. In the middle of the twentieth century, we see a Catholic Church closely aligned with the upper class, dominant in the cities with a smaller and smaller presence in the rural areas, and burdened with an old and crumbling infrastructure. It is a Catholic Church with fewer vocations even as cities grow due to migration from the countryside and small towns. In this context of explosive growth and political and social change, the Catholic Church was identified with the forces of tradition and conservatism.

The modern mission movement in Latin America can be traced to the middle of the twentieth century. It was a new *pachacuti*. In 1942 Maryknoll was asked to go to Bolivia to work in the Pando vicariate. In 1943 Maryknoll began working in Peru, Chile, Guatemala, and Mexico.

In each country Maryknollers went to places that had been abandoned and isolated or to places with large Indigenous populations, like Puno in Peru, southern Chile, and the Yucatan Peninsula in Mexico.

The decades of the 1950s and 1960s witnessed a concerted effort to save the Church in Latin America from communism, to rebuild the infrastructure of parishes, seminaries, and religious institutions, and to foster and train vocations to the priesthood and religious life. The mission paradigm changed again, with a much stronger emphasis on economic development that created both productive and financial cooperatives to bring more people into the emerging national economies and to promote human development through health care and education.

The impact of the Second Vatican Council was seen in the results of the Medellín Conference, which emphasized the importance of the option for the poor, social justice, and the Church of the poor. It would be difficult to overestimate the impact and importance of the development of the theology of liberation both in its direct influence and in the backlash against it that has occurred over the past thirty years. It helped spark a new grassroots participation in the Church among the poor, and this is still a reality in countries like Peru, Bolivia, Brazil, and Ecuador.

Liberation theology also allied itself with movements to promote Indigenous religiosity and theology. The Churches in Peru and Brazil in particular were transformed on all levels during the late 1960s and the 1970s. It was not until the 1980s that the backlash arrived, beginning in Peru, where some very traditional groups extended their presence and influence. Despite some drastic changes in Church leadership liberation theology is still important and continues to impact mission. The option for the poor is no longer questioned, the centrality of justice issues to the Gospel and evangelization is taken for granted, and the base communities are still alive and functioning in the poor areas of Peru and Brazil.

The decade of the 1970s is also noted for the position taken by the institutional Church in defense of the poor and against the many military dictatorships that sprouted up throughout Latin America. The Church became a meeting point, a space in which to struggle against the national security forces and the often antipoor dictatorships in much of Latin America. The Church, formerly seen as the bulwark against the left, was now perceived as its mainstay.

As the dictatorships fell one by one, the Church was no longer needed to act as the voice of those without a voice; the poor found their own voice. At the same time an important anthropological and theological shift occurred. Indigenous peoples began to be seen in a new light. Previously the objective had been to integrate them into the "mainstream," to help them to adapt to modern European culture and join the dominant society. Now there was a new recognition that the Indigenous cultures possessed values and practices that the world needed. In terms of evangelization the shift was away from imposing foreign rituals, forms, and structures to attempting to see how Christian rituals, values, and structures could be better expressed through Indigenous cultural expressions. The word "inculturation," used by Pedro Arrupe, became popular, and there were new efforts to promote expressions of Catholicism that were both in communion with the universal Church and authentic expressions of the different Indigenous manifestations of Catholicism.

The *pachacuti* of mission continues in Latin America as the direction of mission is changing, with a growing number of missioners from the South going to the North. As Latin Americans assume a more active role, the gift is still there: the gift of encounter, the gift of both personal and social growth, and, most of all, the gift of discovering God's presence in the midst of diversity and change.

10

A History of Mission in China

Jean-Paul Wiest

On December 17, 1917, Fr. James A. Walsh telegraphed Fr. Thomas Price from Canton, China, with the long awaited words "Field found!" This brief reflection will focus on the relevance of the China experience for Maryknoll today and tomorrow. Should the experience be reduced to a collection of photographs and narratives of a bygone era? Are the seminary building and the tombstones on the Ossining hilltop no more than silent relics of a past that our rapidly changing times have rendered obsolete?

The answer is no. Photographs, narratives, and the buildings themselves are living memories and monuments that speak of encounters, decisions, and deeds. They bear witness to great achievements but also to missteps and even failures. The three and a half decades spent in China were a time of training and enrichment that severely tested Maryknoll's resilience and adaptability. Maryknoll planted its earliest roots in Chinese soil, and it is there that many of its cherished charisms and traditions were nurtured; Maryknoll gained a sense of identity, a tradition, and a way to look at people and cultures that set it on its present course.

Steadfastness in Pursuit of Goals

When in June 1911 James A. Walsh and Thomas Price petitioned the head of Propaganda Fide for permission to found a missionary society and establish a seminary, they singled out China as where their missionaries "would be most needed."[1] This course of action proved that they, and most particularly James A. Walsh, had accurately read the signs of the time. Walsh's analysis of the international political situation at the beginning of the twentieth century, and of Protestant efforts in China, had convinced him that the time had come for "Americans to bear the banners of Catholicity . . . in China . . . to persuade people that everything American [was] not Protestant."[2] In the first issue of

81

The Field Afar in 1907 news about China spread over six of the sixteen pages.

In 1911 the founders believed that the U.S. Catholic Church stood ready to enter into the worldwide missionary effort. Yet finding a mission territory proved difficult because most of China had already been divided among other missionary organizations. Two years after his first inquiry in October 1915, Walsh's repeated appeals had received mostly polite answers but no invitations or offers of a mission territory. Although most European bishops thought that American missioners were not suited for the hard living conditions of China, Walsh never gave up. In September 1917 he boarded a ship for the Orient to pursue the only real offer he had received. Three months later, on December 17, he and Bishop Budes de Guébriant signed the agreement that finally opened the doors of China to Maryknoll: "I had hardly met the bishop before I realized that Maryknoll's first mission in the Orient had been found, and in few minutes my eyes were on the map of China, riveted to a point marked YEUNGKONG."[3]

What are the signs of the times today? Will Maryknoll display the same perseverance as the founders in answering new challenges? In lieu of Yeungkong, what are the places, peoples, and commitments on which Maryknollers' eyes should focus?

Courage to Stand against Prejudices

In November 1919 the bishops of China felt wrongly chastised by Pope Benedict XV's apostolic letter *Maximum Illud,* in which the pope declared how sad he was for countries where the Catholic faith had been preached for centuries and where civilizations produced distinguished people in the fields of arts and sciences, and yet these countries had no native bishops and the native clergy was still maintained in a position of inferiority.[4] Earlier, Vincentian Antoine Cotta had infuriated the episcopacy of China by his criticisms of the disparaging attitude of Western missionaries toward the Chinese clergy and had written to Rome about it. Foreign bishops in China felt that Cotta and his friend Fr. Vincent Lebbe had misled the pope. Treated as a pariah in China, Cotta was permanently recalled to France by his superiors. At that juncture Walsh began to correspond with Cotta and in 1922 invited him to stay at the Maryknoll seminary. Walsh's decision was bold because Maryknoll was still a junior partner in the league of missionary organizations, and antagonizing the bishops of China could jeopardize its mission there. Walsh, however, sensed that the presence of Cotta as a champion of the Chinese Church would inspire his seminarians. The founder's hopes were fulfilled beyond his expectations as Cotta mingled with the seminarians and spent recreation periods with the Sister-novices, informally sharing with them his love for the Chinese and his hope for an indigenous Chinese Church.

Walsh's path has been followed by other Maryknollers who have stood against the wrongdoings, injustice, intolerance, and bigotry exhibited by some segments of the Church, civil societies, and political regimes. Some Maryknollers were imprisoned because of their stands, and some even gave their lives. It is also worth asking if there were also instances when Maryknoll failed to rise against prejudices and injustices.

The Ultimate Sacrifice and "Thinning of the Blood"

One of James A. Walsh's favorite mottoes was "go the whole way" for Christ. He was well known for his admiration and devotion for the French martyr Théophane Vénard. In his spiritual lectures, he often presented Vénard as the model of a Maryknoller prepared to "go the whole way" for Christ. It was not just a coincidence that the first Maryknoll junior seminary was called the Venard.

By 1927 Walsh was already a realist who had witnessed the death of several Maryknollers, including Thomas Price, Anthony Hodgins, Mary Gertrude Moore, and Daniel McShane. Walsh's reflections on the lives of these four persons led him to transform the lofty slogan of martyrdom into the spiritual force behind each Maryknoller's daily activities. "Very few of us," he told them, "will actually shed blood for Christ, but there is none who will not have the opportunity to thin out his blood for Christ, . . . [the] opportunity to stand and wear [himself] out for Christ."[5]

This thinning of the blood for Christ culminated for some Maryknollers in the sacrifice of their lives, including nine Maryknoll priests whose blood was spilled while serving the poor and the oppressed. Of the four who died in China, Gerald Donovan was the first in 1938. When the news of Donovan's murder arrived, Fr. James E. Walsh, then superior general, wrote to his Council: "Maryknoll is complete, and America is apostolic."[6]

Maryknoll Sisters also shed their blood for Christ, including Ita Ford, who died in El Salvador some thirty years after her uncle, Bishop Francis X. Ford, died in China. Bishop Ford had been charged with spreading American imperialism in China, and Ita Ford was shot for helping alleged Communist-backed revolutionaries in El Salvador. However, in fact both died because their success in gaining the hearts of the people was viewed as a threat by the respective governments. This wearing oneself out for Christ remains at the core of what Maryknoll is all about. This spirituality that sprouted in Chinese soil was transplanted around the world as Maryknoll's mission spread.

Sharing Life, Joys, and Sorrows of the People

A hundred years ago, Maryknoll set out to bring millions of Chinese people into the Catholic Church. In pursuing this goal Maryknollers encountered a diversity of challenges to their bodies, their souls, and their work. The physical surroundings in China were not favorable: the climate was harsh with hot, humid summers and cold winters. In the hot summer months, mold grew overnight and vermin (rats, white ants, cockroaches, mosquitoes, fleas, and bedbugs) proliferated. "The heat stays between 92 and 98 in the shade with no breeze. One just sweats and sweats," writes one missioner. "We are now down to 18 degrees and we shall keep falling to zero and below. How far below?" writes another.[7]

The terrain was mostly hilly and transportation unreliable. Widespread banditry, endemic local feuds, and large-scale wars also hindered their work. The difficulty of the language with its many dialects also prevented many Maryknollers from communicating effectively with the Chinese people. Yet most Maryknollers did not shy away from these challenges; instead, they learned to live with and even overcome them.

Their diaries and letters conveyed the images of the missioners' efforts to adapt to the physical conditions of China but also to share the life, joys, and sorrows of the people. Maryknollers wrote of their travels to contact non-Christians, marry young people, anoint the sick, and bury the dead. Stories from the war and tales of the work in orphanages, dispensaries, and hospitals told of compassionate missioners who cared for those in direst need. Maryknollers became embedded into a historical and human setting of war and peace, good harvests and cataclysms, life and death. The Chinese were not just souls to save for the life hereafter, they were also people who deserved a better life.

Maryknoll's work in China gave priority to the poor and the defenseless. Dispensaries provided free medications and sponsored vaccination programs in rural areas; orphanages countered local aberrations caused by poverty and customs that were unfair to females babies; leper colonies treated as human beings people who lived as outcasts; mission schools offered the first rudiments of literacy to villagers; hostels allowed poor Catholic students to pursue higher studies; and cooperatives protected villagers from local loan sharks.

Maryknollers certainly made their share of mistakes, including a refusal to return children kept in the orphanages to their non-Catholic parents and the occasional manipulations of non-Catholic children in schools. The preoccupation with salvation only through baptism in the Church sometimes blurred Maryknoll missioners' message of Christian charity. Nonetheless, as they gained a deeper understanding of the reality of China and its values—and to a certain extent were transformed in the process—Maryknollers often avoided many of their earlier blunders.

Generally Maryknollers' views of the corporal works of mercy evolved beyond what they had been taught during their formation. Corporal works of mercy, they felt, should be more than a manifestation of Christian charity or a device to attract converts. These works should also be more than temporary measures to alleviate suffering or a means to promote the Church. Many Maryknollers realized that relief work had little value if not accompanied by plans to provide people with the means to improve their living conditions. Gradually the commonly accepted view in today's Catholic Church emerged, namely that the intrinsic value of corporal works of mercy is to prepare for the coming of the reign of God by building a world that is more just and fosters full human development.

This is how Maryknoll, through its Maryknoll China Service Project, successfully reconnected with the people of China when the country finally reopened to the outside world. Maryknoll is there today to serve and help people according to their needs, whether training people suffering from Hansen's Disease to make their own orthopedic shoes, or assisting Chinese Sisters in running clinics, or finding volunteers to teach English to college students, thereby responding to one of the Chinese government's educational priorities.

The Training of Local Leadership among Chinese Clergy and Sisters

The Constitutions of Maryknoll have been a constant reminder that one of the Society's priorities is to foster a native clergy. In each of Maryknoll's five mission territories in China, seminaries were among the first institutions initiated. In the same manner, the Maryknoll Sisters established novitiates to train native Sisters.

Maryknoll's experiment in forming a local clergy and sisterhood went through three overlapping phases of development with its approach somewhat contradictory at times. On the one hand, Maryknollers aimed to become as Chinese as possible; on the other hand, the training provided in their mission seminaries and novitiates tended to Westernize their Chinese recruits. As Maryknollers gained experience, they began to develop new approaches to seminary and novitiate training. In the second phase, they were not just forming priests and Sisters who would work under them, they were also training Chinese replacements who would one day take over the leadership. As the years passed, Chinese priests were given more and more responsibilities as pastors or seminary professors. The Kaying seminary, for instance, reached the point where it was entirely run by Chinese priests and laypeople. In the Fushun mission, where all Americans were interned during World War II and then repatriated, the native Sisters and priests ran the vicariate by themselves until the return of Maryknollers in 1945. The fact that most of the local priests and Sisters persevered despite long years of isolation and persecution is a tribute to the spiritual training they received from Maryknoll.

Although some Maryknollers had difficulty in treating Chinese priests and Sisters on an equal footing, the actual passing of the leadership to native priests and Sisters, the third stage, did occur, although it was cut short by the ousting of foreign missionaries from China in

1949. Prior to their departure, no Maryknoll territory had ever been turned over to a Chinese bishop. The Maryknoll Sisters, however, were more successful, with the Fushun Sisters electing their own mother general in 1949.

Twenty years ago, as part of its China apostolate, Maryknoll launched a project now known as the Chinese Seminary Teachers and Formators Project, which ushered in a fourth stage in training Chinese leadership. Through its project coordinator, Maryknoll acts as a facilitator in selecting and educating trainees as well as in providing for their personal, vocational, and spiritual well-being. Numerous U.S. Catholic orders and universities support this effort in various ways. Over a hundred priests, sisters, seminarians, and laypersons have already completed four years or more of studies in the United States in scripture, systematic and moral theology, philosophy, sociology, pastoral counseling, ethics, church history, and formation.

It is almost impossible to overestimate the influence of this group, which serves the Chinese Catholic community as seminary professors, academic deans, rectors, spiritual directors, novice mistresses, retreat house directors, and bishops' secretaries. Several have already become bishops with the blessing of the pope, and one serves as the superior of a large congregation of Sisters.

The American Catholic: The Role of the Laity

Compared to its Protestant counterpart, the Catholic laity did not fully awaken to its worldwide responsibility until the first decade of the twentieth century. Today, however, the Maryknoll Lay Missioners, the Maryknoll Affiliates, and the Maryknoll China Service Project are prime examples of the various ways in which the laity has become part and parcel of the missionary activity of the Church. These are relatively new organizations, but their roots stretch deep into the Chinese soil of the 1930s.

Medical doctor Paluel Flagg joined the Maryknoll seminary staff in 1912 to give weekly classes on medical practices; he also recruited other doctors to open their clinics and hospitals to provide training opportunities to the seminarians and novice Sisters.[8] Maryknoll's Sister Mary Moore and Brother John Dorsey, the first two registered nurses who studied under Flagg, arrived in China in the early 1920s.

Moore earned the nickname of "Sister Doctor," and Dorsey became known as "the man from Heaven with the big heart."

As early as 1914, Flagg posted a "Doctor's Column" in *The Field Afar*, urging the medical profession to donate supplies and personnel for the missions. In 1930, Harry Blaber, a young doctor from Brooklyn, later joined by his new bride and nurse, was the first to respond to Flagg's call to serve with Maryknollers in China. Others soon followed, including a retired British army surgeon, a doctor from the Canton Medical School, and a doctor from the University of St. Thomas in Manila.

Meanwhile, in 1925, with the encouragement of the Maryknoll founder and the collaboration of Dr. Anna Dengel, Flagg launched the Catholic Medical Mission Board and the Medical Volunteer Program in order to recruit physicians and nurses to volunteer for medical mission service all over the world. By the time of Flagg's death in 1970, the program had staffed over three thousand medical missions in fifty-seven countries. Although he never left the United States, Flagg could well be considered Maryknoll's first Lay Missioner.[9] There is no doubt that he planted the seed that slowly matured and finally in 1994 took the name Maryknoll Mission Association of the Faithful.

Conclusion

For the relatively young Maryknoll Society and Congregation, the three and a half decades spent in China were a time of training and enrichment. The experience gave them a sense of identity, a tradition, and a way to look at people and cultures that have set the two communities on the course they follow today.

In spite of setbacks, the Maryknoll Society and Congregation never relented in their efforts to found an indigenous Catholic Church in China. This drive, more than the conversion movement after World War II or even the success of its missionary methods, constitutes Maryknoll's greatest achievement and contribution. Maryknoll went to China to save souls and was, in turn, saved from the false belief that everything outside the realm of Christianity and the West was necessarily bad or wrong. Maryknollers became increasingly aware that the Chinese philosophy of life, culture, and traditions compared favorably to those of the Christian West. From its beginnings in China,

Maryknoll has learned to transmit the heartbeat of many peoples from around the world through their own authentic indigenous expressions of Christian faith, practices, and theological interpretations.

Notes

1. Maryknoll Archives, Letters of Importance 1901–40, Petition of Fathers James A. Walsh and Thomas F. Price, June 1911, 348–50.

2. *The Field Afar*, January 1907, 2.

3. James A. Walsh, *Observations in the Orient by a Maryknoller* (Catholic Foreign Mission Society of America, 1919), 184.

4. See Apostolic Letter *Maximum Illud*, 13.

5. Robert E. Sheridan, *Discourses of James Anthony Walsh, 1890–1936* (Maryknoll, N.Y.: Maryknoll Fathers, 1981), July 1, 1928, 269–70. See also June 29, 1928, 266; and June 29, 1927, 230.

6. Letter of James E. Walsh to Council members, June 19, 1939.

7. Maryknoll, Archives, Pingnam Diary, Fr. Thomas Kiernan, July 19, 1930; Linkiang Diary, Fr. Michael Henry, November 1940.

8. Maryknoll Mission Archives, Maryknoll Chronicle, 227; interviews of James Smith, 6, and Sister Mary Gerard Gallagher, 13. *The Field Afar*, April 1914, 14; February 1915, 29; May 1921, 124; February 1922, 38; June 1924, 188.

9. As early as 1922, James A. Walsh had advocated for an organism for training and financing lay missionaries, but his plea met no response. See *The Field Afar*, April 1922, 100.

11

Islam and Mission:
Reflections for Twenty-First Century
Missioners

Scott C. Alexander

The fact that this presentation was scheduled for October 7—the Feast of the Holy Rosary—was undoubtedly a coincidence of planning logistics and of historical memory in Catholic-Muslim relations. Nonetheless, it seems opportune to call attention to this happy coincidence for the purpose of exploring the topic of Islam and mission in the twenty-first century. The reason for this is that the feast commemorates the victory of politically "Christian" (Holy League) naval forces over their politically "Muslim" (Ottoman Turkish) counterparts on this day at the Battle of Lepanto in 1571. The Roman Catholic Church officially attributed the victory to the intercession of the Blessed Virgin Mary.

In addition to the irony in this attribution (given the degree to which the Blessed Mother is revered by Muslims the world over), this feast stands as a liturgical monument to a long history of mutual triumphalist imperialism between the various states of the Muslim Middle East and North Africa, on the one hand, and the Byzantine and Latin Christian East and West, on the other. This is significant because it was precisely this history of mutual triumphalism that shaped so much of Roman Catholic (and certainly other Christian) missionary activity throughout much of the modern period. Indeed, Christian missionaries were willy-nilly participants in the European colonial domination of the Muslim world, which reached its apex in the late nineteenth century. This is also significant because twenty-first-century Catholic missioners are, for the most part, deeply aware of the complicity of their mission forebears in the colonial project and the degree to which this complicity has, for all its positive contributions to the lives of so many, also severely compromised the essence of Christian mission: witness to Christ's Gospel of redeeming love. The Feast of the Holy

Rosary, therefore, continues to awaken our memories of the complex historical contours of Catholic-Muslim relations but now in a way that subverts its original design by encouraging missioners consciously to abjure the will to dominate and instead seek out new paradigms for mission among our Muslim sisters and brothers.

One such paradigm is embodied in the life and work of Dom Christian de Chergé, OCSO (d. 1996), whose mission among Muslims has been documented in two powerful forms: the excellent account of *The Monks of Tibhirine* (2002) by John Kiser, and the masterful film by Xavier Beauvois, *Des hommes et des dieux* (2010; Eng., *Of Gods and Men*). In his now famous "Last Testament," Dom Christian speaks—in anticipation of his martyrdom—of a distinctly antitriumphalist missionary vocation rooted in both the awareness that Muslims have many things to teach him about God, and an eschatological beatific vision of God the Father and "his children of Islam just as he sees them, all shining with the glory of Christ, the fruit of His Passion, and filled with the Gift of the Spirit, whose secret joy will always be to establish communion and to refashion the likeness, playfully delighting in the differences."

In many ways, the life and work of Dom Christian is a living expression of the dialogic nature of authentic Christian mission. It is a living expression of the stirring words regarding the "dialogue of salvation" by Paul VI in his 1964 encyclical *Ecclesiam Suam* (70ff.) and their echo in the teachings of *Dialogue and Mission* (1984, Vatican Secretariat for Non-Christians) that dialogue is characterized by mutual respect and concern and thus is "the norm and necessary manner of every form of Christian mission, as well as of every aspect of it" (DM 29).

In faithfulness to this more authentic understanding of mission, it is crucial for twenty-first-century missioners to deconstruct, and replace with the fruits of sound contextual analysis, the many stereotypes regarding Islam and Muslims that abound in the form of media sound bytes. These include, but are not restricted to:

- treating Islam and Muslims as monolithic entities defined by a negative essentialism that takes the abhorrent actions of a few and uses them to make purportedly definitive claims about the many;

- failing to understand the actual historical and political context of perceived "religious" motivations for political action (for example, sectarian conflict between Sunnis and Shiites in Iraq);

♦ failing to understand that many exercises in comparative Christian/ Muslim theology need a much greater degree of sophistication, especially in the area of making proper analogies , for example:

Christ : Christians :: Qur'an : Muslims

Mary : Catholics :: Muhammad : Muslims

♦ failing to appreciate that democracy and Islam are not only compatible, but in those cases where one finds a viable democracy in postcolonial Muslim societies (for example, Turkey under Justice and Development Party reforms), Islamic ideals and values have played a key role in its establishment.

12

Dying to Live: Migration and the Mission of Reconciliation

Daniel G. Groody, CSC

A few years ago I was working in Mexico at a border outreach center that offered material and pastoral support to those on the move.[1] Some were traveling north in search of better lives, and others had tried to enter the United States but failed and were subsequently deported back to Mexico. One day a group of forty immigrants arrived at the center. It had been a long night for them, and an even longer week. For three days they had crossed through the Arizona desert in temperatures that reached up to 120 degrees in the shade. Amid the challenges of the desert terrain, the physical demands, and their personal vulnerability to everything from heat stroke to poisonous snakes, they braved a perilous journey and tried to make their way to the United States, often under the cover of darkness. They were walking remote and diffuse trails that have taken the lives of thousands of immigrants over the last decade. When I asked them why they were willing to take such risks, some said they had relatives back home who needed medication they could not afford. Others said the $3 or $5 a day they earned after a twelve-hour work day was not enough to put much more than beans and tortillas on the table. Still others said that potato chips had become a luxury they could no longer afford, and they could not stand to look their children in the eyes when they complained of hunger. "We are migrating not because we want to but because we have to," said Mario. "My family at home depends on me. I'm already dead in Mexico, and getting to the United States gives us the hope of living, even though I may die."

Today there are more than 214 million people migrating around the world, or one out of every thirty-five people on the planet, which is equivalent to the population of Brazil. Approximately 42 million of these migrants are forcibly uprooted, including 16 million refugees outside their countries and 26 million who are internally displaced.[2]

93

For many reasons some scholars refer to today as the "age of migration."[3] It has become one of the defining issues of our time, touching upon every area of human life. It has also become one of the most complex and controversial issues. It brings us not only to the areas of conflict at geographical borders but to the crossroads between national security and human insecurity, sovereign rights and human rights, civil law and natural law, and citizenship and discipleship.[4] Here I would like to highlight the issue of migration in light of a mission of reconciliation.

Crossing the Inhuman-Human Divide

In the first pages of Scripture we read that we are created in God's image and likeness (Gen. 1:26–27). No text is more foundational nor more significant in its implication for the immigration debate than the *imago Dei*. In listening to stories of immigrants along the U.S./ Mexico border, as well as the borders between Slovakia and Ukraine, Malta and Libya, and Morocco and Spain, I have discovered that the common denominator among all who migrate around the world is the experience of dehumanization. I was recently speaking with a group of refugees in the Spanish-occupied territory of Ceuta on the Moroccan coast. They took me up to the mountains to meet some people from India who were hiding out in cardboard shacks in the mountains. The only place available to them was a small area located above an animal shelter that had a few hundred dogs that barked all through the night. "Even many of the animals here live better than we do here," said one refugee. "It is as if we are worth nothing to the people who live here, and if we die, it won't matter."

The insults they undergo are not just a direct assault on their pride but on their very existence. Their vulnerability and meaninglessness weigh heavily on them, and they often feel that the most difficult part of being an immigrant is to be no one to anyone. The *imago Dei* brings to the forefront the human costs that are part of the immigration equation, and it challenges a society more oriented toward profit than people with the awareness that an economy is made for people, and not people for the economy. The *imago Dei* holds out the challenge that immigrants are not just problems to be dealt with but rather people to be healed and empowered.

Crossing the Divine-Human Divide

The incarnation itself is a migration narrative that speaks of God crossing over the divine-human divide. In becoming human God migrates to the human race and, as Karl Barth notes, makes his way into the "far country."[5] This far country is a country of human discord and disorder, a place of division and dissension, a territory marked by death and the demeaning treatment of human beings. The Gospel of Matthew says that God in Jesus not only takes on human flesh and migrates into our world but he actually becomes a refugee himself when he and his family flee political persecution and escape into Egypt (Matt. 2:13–15). The divine assumes not just any human narrative but that of the most vulnerable of the human race.

This movement toward the human race takes place not because of human initiative or any form of human accomplishment but because of divine gratuity. In walking the way of the cross and in overcoming all the forces of death that threaten human life, Jesus gives hope to all who go through the agony of economic injustice, family separation, cultural uprootedness, and even a premature and painful death. Certainly migrants who cross the deserts in search of more dignified lives see their own story in the Jesus story, and Jesus opens up a reason to hope amid some of the most hopeless of circumstances. Surprisingly, amid such diversity, many find the ability to believe in God; amid some of the most godless of situations, many find the ability to speak about trusting in God after all has been taken away and to affirm God's goodness when their lot has been marked by such suffering in pain.

Crossing the Human-Human Divide

At the heart of the mission of the Church is to proclaim a God of life and to make our world more human by the building up of, in Paul VI's words, a "civilization of love." In imitation of Jesus, a "civilization of love" seeks to make real the practice of table fellowship. The significance of Jesus' table fellowship with sinners is that Jesus crosses over the human borders that divide one human being from another. If the incarnation is about God crossing over the divine-human divide, the mission of the Church is to cross the human-human divide.

This is fundamentally a mission of reconciliation, a realization that the borders that define countries may have some proximate value but they are not ultimately those that define the Church. On the contrary, the Church affirms in its mission and creed that it is one body in Christ. In uniting people beyond the political constructions that divide us, it gives tangible expression to the moral demands of the reign of God, the ethical possibilities of a globalization of solidarity, and the Christian vision of a journey of hope.

The Gift and Challenge of Mission: Crossing the Life-Death Divide

Immigration is arguably the most complex and challenging issue of our times, but this need not blind us from the core issues that lie at the heart of every one of us. How we respond to those most in need says more about who we are individually and collectively than it does about those on the move. Theology offers a way of thinking about migration that keeps the human issues in the forefront of the debate and reminds us that our own existence as a pilgrim people is migratory in nature.

Theology also offers not just more information but a new imagination, one that reflects at its core what it means to be human before God and live together with each other in community. In seeking to overcome all that divides us in order to reconcile us on all levels of our relationship, Christian discipleship in mission reminds us at the same time that the more difficult walls to cross are the ones that exist in the hearts of each and every one of us. Unable to cross this divide by ourselves, Christian faith rests ultimately in the one who migrated from heaven to Earth and through his death and resurrection passed over from death to life. From a Christian perspective, the true aliens are not those who lack political documentation but those who have so disconnected themselves from the needs of their neighbor in need that they fail to see in the eyes of the stranger a mirror of themselves, an image of Christ and a call to human solidarity.

Notes

1. This article is drawn in part from an essay entitled "Dying to Live: Theology, Migration, and the Human Journey," *Reflections* (Fall 2008): 31–33.

2. http://www.unhcr.org/4a3b98706.html (accessed November 29, 2011).

3. Stephen Castles and Mark J. Miller, *The Age of Migration: International Population Movements in the Modern World* (London: Guilford Press, 2003).

4. Daniel G. Groody and Gioacchino Campese, eds., *A Promised Land, A Perilous Journey: Theological Perspectives on Migration* (Notre Dame, Ind.: University of Notre Dame Press, 2008).

5. Karl Barth, "The Doctrine of Reconciliation," *Church Dogmatics*, IV.1, trans. G. W. Bromiley, ed. G. W. Bromiley and T. F. Torrance (London: T & T Clark International, 1956/2004), 157–210.

13

Mission in the Global Context: Challenges and Opportunities

Dana L. Robert

The story of Christianity as a worldwide faith is being written before our eyes. As Professor Robert Schreiter has pointed out in his address, we have entered a new global era for mission mobilization. Given the amazing diversity among Christ's followers in the twenty-first century, what are the key challenges and opportunities for mission *ad gentes* today?

As a professor of mission in a United Methodist seminary, I believe that my best contribution to this discussion is to reflect upon mission *ad gentes* from a North American Protestant perspective. Mainline Protestant experience is unlike the Catholic experience because we traditionally do not have vowed religious communities as the backbone of our mission force. But we are experiencing similar transitions from the twentieth century's "age of mobilization." Our denominational mission boards are either downsizing or have already collapsed. Younger full-time missionaries are often of Asian, Latin American, or African origin, even though sent by mission structures based in North America.

Among the North American laity, globalization means that interest in mission has burst out of the traditional categories. It has moved beyond denominational structures into multiple shifting networks and alliances, parachurch groups that recruit through the Internet, and international NGOs. Because people are having personal religious experiences in a multitude of places (and often in multiple churches), they no longer necessarily channel their mission commitment through their current denomination or into lifetime vocations. On a grassroots level, global migration of believers from everywhere to everywhere and the proliferation of church-to-church partnerships have increased the commitment of ordinary Christians to global outreach—even though laity may lack the theological language of "mission." Global/local interactions crafted by the grassroots membership are pressing on church leadership. Bureaucratic denominational structures crafted in the mid-twentieth century are not flexible enough to keep up with rapidly changing contemporary realities.

And yet, despite the changing terrain for traditional denominational mission structures, North American Protestants are supporting more missionaries than at any time in U.S. history—an estimated 127,000.[1] What do all these changes mean for mission *ad gentes*?

Mission from a New Direction

Mission *ad gentes* is alive and well among evangelical Protestants worldwide, but today the mission force is streaming through megachurch and parachurch channels and is heavily mobilizing Asians, Africans, and Latin Americans.

The great European migration reversed itself in the mid-twentieth century: by the 1960s, emigration from Asia, Africa, and Latin America into Europe and North America had become more significant than the opposite. Mission *ad gentes* remains a high priority for majority-world evangelicals and Pentecostals on the move. The classic mission text, the "Great Commission," (Matt. 28:16–20) still functions today as a divine charter within a social context of migration. For example, in 2010 Brazilians sent thirty-four thousand foreign missionaries. The number of Korean missionaries today is estimated upward from twenty thousand, and Koreans send a larger percentage of missionaries to the "unreached" than do North Americans.[2] Korean and Chinese evangelicals share the vision of a "Back to Jerusalem" movement, whereby they seek to travel the Silk Road westward and evangelize in the ancient holy land.[3] Nigerian evangelicals have declared support for *Vision 2015*, with its goal of sending fifty thousand missionaries *ad gentes* within fifteen years.[4] Many majority world missionaries prioritize work among Muslims, including holding large strategy meetings at which theological and cultural issues around Muslim Based Believers (MBBs) are explored.

These examples underscore the importance of recognizing that even if the Roman Catholic Church and the older Western denominations abandon the mission *ad gentes* in favor of mission practices that downplay conversion, there are thousands of majority world

Christians who are mobilizing to fill the gap. One of the goals of today's mission *ad gentes* is to convert secularized Westerners who no longer believe in religion. In the United States today, "none" is the second largest religious group. If historic denominations stop paying attention to the mission *ad gentes*, they will soon find themselves outnumbered by vigorous new movements, some of which deny that Roman Catholics and mainline Protestants are saved.

The contemporary migratory patterns endemic to globalization are creating new interest in the Great Commission on the part of Asian, African, and Latin American Christians. One of the centennial anniversary meetings for the World Missionary Conference of 1910 was held in Tokyo. Mission *ad gentes* held center stage, as the heads of hundreds of Asian mission societies discussed their strategies for world evangelization. Since the Tokyo 2010 meeting, evangelical Asian mission societies have launched the Global Great Commission Network to disciple all peoples "in our generation."[5] As new churches proliferate, so do competition and the potential for inter-Christian conflict.

The Meaning of Mission in the Twenty-First Century

Among ordinary Christians, interest in outreach and service is widespread. But laypeople are struggling with how to define mission theologically for the twenty-first century. Fr. Steve Judd is right on target here when he comments that finding a vocabulary to translate mission across parishes is one of our biggest challenges today. For both Catholics and Protestants, mission formation must take center stage: our people in mainline churches have lost the old familiar language of mission, but not the desire for it. Thus mission leaders need to build bridges from where people are toward a full-blown concept of mission as boundary crossing for the sake of witnessing to the Gospel and movement toward the reign of God.

I faced this reality in my own denomination by writing a mission study for United Methodist laypeople that has sold fourteen thousand copies. The approach I took in the study was to start with the contemporary context and help people see that many of the good things they are already doing can be framed theologically as mission and that the laity can claim their own apostolic identities as part of what it means to be a follower of Christ.[6] I realize that the issues in Catholicism are somewhat different, in that apostolic vocations have traditionally been seen as a special responsibility of religious communities. But the lay upsurge is increasingly important in Catholic as well as Protestant parishes. Perhaps one of the most important roles for experienced Catholic missioners today is to focus anew on parish-level lay mission formation. As do mainline Protestants, Catholics need to build a new generation of missioners from the ground up. Renewed commitment to the mission *ad gentes* will burst forth with the rebuilding of mission theology and vocabulary among the laity.

The openness of ordinary Americans to missional issues can be demonstrated by the following statistics from Robert Wuthnow's book *Boundless Faith:*

◆ 81 percent of Americans are concerned about human rights issues (e.g., human trafficking, religious freedom, HIV/AIDS, women. and children)

◆ 68 percent are interested in relief and development (fighting poverty— including microlending, disaster relief, medical clinics)

◆ 29 percent of churches support refugees

◆ 23 percent of churches hold meetings on peace issues.[7]

Western mission leaders need to help people link these popular commitments with the theological language and deep missional spiritualities within Christian tradition.

The Importance of Relational Mission

A chief motive for mission among young people in the West today is the desire to build relationships across boundaries—not necessarily to spread doctrine, or to save people, or even to help others. Relational mission, including hospitality, is essential in the twenty-first century. For many American youth of today, globalization has normalized the idea of cross-cultural movement, travel, and communication. Thus young people often shape their understanding of mission through deep desires for relationships with the "other." Often these relationships begin with short-term mission trips. In 2005, an estimated 1.6 million U.S. American adults went on short-term mission trips.[8] This figure does not include the many youth who go on such trips or are involved with cross-cultural activities within their own parishes. I often ask the students in my introductory mission class whether they have gone on a short-term mission trip. At least half the class raises its hand. And then when I ask how many felt called to seminary through such trips, many leave their hands up. For the youth of the early twenty-first century, the short-term mission trip has become as important in spiritual formation as camping ministry was to the baby boomer generation.

The rediscovery of "radical hospitality" is foundational for relational mission today. Hospitality is an often overlooked, hidden dimension of relational mission. Henri Nouwen called the movement from hostility to hospitality as creating "a free space where the stranger can enter and become a friend instead of an enemy."[9] Hospitality proclaims God's love to all and crosses bridges of difference. Without it, Christian community does not exist.

Through hospitality, commitment to mission *ad gentes* is being rediscovered. Because of the mobility of migrants in the age of globalization, local Churches in North America have opportunities for cross-cultural mission relationships without even leaving their neighborhoods. On average, 13 percent of Americans move every year. The vitality of the local parish requires welcoming those who move into the community. Often the commitment to mission of the immigrants themselves can reenergize the older North American congregation that partners with an immigrant church.

Paradoxically, another essential aspect of relational mission in the age of globalization is the gift of staying in place and refusing the temptation to be a globe trotter who lacks commitment to real people in a particular location. Being sent in mission is not the same thing as aimlessly wandering the globe, seeking one's own spiritual enlightenment. Rather, being sent often calls us to seek the lowest place, in solidarity with people who are either forced to move against their will (such as refugees or the jobless) or who lack the luxury of free movement (including the poor, slave laborers).

In her remarks, Sister Janice McLaughlin spoke of the Maryknoll Sisters who gave their lives to the people of Sudan and of those who lived and died in Japanese internment camps on American soil during World War II. Even though their churches and community were destroyed, after the war Japanese Catholics did not forget the loyalty of the Sisters during their incarceration. The Sisters' ministry of remaining in one place, of giving and receiving the hospitality of the communities they went to serve, was the beginning point of authentic mission. The virtue of staying in place is being rediscovered by young people in the movement called the "New Monasticism," which consists of intentional communities of young Christians who move into the inner city or live communally among the poor.[10] Without long-term commitments to particular groups of people, mission *ad gentes* will not succeed.

For relational mission, the experience of the Maryknollers is invaluable as a guide and model for future generations of missioners. As Fr. Gustavo Gutiérrez has noted in his brief remarks, the important thing to him about Maryknollers is that they became his friends. Being a friend, being in relationship, requires cultivating the discipline of a long-term commitment to others unlike ourselves. Stanley Skreslet points out that the Gospel of John shows us a Jesus whose ministry flowed through personal relationships.[11] Jesus prayed, "As you, Father, are in me and I am in you, may they also be in us, so that the world may believe that you have sent me" (John 17:21). And as Jesus said in John 15:13, "Greater love has no one than this, than to lay down one's life for his friends." Along with these wonderful texts I think we should take seriously John 1:38–39 as a guide for the missional discipline of remaining in place, in solidarity with others: "Rabbi, where are you staying? He said to them, 'Come and see.' They came and saw where he was staying, and remained with him that day."

Mission Must Include Christian Unity

The worldwide spread of Christianity requires that mission be integral to unity. Today a widespread desire for faithful mission is leading the way toward new possibilities of Christian unity. In the 1980s, convergence grew around basic issues of mission theology among Catholics, mainline Protestants, and Evangelicals.[12] This momentum culminated in 2010, the centennial of the World Missionary Conference at Edinburgh. Although the original Edinburgh 1910 conference had involved only Protestants, the hundredth anniversary of the meeting inspired mission leaders around the world to reflect upon the meaning of mission for the twenty-first century. The energy behind meetings in Aarhus, Tokyo, Edinburgh, Cape Town, Boston, and elsewhere demonstrated the tremendous vitality of multicultural, multiecclesial Christianity in the early twenty-first century. The 2010 meetings also revealed the deep longing to witness to Christ that characterizes believers from all continents.

In June of 2011, the Pontifical Council for Interreligious Dialogue (PCID), the World Council of Churches (WCC), and the World Evangelical Alliance (WEA) issued their first common agreement, called "Christian Witness in a Multi-Religious World."[13] Despite ongoing theological differences, the combined weight of these developments, including acceptance of the right to change one's religious affiliation, implies a new willingness to accept the validity of each other's faith. Thus at a formal level, a shared commitment to witness provides a common ground for bridging differences.

Even as we are meeting here in Chicago, the second Global Christian Forum (GCF) is convening in Manado, Indonesia.[14] This gathering includes the full range of Christian denominations, communions, and traditions worldwide: Catholic, Orthodox, Protestant, Pentecostal, Evangelical, and Indigenous churches. The premise of the GCF process is to build a respectful Christian community through listening to each others' experiences of Jesus Christ. Because affirmation of the mission *ad gentes* is thriving among newer churches worldwide, including record numbers of missionaries being sent by Brazilians, Koreans, Nigerians and others, work for ecumenism is essential. The process behind the GCF is extremely important because of the competitive anarchy that often takes place among Christian groups, especially where Christianity is expanding. The GCF approach begins with relationships, not with doctrine or even service as the touchstone for Christian cooperation.[15]

At the end of the day, shared commitment to mission *ad gentes* reminds us that "World Christianity" is a theological vision that guides us toward God's reign, in continuous expanding and deepening fellowship across human boundaries. The plurality of Christian churches is creating global networks. To be a worldwide church means reaching across geography and ethnicity. It also means connecting across the generations to the martyrs and saints, through the living, and onward to the blessed future when believers will gather before the throne of the lamb, lifting their voices in celebration.[16]

Notes

1. Todd Johnson, Kenneth Ross, and Sandra S. K. Lee, eds., *The Atlas of Global Christianity, 1910–2010* (Edinburgh: Edinburgh University Press, 2010), 282.

2. Ibid., 271, 279.

3. Tobias Brandner, "Mission, Millennium, and Politics: A Continuation of the History of Salvation—from the East," *Missiology* 37, no. 3 (July 2009): 317–32.

4. Sang-Bok David Kim, "Trends and Changes in World Christianity," see online Global Christian Forum, http://globalchristianforum.org/manado_updates/trends_in%20worldchristianity_sangbokdavidkim.php (accessed February 28, 2012).

5. http://www.tokyo2010.org/news.htm.

6. See Dana L. Robert, *Joy to the World! Mission in the Age of Global Christianity* (New York: Women's Division, United Methodist Church, 2010).

7. Robert Wuthnow, *Boundless Faith: The Global Outreach of American Churches* (Berkeley: University of California Press, 2009).

8. Ibid., 170.

9. Henri Nouwen, *Reaching Out* (New York: Bantam Dell, 1986), 71.

10. On the New Monasticism, see Jonathan Wilson-Hartgrove, *New Monasticism: What It Has to Say to Today's Church* (Grand Rapids: Brazos Press, 2008).

11. Stanley H. Skreslet, *Picturing Christian Witness: New Testament Images of Disciples in Mission* (Grand Rapids: William B. Eerdmans, 2006).

12. The Lausanne Movement, "The Lausanne Covenant," published in 1974,http://www.lausanne.org/en/documents/lausanne-covenant.html (accessed on February 28, 2012); World Council of Churches, "Mission and Evangelism, an Ecumenical Affirmation," published in 1982, now available in *You Are the Light of the World: Statements on Mission by the World Council of Churches, 1980–2005* (Geneva: WCC Publications, 2005); John Paul II, *Redemptoris Missio*, encyclical letter on the permanent validity of the Catholic Church's missionary mandate, Vatican website, July 12, 1990, http://www.vatican.va/holy_father/john_paul_ii/encyclicals/documents/hf_jp-ii_enc_07121990_redemptoris-missio_en.html (accessed February 28, 2012).

13. World Council of Churches, Pontifical Council for Interreligious Dialogue, and World Evangelical Alliance, "Christian Witness in a Multi-religious World: Recommendations for Conduct," June 28, 2011, http://www.worldevangelicals.org/pdf/1106Christian_Witness_in_a_Multi-Religious_World.pdf (accessed on February 28, 2012).

14. I have come straight from Manado to the Maryknoll celebration here in Chicago.

15. "About Us," Global Christian Forum, http://www.globalchristianforum.org/ (accessed February 28, 2012).

16. Cf. Revelation 7:9–12.

14

Being Christian under Communist-Socialist Regimes

Peter C. Phan

It is one of history's ironic twists that after the fall of the Berlin Wall, communism, a political and economic system that originated in the West, now survives, at least officially, only in the East (that is, excluding Cuba), and more specifically, in mainland China, Myanmar (Burma), North Korea, and Vietnam. Furthermore, its future as a state-controlled economic system is currently under severe threat as China and Vietnam have become members of the World Trade Organization and increasingly adopt the free-market economy (Deng Xiaoping famously declared: "Poverty is not socialism. To get rich is glorious."), while Myanmar and North Korea are languishing under widespread destitution and brutal military dictatorship. Nonetheless, any prediction of the imminent demise of communism and its socialist economic system in Asia will prove vastly premature since the Communist Party in China as well as Vietnam still manages to hold on to power in spite of frequent and insistent, both internal and external, challenges to its monopoly.

Christianity in Asian Communist-Socialist Regimes

Meanwhile Christianity in Asia continues to cope with the Communist-Socialist regimes of its host countries. Fortunately, by now after over half a century of coexistence with communism in the four above-mentioned countries, Christianity has developed a modus vivendi that, while not ideal, has permitted the Christian churches not only to survive but also to expand beyond all expectations. Being a Christian under a Communist-Socialist regime no doubt has its peculiar challenges and opportunities, and to understand them it would be neces-

106

sary to survey the current situation of Christianity in each of these four Asian countries.

North Korea

Christianity, or more precisely, Roman Catholicism, was introduced to Korea in 1784, not by foreign missionaries but by a layman, Peter Yi Sŏnghun (Ri Syeng Houn or Seng-Hoon Lee), who after his baptism in Beijing returned to his country to start a church. The new religion spread rapidly; by 1857 it had around fifteen thousand members. Perceived to be a threat to Confucian social stability (especially due to the Catholic Church's prohibition of ancestor veneration), Buddhist beliefs and practices, and national sovereignty, it was soon subjected to severe persecutions, especially in 1839, 1846, and 1866. About eight thousand Catholics were killed. (In 1984 Pope John Paul II canonized 103 martyrs, the most famous among whom is Andrew Kim Tae-gon, decapitated in 1846.) The Protestant churches (especially Presbyterian, Methodist, and Baptist) started evangelism in Korea in 1885 and, like the Roman Catholic Church, enjoyed spectacular growth, especially through revival movements, in particular in P'yŏngyang, the current capital of North Korea.

The history of Korean Christianity has been closely tied to the nation's political fortunes. After the five-century-long rule of the Yi (Joseon) dynasty (1392–1910), Korea was occupied for thirty-five years by Japan (1910–45), which imposed Shintoism on Koreans as the national religion and systematically persecuted the Christian churches. After the Second World War, the Korean peninsula was provisionally divided along the thirty-eighth parallel by mutual agreement between the United States and the U.S.S.R. Reunification of the country was to be decided in an election in 1948, but it was never held. In that year the South was formed into the Republic of Korea (ROK) under President Syngman Rhee (1875–1965), and the North into the Democratic People's Republic of Korea (DPRK) under Kim Il Sung (1912–94). During the Korean War (1950–53) Christians were again persecuted, this time by the Communist-led DPRK, with hundreds of Christian leaders killed and churches destroyed or confiscated.

While the Christian churches have been languishing in North Korea from the 1950s until today, Christianity, both Catholic and

Protestant, in the Republic of Korea (South Korea, ROK) experienced a phenomenal expansion in both number and influence in the fields of education, health care, and social work. Today in South Korea Christianity is a major religion, along with Buddhism, Confucianism, and Shamanism. According to the 2005 census, 29.2 percent of the South Korean population is Christian, with Protestantism at roughly 20 percent and Roman Catholicism at 10 percent.

Korean Protestantism is grouped into two organizations, the liberal Korea National Council of Churches and the conservative Christian Council of Korea. In addition to mainline Protestant churches, Evangelicals have had a spectacular rise, as witnessed by the Yoido Full Gospel Church, founded by David Yonggi Cho and his mother-in-law Choi Ja-Shil, now the largest Protestant congregation in the world, with almost a million members. Thanks to South Korea's open society, information on South Korean Christianity is readily available. Our focus here is, however, not on South Korean Christianity but on North Korean Christianity. Yet, ironically, as will be explained shortly, the issue of Christian identity in the Communist DPRK cannot be broached apart from the activities of the Christian churches in the capitalist ROK.

One of the disastrous results of the Korean War was mass migration from the North to the South, causing the separation of over ten million families and the decimation of Christianity in the North. Prior to the war, two-thirds of Korean Christians lived in the North, most of whom fled to the South to escape communism. Since 1945 North Korea's political leadership has adopted the militant atheism of Stalinist communism and aggressively repressed all religious practices and organizations, including Christianity. In the 1960s, in an attempt to achieve self-reliance (*juche*), North Korea moved away from the Soviet and Chinese spheres of influence. With the collapse of the Soviet Union and the Communist regimes in Eastern Europe in 1989, however, Korea suffered severe economic setbacks. Toward the end of his life Kim Il Sung sought to open a dialogue with South Korea. Unfortunately, the prospect of the reunification of the Korean peninsula by peaceful means was dashed with his death in 1994. In 1998 the president of South Korea, Kim Dae Jung, initiated the "Sunshine Policy" toward the North. In 2000 he visited its capital, P'yŏngyang, and met

with its president, Kim Jong Il. In recent years, however, political relations between North Korea and the outside world have badly deterio-
rated due to its attempt at developing nuclear weaponry.

Until recently nothing much was known about Christianity in the
isolationist DPRK, which gave new meaning to the old description of
Korea as "The Hermit Kingdom." In 1945 the Roman Catholic Church
had three dioceses in the North. After the 1953 emigration, there were
only some twenty-five thousand Catholics left. Since the 1980s visits by
Roman Catholic authorities, from both the Vatican and South Korea,
were permitted, and in 1988 a church was erected in P'yŏngyang,
where masses are regularly celebrated by visiting South Korean clergy.
As for the Protestants, in 1946 the Communist government created the
Korean Christian Federation (KCF) into which all Protestant denominations were grouped. The KCF claims a membership of a hundred
thousand, though the actual number is believed to be much lower,
existing mostly in house churches. In 1972 the KCF was permitted to
reconstitute its seminary (P'yŏngyang Theological Seminary) and in
1988 and 1992 to build two churches in P'yŏngyang. In 1974 the KCF
approached the World Council of Churches with an inquiry about the
possibility of membership, and in 1976 it joined the Christian Peace
Conference. In early 1985 the National Council of the Churches of
Christ in the USA sent a delegation of representatives to North Korea.
The following year, the leaders of the KCF and the National Council of
Churches in Korea (NCCK) met together for the first time since 1945 at
a conference on peace in Glion, Switzerland. They met again in 1990,
1995, and 1996. Subsequently, the KCF and the NCCK met in North
Korea itself and laid plans for national reunification. International
humanitarian aid to North Korean flood victims in the 1990s was partially channeled through the KCF, a remarkable measure of recognition of North Korean Christianity by the government.

Burma/Myanmar

Known as Burma until 1989, this country between South and South-
east Asia on the Bay of Bengal was colonized by Britain between 1824
and 1885 and occupied by Japan during World War II. It achieved
independence in 1948, and free elections were held in 1960. In the
1990 national elections the opposition party (the National League for

Democracy), led by Aung San Suu Ky (later a Nobel Peace Prize win-
ner), won a decisive victory. However the ruling military junta refused
to hand over power and placed Aung San Suu Ky under arrest. Though
rich in natural resources, due to the greed and mismanagement of the
military rulers, Myanmar (together with North Korea) is now one of
the world's poorest countries.

Roman Catholicism arrived in Myanmar in 1554 with Portuguese
Franciscan missionaries, later joined by other religious societies such
as the Paris Foreign Missions and the Milan Foreign Missions. Currently there are about half a million Catholics, especially among the
ethnic groups such as the Chins, Kachins, Karens, and Shans. There
are twenty-three dioceses, with three archdioceses, constituting the
Episcopal Conference of Burma.

Protestantism arrived in Myanmar in 1812 with Adoniram and
Ann Judson of the American Baptist Mission. The Anglican Church
came on the heels of British colonization, and the Anglican Church
of Burma was founded in 1877. Later, other denominations arrived,
including the Assemblies of God, Church of Christ, Methodists, and
Presbyterians. The Protestant churches form the Burma Council of
Churches, which is also a member of the Christian Conference of Asia.

As with North Korean Christianity, Myanmar Christianity's fortunes have been tied with the country's political vicissitudes. After
independence in 1948, the government of U Nu (1948–58, 1960–62)
established Buddhism as the state religion, creating disadvantages for
the Christian tribal groups. The government of Ne Win (1958–60 and
1962–88) abolished such privileged status for Buddhism and granted
equal rights to all religions. However, Ne Win (1910–2002), who had
founded the Burma Socialist Program Party, ruled Burma as a one-
party state. Furthermore, he established the "Burmese Way to Socialism," which included Marxist, anti-Western, Socialist tendencies and
concentration of power in the military. As a result, all the churches'
educational, medical, and social institutions were nationalized and
foreign missionaries expelled. This situation forced the local Christian
churches to learn how to survive on their own, without external personnel and financial assistance.

Vietnam

Along with the Philippines, South Korea, and East Timor, the Socialist Republic of Vietnam has a significant Christian presence. The Vietnamese Catholic Church currently has twenty-six dioceses and makes up about 7 percent of the population of eighty million. The Jesuits, the most celebrated among whom was Alexandre de Rhodes (1593–1660), began missions in Vietnam at the beginning of the seventeenth century under the Portuguese *padroado* (patronage). Vietnam, then known as Annam, was divided into two parts, Tonkin (the North or "Exterior Part") and Cochinchina (the South or "Interior Part"), the former ruled by the Trinh family and the latter by the Nguyen family. Rivalry and wars between the North and the South vastly complicated the work of missionaries, who were suspected of being spies by both sides. Furthermore, the prohibition of the cult of the ancestors (the so-called Chinese Rites Controversy) made Christianity liable to the charge of being inimical to Vietnam's cultural and religious traditions. These obstacles notwithstanding, by the middle of the seventeenth century the Catholic Church had grown substantially, but its expansion was drastically reduced by persecutions, particularly after France's colonization of Vietnam in the mid-nineteenth century. About 130,000 Catholics were killed from the middle of the seventeenth century to the end of the nineteenth century. (In 1988, Pope John Paul II canonized 117 of them, 96 of whom were Vietnamese.)

As regards Christians under a Vietnamese Communist-Socialist regime, of great interest are the periods between 1954 and 1975 for the Roman Catholic Church in the Communist North (then known as Democratic Republic of Vietnam) and between 1976 till today for Christianity as a whole in the Socialist Republic of Vietnam (after the reunification of the North and the South, the latter known before 1975 as the Republic of Vietnam).

The armed struggle for independence from France, led principally by Ho Chi Minh, ended with the Geneva Accords (July 21, 1954), which temporarily partitioned the country into two zones, with the seventeenth parallel as "the provisional military demarcation line." According to the accords, the North was to be ruled by the Communist Viet Minh and the pro-Western South by Emperor Bao Dai until national elections, stipulated for 1956, that would establish a unified government. Meanwhile, within three hundred days from the signature of the accords, people of each zone could move north or south, according to their political preferences. About one million northerners, of whom about half a million were Catholics, moved south, whereas about fifty-two thousand southerners moved north. This migration would prove to be a disaster for Christianity in the North, as had been the case with North Korean Christianity about a decade earlier.

The stipulated elections, opposed by the Catholic leader Ngo Dinh Diem and the United States, were never held, and in October 1955 Diem held a referendum on the future of the State of Vietnam; as a result he became president of the newly proclaimed anti-Communist Republic of Vietnam. Soon, with the authorization and support of the Communist-led Democratic Republic of Vietnam, insurgency against the Diem regime began under the banner of the National Liberation Front, which the Diem government sought to deride by calling it "Viet Cong" (Vietnamese Communists). The ensuing war between the North and the South was part of the Cold War, with the former assisted by the People's Republic of China and the Soviet Union, and the latter by the United States. The twenty-year war ended with the victory of the Communist North on April 30, 1975, and the country was reunified the following year as the Socialist Republic of Vietnam. Since then Christianity, both Roman Catholic and Protestant, began the hard task of coexisting with the Communist-Socialist government.

As mentioned above, during the 1954 migration two-thirds of Catholics in the North fled south with their clergy, thereby decimating the Catholic Church in the North. Persecuted by the Communist government, its institutions confiscated, and the remaining clergy practically under house arrest, the Church limited itself to sacramental celebrations and popular devotions. The rabid anti-Communist ideology of the Roman Catholic Church at the time prevented any form of collaboration between the Vietnamese Church and the government. Cut off from other Catholic communities, the northern Church was for all practical purposes moribund. Ironically, its condition was significantly ameliorated after the Communist North's victory over the South and the reunification of the country in a single state. The Vietnamese Catholic Church began functioning as one Church, with a single episcopal conference. Regular contacts between the two parts of the Church were now possible (some southern clerics were even appointed bishops for the northern Church), and the northern Church was able to establish communications with other centers of the Roman Catholic Church, especially the Vatican. These changes enabled the northern Church to adopt the ecclesial reforms begun since the Second Vatican Council (1962–65).

However, as a whole, Vietnamese Christianity has faced a different set of challenges under the Socialist Republic of Vietnam since 1975. Flushed with an unexpectedly quick and easy victory over the South, the Communist North reunified the country and installed the Vietnamese Communist Party (VCP) as the only legal organization with the power to decide all policies and activities, including religious ones, of the state. Soon after, the VCP adopted the Socialist model of development, with state control of the major sectors of the economy, bringing the country to the brink of economic disaster. The meltdown in the 1980s forced the government to initiate a program called *Doi Moi* (renovation), introducing a "socialist-oriented market system," thanks to which the country enjoyed an unprecedented economic boom since the 2000s.

As in North Korea and Burma, the fortunes of Vietnamese Christianity have been deeply entwined with the country's political upheavals. Mention has already been made of the near-destruction of the northern Catholic Church during 1954–75. Furthermore, in 1975, after the Communist victory, hundreds of thousands of Catholics with a great number of clergy emigrated abroad, once more reducing the presence of the Catholic Church in Vietnam. Meanwhile, the VCP applied the same oppressive measures against Christianity in the South that it had in the North: all church-owned institutions were abolished or confiscated, religious activities severely limited, priestly ordinations and religious vocations regulated, and episcopal appointments controlled.

Since the *Doi Moi* reform, however, the government began relaxing its control of religious affairs, though with notorious relapses into repression. With regard to the Catholic Church, steps have been taken by the government toward establishing diplomatic relations with the Holy See. The 1992 Constitution of the Socialist Republic of Vietnam, amended in 2001, recognizes "the right to belief and religion" and the equality of all religions before the law. In spite of these significant improvements, the road toward full religious freedom and total noninterference in the Church's internal matters remains long and arduous.

China

Along with India, Christianity in China can boast an ancient history. In 635 a group of Christians of the Church of the East (or Assyrian, sometimes misnamed as "Nestorians") came to the Middle Kingdom under the Tang dynasty, and their communities enjoyed imperial favors and flourished (except under the empress Wu Zong since 845) until the Tang's fall at the beginning of the tenth century. The Catholic Church came with the Franciscans in the thirteenth century when China was ruled by the Mongols (the Yuan dynasty), and in spite of a favorable reception by various khans and some success at conversion (there were some thirty thousand Christians), Christianity faded after the Yuan's collapse in 1368. The Catholic Church returned in the sixteenth century during the Ming dynasty (1368–1644), especially with the Jesuits, who were followed by other religious societies, notably the Dominicans, Franciscans, Augustinians, and the Society of Foreign Missions of Paris. The Church flourished during the following Qing dynasty (1644–1911) until its growth was arrested by the Chinese Rites Controversy (begun in 1643), after the rituals of ancestor veneration were proscribed by Popes Clement XI (1715) and Benedict XIV (1742). This debacle was worsened by colonialist interventions in China (the Opium War in 1840). In 1842 the Treaty of Nanking brought the Catholic missions into a French "protectorate" and had the unfortunate effect of isolating Chinese Catholics from their fellow countrymen. Antiforeign and anti-Christian sentiments culminated in the Boxer Rebellion (1900) in which nearly thirty thousand Catholics were killed. (In 2000 Pope John Paul II canonized 120 Chinese martyrs.)

In terms of our theme, the most fateful event for Chinese Christianity is the victory of the Communist Party over the Nationalist Party, the Kuomintang, and the establishment of the People's Republic of China under Mao Zedong on October 1, 1949. The new country adopted atheistic materialism as its ideology and aimed at controlling all religions to achieve its Socialist goals. To achieve these objectives the Communist government promoted the so-called Three-Self Movement for Chinese Christianity (self-governance, self-support, and self-propagation), a program already put forward by the Protestant churches in 1922. When Protestantism arrived in China in the nineteenth century, its missions were operated mostly along denominational lines. In 1954, to rally the Protestant churches in a fight against Western imperialism and to foster patriotism, the Communist Party sought to abolish denominationalism and established the Three-Self Patriotic Movement (TSPM) to bring all the Chinese Protestant churches under its control. In the same year it also founded the China Christian Conference (CCC) as an ecclesiastical organization.

The same strategy was applied to the Catholic Church. In 1957 the Chinese Catholic Patriotic Association (CCPA) was officially established. The Communist anti-Christian policies reached their peak during the Cultural Revolution launched by Mao Zedong (1966–76), with all places of worship closed and religious leaders sent to labor camps.

Since the 1980s, as a consequence of Deng Xiaoping's policy of economic reform and modernization, there has been a more open attitude toward Christianity. Two changes deserve notice. First, both the Catholic Church and the Protestant churches were permitted a wider range of activities. In 1982 and 1983 Catholic seminaries were opened in Shanghai and Beijing respectively. In 1985 the Protestants organized the Amity Foundation to promote contacts with international Christian institutions. There has also been a spectacular rise of independent house churches, mostly among Protestants, with large memberships in both rural and urban areas. These house churches do not want to have anything to do with the TSPM and refuse official registration with the Religious Affairs Bureau. By and large these house churches are Pentecostal/Charismatic in orientation, emphasizing personal salvation and charismatic gifts such as *glossolalia*, prophecy, and healing. With the return of Hong Kong (1997) and Macau (1999) to China within the framework of "one country, two systems," the issue of religious freedom, and consequently of the role of Christianity, within the People's Republic of China is bound to arise for further discussion and action.

Being a Christian under
Communist-Socialist Regimes

As is clear from this historical overview, it is not impossible to remain a Christian under Communist-Socialist regimes. Indeed, in spite of severe and repeated persecutions and oppression, Christianity in all its branches, Catholic, Protestant, and to lesser extent Orthodox, has not only survived (for example, in North Korea and Vietnam) but also prospered in some places such as China and Myanmar—and spectacularly so. Curiously, given the precipitous decline of Christianity in many capitalist and democratic countries and in formerly Communist and now capitalist ones, it may be asked whether socialism and communism are not blessings in disguise for Christianity. Tertullian's dictum about the blood of martyrs being the seed of Christians comes to mind.

This of course does not mean that socialism and communism are to be preferred to other political and economic systems or that they do not present difficult challenges to being Christian in the four Asian countries under discussion. Different as they are for each country, these challenges can be grouped in clusters. The first challenge concerns the relationship between Christianity and the state. In all four countries, Christianity was and to a certain extent still is perceived as a Western religion that has colluded with Western colonialism and is associated with foreign powers. This is particularly true of Roman Catholicism, which is seen as identical with the Vatican City State (whose nature as a sovereign state distinct from the Holy See is recognized under international law). No doubt the colonialist legacy remains heavy and scandalous baggage for Asian Christians; they must honestly acknowledge this, even if historically Christian missions have made and continue to make significant contributions to their countries, especially in the fields of education, health care, and social welfare. As for Roman Catholics, they must demonstrate by word and deed that their membership in the Catholic Church does not make them citizens of the Vatican City State and that patriotism—though not nationalism and loyalty to a particular political party—is a fundamental Christian duty.

The second challenge to Christians under Communist regimes concerns religious freedom. Christians must continue to press their governments for religious freedom as an inalienable human right and not a special favor to be secured through under-the-table deals or through diplomatic negotiations between their governments and the Holy See in the case of Roman Catholics. Furthermore, this struggle for religious freedom must be carried out on behalf of all believers and not just for Christians. It should be pursued in concert with the followers of other religions, in particular Buddhism, as well as with nonbelievers, since religious freedom is also their concern.

The Communist Party's current attempt at controlling religion, especially Christianity, through various "organizational weapons" and by means of the Three-Self Movement seems to be motivated not so much by atheistic-Marxist-Leninist-Maoist ideology or a concern for national independence as by the desire to perpetuate its monopoly on power with all its attendant privileges. This is true especially of China, North Korea, and Vietnam. Such total control of religion, however, requires impossible political acrobatic skills. On the one hand, in order to achieve a minimum level of economic well-being for all citizens, the Communist Party in China as well as in Vietnam have found it necessary, especially since the 1980s, to introduce economic reform as they began trade with the capitalist world, particularly with the United States.

On the other hand, such economic liberalization inevitably brings in its wake widespread demands for democracy and religious freedom (witness the June 1989 Fourth Pro-Democracy Movement in the Tiananmen Square). The Communist leaders are well aware of this dilemma. They want economic reform without loosening their political monopoly. In this context Christians should remind government officials, especially in China and Vietnam, that internal Church matters such as the appointment of bishops do not pose a threat to the well-being of the Communist Party and the nation, as the last fifty years have convincingly shown. Government control of and interference in these matters is arguably based on unfounded fear and is unnecessary and harmful to the common good.

The third challenge is internal, albeit originally caused by the Communist governments' religious policies, and that is the need for reconciliation between the various groups and divisions in the Church itself. This may take the form of patriotism vs. allegiance to a foreign power (the "patriotic church" and the "underground church") or competition among different Christian denominations (for example, between Catholics and Protestants), or theological differences (such as mainline Christianity vs. Pentecostals/Charismatics). It is incontro-vertible that these intraecclesial disputes have been exploited by the Communist governments. Fortunately, in recent times these divisions have been partially bridged through mutual recognition and collabo-ration, but much work remains to be done. Authentic and full Christian identity depends largely on the success of this ecumenical enterprise.

Within this context it would be helpful to ask whether the tradi-tional missionary method of propagating Christianity along denomi-national lines is still appropriate. Once again we may wonder whether the Communist policy of uniting all Protestant denominations under one umbrella organization, especially in North Korea, China, and Viet-nam, has not been a blessing in disguise for Christianity inasmuch as it has forced different Christian denominations and communities to work together, a "unity" now being torn apart by the rivalry between the "registered" and "unregistered" churches, surely a *skandalon* to the credibility of the Christian message itself.

Raising this question is of course not tantamount to committing oneself to pan- or postdenominationalism, but rather highlights, over against the general indifference if not skepticism toward church unity in the West in recent years, the urgency of ecumenical unity for Christian identity in Asia. Christian unity, it is to be noted, has become a burn-ing issue, especially in China, with the spectacular rise of Evangelicals and the so-called indigenous and independent churches (for exam-ple, the True Jesus Church, the Jesus Family, and the Little Flock) and innumerable house churches. These "unregistered" churches, whose membership likely will outstrip that of the "registered" churches, will remain as one of the greatest challenges to Christian identity in Asia in the foreseeable future.

A fourth issue concerns the role of Asian Christians outside China and North Korea for the Christian Churches of these countries. As has been pointed out above, Christians in South Korea have played an important role in the project of national reunification. Given the large number of Christians in Korea (some 30 percent of the pop-ulation) and their enormous influence, it is unlikely that national reunification will occur without the contribution of South Korean Christians. Similarly, Chinese Christians in Hong Kong, Taiwan, in the diaspora, and to a lesser degree in Macau, are equipped to play a key role in promoting a theologically educated and renewed Christianity in mainland China. Similarly, Christians in the South of Vietnam possess greater material, academic, and personnel resources than their fellow Christians in the North and could assist them. What is being advocated here is not old-style financial support and control by mission boards (for Protestants) or the Congregation for the Propagation of the Faith (for Catholics). The Three-Self Movement, whatever the Communist Party's exploitation of it, must remain the norm for Asian Christianity. Rather, what is being suggested is that the Christian churches that enjoy political freedom and economic prosperity have a particular responsibility toward their counterparts in North Korea, China, and Vietnam (and Myanmar for that matter). Indeed, being a Christian in Asia demands solidarity with the churches under the Communist-Socialist regimes.

A fifth challenge to Christian identity for Christians in the four Asian Communist countries as well as in Asia in general is the encounter with other religions. Mention has been made of the negative attitude of the Christian churches toward the practice of ancestor veneration in the past and its deleterious impact on Christian missions. Though there has been a remarkable change in the position of the Roman Catholic Church toward non-Christian religions, at least since the Second Vatican Council, interreligious dialogue is still in its infancy, especially in these four Communist countries. An adequate theology of religions remains to be developed that acknowledges the positive role of non-Christian religions for the spiritual well-being of their adherents beyond the so-called exclusivist, inclusivist, and pluralist categories made popular in recent decades. In Asia, more than anywhere else, being religious is being interreligious, and Christian identity cannot be formed apart from a sincere and humble dialogue with the believers of other faiths and within the reality of multiple religious belonging. This dialogue is not only theological but must involve a sharing of life, activities, and religious experiences.

The sixth, and perhaps the hardest, challenge to being Christian in Communist countries today is, ironically, the rapid encroaching of the market economy, especially in China and Vietnam, and the attendant rampant materialism and consumerism, especially among the young.

Communism as an ideology, though still spouted and propped up by the Communist Party, is fast becoming an empty shell; party leaders are quite cognizant of this state of affairs and are busy preserving their interests in an eventual postsocialist state. Today the greatest threat to Christianity in the Asian Socialist countries is not (or no longer) the oppressive religious policies of the Communist Party or the cultural "dictatorship of relativism" for that matter. Rather it is a complete indifference to Christianity as well as to any other religious way of life as the result of a relentless pursuit of wealth and all the pleasures it promises. Religious oppression produces faithful resistance, martyrdom sows seeds of conversion, and relativism at least still takes religion into account by declaring that all religions are equally effective. The threat to Christianity now comes from the newfound faith in the unbounded and unparalleled power of capitalism, whose sole creed is "Greed is good," as the panacea for all ills, the faith that swallows up all other faiths.

After half a century of coexistence with communism Christians have devised effective strategies for survival; when persecuted, they know how to resist and preserve the faith and have even found in communism a kindred quest for social justice. Now faced with the near universal dominance of capitalism, the Christian churches are at a loss of what to do to help their members, especially the young, resist the call of its sirens. It comes as no surprise that the so-called Prosperity Gospel has proved as attractive in Asian Communist countries as in the United States. Consequently, the most difficult challenge to being Christian in Asian Communist countries and in Asia as a whole may no longer be the suppression of religious freedom but a complete indifference to it.

Bibliography

Clark, A. D. *A History of the Church in Korea*. Seoul, 1971.

Fox, Thomas. *Pentecost in Asia: A New Way of Being Church*. Maryknoll, N.Y.: Orbis Books, 2002.

Leung, Beatrice, and William T. Liu. *The Chinese Catholic Church in Conflict: 1949–2001*. Boca Raton, Fla.: Universal Publishers, 2004.

Park, K. S. *Reconciliation-Reunification: The Ecumenical Approach to the Korean Peninsula*. Hong Kong: Christian Conference of Asia, 1998.

Phan, Peter C. "The Roman Catholic Church in the Socialist Republic of Vietnam, 1989–2005." In *Falling Walls: The Year 1989/1990 as a Turning Point in the History of World Christianity*, ed. Klaus Koschorke 243–57. Wiesbaden: Harrassowitz Verlag, 2009.

Tang, Edmond, and Jean-Paul Wiest, eds. *The Catholic Church in Modern China: Perspectives*. Maryknoll, N.Y.: Orbis Books, 1993.

Uhalley, Stephen, and Xiaoxin Wu, eds. *China and Christianity: Burdened Past, Hopeful Future*. Armonk, N.Y.: M. E. Sharpe, 2001.

Wickeri, Philip L. *Reconstructing Christianity in China: K. H. Ting and the Chinese Church*. Maryknoll, N.Y.: Orbis Books, 2007.

Part III

Pivotal Areas
for Mission Today

15

Mission as Proclamation and Dialogue

Roger Schroeder, SVD

The centennial of the Maryknoll Society is an opportunity for remembering the past and moving into the future. Both actions revolve around the celebration and challenge of the "Gift of Mission," not just for Maryknoll, but for all Christians, whose baptism by nature is a call to receive and share that gift of God's mission. While this call to mission is *constant*, the theory and practice of mission have always been shaped by particular *contexts* throughout history. The Second Vatican Council was a breakthrough moment for the Catholic Church as it embraced its fundamental missionary nature and engaged the contexts of our world and all creation today. Among other things, the Council had a much more positive appreciation of all religions, which led eventually to the inclusion of interreligious dialogue as a necessary component of mission. While this has opened the door for mutual respect and collaboration, others wonder if it has diluted the essential dimension of mission to proclaim the Gospel and invite people to become members of the Church. We shall address this challenging issue of mission as *both proclamation and dialogue.*

Before Vatican II, the primary motivation for mission was "ransoming 'pagan' babies" and establishing the visible Church, which primarily saw itself as a "perfect" society in opposition to an evil world. During the Council, the Church reaffirmed that God's omnipotent grace and presence extended beyond the Church, and the Church needed to recognize and engage these "signs of the times" (*Gaudium et Spes* 4). The understanding of mission shifted from bringing God to "pagans" and the world, to meeting God already present in human experience, culture, Christian churches/denominations, and all religions. After Vatican II, the understanding and practice of mission expanded, so that twenty-five years later Pope John Paul II described it as a "single, but complex reality" (*Redemptoris Missio* 41). Mission can be defined today as "proclaiming, serving, and witnessing to God's reign of love, salvation, and justice."[1]

Stephen Bevans and I have proposed that mission in general and every aspect of it can be understood and practiced as "prophetic dialogue."[2] Just as the Trinitarian God is dialogical in Godself and is present as the *missio Dei* in all creation, so the Church needs to learn from and be in *dialogue* with these unfathomable riches of God. Just as God "humbled" Godself in the incarnation, so the Church needs to do mission not out of superiority, but in humility and vulnerability.[3] "Each member of the faithful and all Christian Communities are called to practice dialogue" (RM 57).

An image of this dimension is found in the well-known phrase of Max Warren—taking off one's shoes before approaching another, lest one risks trampling upon where God is already present.[4] At the same time, mission is *prophetic* in two senses. It is a denunciation of or "speaking against" (with or without words) that which is contrary to God's reign and an annunciation of or "speaking forth" (with or without words) the message of God's reign, particularly in and through Jesus Christ.[5] As an image, one knows that every garden (culture, ecclesial body, religious institution, community, and so on) is in need of weeding. Similar to the term of "prophetic dialogue," South African missiologist David Bosch spoke in terms of "bold humility": "It is . . . a bold humility—or a humble boldness. We know only in part, but we do know."[6]

Within this general framework, two components from a number of particular components of the "single, but complex reality" (RM 41) of mission today are witness/proclamation and interreligious/secular dialogue,[7] the activities of our focus here. It is important to maintain the distinction in the two uses of the term "dialogue": (1) one of two dimensions of "prophetic dialogue," that serves as the overarching umbrella/framework for understanding mission in general; and (2) one particular activity of mission, as "interreligious and secular dialogue." We shall now briefly look first at witness/proclamation and interreligious/secular dialogue, and then at their relationship.

To begin with, witness and proclamation belong together. "The first means of evangelization is the witness of an authentically Christian life" (*Evangelii Nuntiandi* 41). Such witness can be personal, communal, institutional, and/or ecumenical. Witness is dialogue in that it is never imposing, and it is mutually inspiring. Witness is prophetic in that it is often countercultural and inclusive rather than exclusive in its invitation to the reign of God. As a close companion to witness, proclamation is "the permanent priority of mission" (RM 44). The prophetic dimension of proclamation is quite obvious in that it consists of an authentic presentation of the Good News and a call to conversion.

At the same time, the secretary for the Congregation of the Evangelization of Peoples, late Archbishop Marcello Zago, highlighted the dialogical dimension: "Proclamation presupposes and requires a dialogue method in order to respond to the requirements of those to be evangelized and to enable them to interiorize the message received."[8] In contrast to an old bumper-sticker stating "Jesus is the answer but what is the question?" proclamation needs to provide an answer for the spiritual and human yearnings that people have in today's multiple contexts. At the same time, witness and proclamation together should reflect the Gospel as authentically as possible.

As mentioned above, the Second Vatican Council presented a positive attitude toward other religions and secular society. It avoided the use of the phrase "Outside the church, no salvation," and rather talked about the possibility of salvation for people of good will, whether they have faith in God or not (*Lumen Gentium* 2) and the presence of the Holy Spirit who "in a manner known to God, offers to every man [sic] the possibility of being associated with this paschal mystery" (*Gaudium et Spes* 22). Interreligious and secular dialogue can take the form of a respectful and mutual dialogue of life, action, spirituality, and theological exchange. While the dialogical dimension is quite obvious, such dialogue also needs to be prophetic in that the Christian must witness to and speak the truth of the Gospel with honesty, conviction, and faith. Theologically, the Christian needs to hold two basic principles in a balance: Christ is the "face" of God and the means of salvation for all, *and* God is drawing all peoples back to God in ways we do not understand. A focus on the first principle without the second leads to fundamentalism, while an exclusive focus on the second without the first leads to the other danger of relativism.

Having looked at these two components of mission individually, we now come to questions of the relationship of witness/proclamation and interreligious/secular dialogue—proclamation and dialogue, for short. Do they have conflicting purposes? Does dialogue water down proclamation? Is dialogue a "disguise" for proclamation? Can they be complementary?

The 1990 encyclical letter *Redemptoris Missio* emphasized the role of the Church and salvation through Christ, the universal savior, and declared that "proclamation is the permanent priority of mission" (44). At the same time, the document recognized God working outside the Church and stated that interreligious dialogue is "part of the Church's evangelizing mission" (55). The encyclical letter also maintained that dialogue does not dispense with proclamation (55) and "does not originate from tactical concerns or self-interests," but rather is founded on "deep respect" for the movement of the Spirit in the other (56), and "dialogue can enrich each side" (56).

In 1991 the Pontifical Council for Interreligious Dialogue and the Congregation for the Evangelization of Peoples published a joint document, entitled *Dialogue and Proclamation*, to address the relationship between these two activities of mission more explicitly and in more depth. Dialogue requires balance, religious conviction, and openness to truth, and it promises rich rewards (47–50). Proclamation should be confident and faithful, on the one hand, and humble and dialogical, on the other (70). In terms of their interrelationship,

> Interreligious dialogue and proclamation, though not on the same level, are both authentic elements of the Church's evangelizing mission. . . . They are intimately related, but not interchangeable; true interreligious dialogue on the part of the Christian supposes the desire to make Jesus Christ better known, recognized and loved; proclaiming Jesus Christ is to be carried out in the Gospel spirit of dialogue. (77)

One can see the foundation for prophetic dialogue in both dimensions in this statement.

In a seminal article published in 2000,[9] Archbishop Zago addressed the complementarity of proclamation and dialogue. He states that while interreligious dialogue is a necessity, duty, and benefit, it "does not exonerate the Christian community from the proclamation of Christ" (16). At the same time, proclamation is not the only way of mission. Zago then points to the distinction in purpose: "Of course, dialogue is often a witness to one's own faith. The aim, however, is different. Dialogue is a search for mutual knowledge and enrichment, while proclamation incorporates the idea of a challenge to accept the message" (17). He also indicates the contextual nature of mission, in that some contexts call for proclamation, while others call for dialogue and human promotion. Furthermore, some Christian individuals, movements, and congregations focus on proclamation and others on dialogue. However, Zago asserts that all must acknowledge the right and the duty of the Church to undertake both proclamation and dialogue (17).

The approach of prophetic dialogue and its ensuing spirituality for all aspects of mission is evident in his closing comments. On the one hand, he states that "the dialogue method should be characteristic of all the activity of the Christian community and its leaders" (17–18). But at the same time, there needs to be "a constant deepening and strengthening of one's own Christian identity . . . [and] one's faith" (18).

An overview of prophetic dialogue is helpful in avoiding any tendency to set witness/proclamation and interreligious/secular dialogue in opposition, with the former as only prophetic and the latter as only dialogical. Rather, proclamation and dialogue, in theory and practice, should be seen as necessary complementary aspects of the "Gift of Mission" in its richness and complexity.

Notes

1. Roger P. Schroeder, *What Is the Mission of the Church? A Guide for Catholics* (Maryknoll, N.Y.: Orbis Books, 2008), 3.

2. See Stephen B. Bevans and Roger P. Schroeder, *Constants in Context: A Theology of Mission for Today* (Maryknoll, N.Y.: Orbis Books, 2004), 348–95; Stephen B. Bevans and Roger P. Schroeder, *Prophetic Dialogue: Reflections on Christian Mission Today* (Maryknoll, N.Y.: Orbis Books, 2011).

3. See Bevans and Schroeder, *Prophetic Dialogue*, 19–39.

4. Max Warren, Preface to John V. Taylor, *The Primal Vision* (London: SCM Press, 1963), 10.

5. See Bevans and Schroeder, *Prophetic Dialogue*, 40–55.

6. David J. Bosch, *Transforming Mission: Paradigm Shifts in Theology of Mission* (Maryknoll, N.Y.: Orbis Books, 1991), 489.

7. See the total of six components proposed and described in *Prophetic Dialogue*, 64–71.

8. Marcello Zago, "The New Millennium and the Emerging Religious Encounters," *Missiology* 28 (January 2000): 17.

9. Ibid.

16

Mission as Peacemaking

Marie Dennis

Woven into the fabric of the Jesus story from beginning to end is an identification of his mission with peace on Earth—deep peace, peace rooted in justice, *shalom*, and a call to the task of peacemaking for those who would be disciples.

We say the words often and easily: "Peace be with you." We call Jesus the Prince of Peace. We listen to the promise, "Blessed are the peacemakers, for they shall be called children of God." We struggle to follow his mandates: "Love your enemy" and "Leave your gifts at the altar and go be reconciled with a brother or sister who has something against you." And we are deeply puzzled by his warning, "I come not to bring peace, but the sword."

To seek peace, deep peace rooted in justice, *shalom*, and not a mere absence of war, but the fullness of life for all is the Christian vocation. As followers of the One who is peace, who on the cross overcame the violences of our world, we are called to mission—to proclamation and witness, dialogue, inculturation, spirituality, and transformation of the world that is contextualized as violent and unstable.

Mission as Peacemaking

It seems to me that mission as peacemaking is an exceptionally appropriate theme for consideration at this time in history. While the theme of peace is woven into the words and witness of Jesus—and there has been excellent work done in this area, especially in the past twenty years by Robert Schreiter, Michael Amaladoss, and others—I believe that the development of a deep and rich reflection on mission as peacemaking is one of the greatest challenges for the future of missiology.

Furthermore, I believe that this crucial missiological reflection is coming more and more into focus because Christian theology bearing on peace has evolved so dramatically (at a snail's pace for centuries and much more rapidly in the last three decades), making Christian witness in this area much more in harmony with the Good News than it was, for example, during the Crusades or during the era of colonization. Then, the Church itself as a public institution was desperately in need of evangelization (not that divisions in the Church do not still cry out for evangelization)! The Christian community's sociopolitical location and the history of our response to war and violent conflict have had a huge impact on the Church's mission for peace. Christians moved from a refusal to serve in the Empire's military to self-identification with the Empire; from a dominant, crusading majority to a repudiated, oppressed minority.

In the second half of the last century the Catholic ethical framework for evaluating the actions of nation-states in terms of war and threats of war has evolved from the classical "just war theory" to the "just war theory with a presumption against the use of violent force," to embracing nonviolence as a potentially legitimate option for states to adopt. Previously, nonviolence and pacifism were considered to be a legitimate personal commitment but an impossible or inappropriate stance for governments responsible for the security of their citizens. More recent thinking about the positive work of "just peacemaking" and the possibility of waging "nonviolent conflict" has begun to shift the location and parameters of Catholic/Christian contributions to peace work.

As the very nature of war and destructive violence has changed and the futility and negative consequences of war have become more evident, the role and importance of peacemaking has come into focus. I will say more a little later about the content of Catholic peacemaking as mission.

Context for Mission

To begin, it is necessary to describe the context for mission as it has changed and is changing dramatically. We now live in a world wracked by violence. It is both intensely integrated and controlled (as perpetrated by powerful nations and transnational powerbrokers) and disintegrated, unpredictable, and random (as defined by terrorists and non-state actors, street violence, and organized crime), even as the capacity for viciousness escalates. On the one side we have a highly centralized so-called war on terror with drones and approved assassination lists mocking international law and, on the other, the very common experience of intense insecurity at a local level where fear, especially fear of the "other," is the dominant emotion in many peoples' lives. Maryknollers in Latin America speak often about this latter kind of violence and insecurity, and we see similar patterns in Afghanistan, Iraq, Yemen, and Somalia.

In this context, peace is inseparable from social and economic justice and respect for the integrity of creation. Desperate poverty, lack of access to a dignified life, hunger, food and water insecurity, climate change, environmental degradation, the growing chasm between a small number of people with access to excessive wealth and power and a majority who barely survive, massive global migration, and on and on—*are themselves violent*, and are *fed by* violent conflict, war, and preparations for war. And simultaneously they *lead to* destructive violence, repression, and war, declared as such or not. Bob Schreiter describes the "deep churning of the social, cultural, and political matrix in which Christian mission finds itself" (Foreword to Müller et al., *Dictionary of Mission: Theology, History, Perspectives* [Marykoll, N.Y.: Orbis Books, 1997]).

Proclamation

Proclamation of the Good News in a broken and violated world—in other words, to speak the word "peace" in this context, to *give witness* to the possibility of lived peace—is naïve, necessary, profound, and enormously complex. But I believe that the evangelization of the cultures of death now dominant in our broken world is one of the most urgent tasks of mission today. It is, I think, a very real participation in God's work through the passion, death, and resurrection of Jesus Christ and, in that sense, a source of hope in an otherwise hopeless world.

To make the nonviolent Jesus present and visible in a world that is convulsed in violence is a demanding and multidimensional vocation that requires tremendous creativity and persistence. Often it will be dismissed as naïve, not up to the task, not politically useful or pertinent; at other times, as in war-weary Sudan or drug-lord-controlled Juárez, it will be welcomed. But far too often the gospel of peace will be considered dangerous, and those who pursue peace will pay a price.

In these times much too often the roots of repeated or unrelenting violence are planted in religious extremism. Schreiter talks about religious differences being "used to inflame populations and foster violence" (*Mission in the Third Millennium* [Maryknoll, N.Y.: Orbis Books, 2001], 158). In that same volume Mercy Amba Oduyoye describes conflicts based on fear and feelings of superiority in Africa that have arisen out of confrontations between Christianity and Islam, and between either of the two Abrahamic faith communities and African religion (44).

Dialogue

Dialogue, then, is essential to mission. Michael Amaladoss defines dialogue as "a way of acknowledging and accepting the other's identity shown in the readiness to listen, to change, and to collaborate" (*Mission in the Third Millennium*, 34). He quotes Asian theologians from the document "Asian Christian Perspectives on Harmony":

> Jesus Christ is continuing his Spirit-filled mission of restoring peace and harmony with God and among humans. . . . His disciples are called to be effective signs of union with God and unity of humankind. . . . It is through triple dialogue with cultures, with religions, and with the poor, through a mutually-enriching interchange in its various modes and at various levels, not the least in the dialogue of life with people of other faiths and religious traditions, that Asian Christianity is to strive for human and cosmic harmony in Jesus Christ. (Amaladoss, 34–35)

In that same volume Sung-Hae Kim, SC, quotes from *Ecclesia in Asia*:

> The desire for dialogue . . . is not simply a strategy for peaceful coexistence among people; it is an essential part of the Church's mission because it has its origin in the Father's [Creator's] loving dialogue of salvation with humanity through the Son in the power of the Holy Spirit. . . . The dialogue which the Church proposes is grounded in the logic of the Incarnation. (John Paul II, *Ecclesia in Asia*, 29)

Inculturation

Inculturation is also an important concept in terms of mission as peacemaking. On the one hand, inculturation is essential for any Christian praxis of peacemaking to learn, for example, (1) from the deep, rich experience of Eastern traditions, especially in pursuit of harmony and benevolence; (2) from the many different African traditional rituals for reconciliation and healing; (3) from the indigenous understanding of right relationships with others, including ancestors, future genera-tions, and the natural world; and (4) to make operational our belief in the agency of people and the presence of grace and the seeds of peace present in local communities, even in the midst of war.

The practice of respectful encounter with difference that is integral to the process of inculturation is itself valuable to mission as peacemaking, since one of the most pervasive strategies of those perpetrating violence is to orchestrate fear of the "other": fear of Muslims, fear of the "West," fear of immigrants, fear of Palestinians, fear of Israelis, fear of China, and so on. To experience diversity as a gift and not a threat may be one of the most important tasks of peacemaking in the coming period of time.

On the other hand, I believe that inappropriate inculturation has been a serious obstacle to mission as peacemaking. This is particularly evident if we take seriously the Church's emphasis on a new evange-lization, by which the Church's mission will no longer be perceived as a "north-south or west-east dynamic but one which transcends the geographic confines of past missionary activity," making all five conti-nents fields of missionary activity (*Lineamenta* for the 2012 Synod on New Evangelization).

"Inappropriate inculturation," it seems to me, has so tightly tied together the Church in mission and a given culture that the Church assumes as normative or necessary (beyond evangelization?) some of that society's most egregious and violent cultural practices. Some would say that is the case in our own country, where chaplains to the military are themselves members of the military; or when the U.S. Church, having declared the Iraq War unjust, was silent once the United States went to war so as not to create a crisis of conscience for military personnel; or when Catholic pulpits are silent about a $700 billion military budget that robs from the poor.

Transformation of the World

Thus mission as peacemaking is proclamation and witness, dia-logue, and inculturation. It must also be transformation of the world:

engaging the roots of war, the drivers of violent conflict, and the consequences of "peace-less-ness."

The roots of war and destructive violence are many and varied: the pursuit of natural resources, including oil, land, water, and all the minerals that drive development; economic injustice; concentrated power; the reality and/or excuse of terrorism; huge profits from military contracts; geopolitical or territorial advantage; environmental destruction and climate change; religious, cultural, and ideological intolerance; arms traffic, and on and on.

Transformation of this reality toward the New Creation will engage the institutional, theological, and spiritual resources of our tradition in the great task of creating a culture of peace. It will include at least conflict resolution, conflict transformation, the prevention of violent conflict, the transition to a stable, just, peaceful society after war, and the transformation of cultural practices or political and socioeconomic structures and systems that promote or perpetuate violence.

The characteristics of Catholic peacebuilding are very effectively discussed in a recent book, *Peacebuilding: Catholic Theology, Ethics, and Praxis* (2010), published by Orbis for the Catholic Peacebuilding Network (Scott Appleby, Jerry Powers, and Robert Schreiter, eds.). They include, for example,

- practicing of *presence and accompaniment*; connecting with and supporting local efforts for peace;

- using *political and ecclesiastical networks*, including existing Catholic parish, diocesan, and international networks, to promote peace;

- recognizing the pervasiveness of grace and the agency of local people; in other words, seeds of peace are often found within the conflicted community, or even among those working within destructive structures or agencies;

- promoting *nonviolence* and *social justice* as necessary building blocks for lasting peace through ecumenical efforts to identify building blocks of *just peace* (beyond the just war/pacifism debate) or to explore the concept of *waging nonviolent conflict*;

- giving witness to our belief in *mediation* and to our rich *sacramental life*, which speaks to the spirituality of mission as peacemaking.

Transitional Justice and Reconciliation

Of particular concern in these times is the relationship of peace and social justice in countries transitioning out of war or violent repression—what Dan Philpott calls the "agenda of a Catholic ethic of transitional justice," an ethic rooted in reconciliation, a "concept of justice and peacebuilding that envisions a holistic, integrated repair of the wounds that war. . . . leaves behind." Robert Schreiter's several important works point to *reconciliation* itself as a model for mission.

> Reconciliation is about all of these things—making peace, seeking justice, healing memories, rebuilding societies. . . .
>
> Reconciliation is first and foremost the work of God in our lives. . . . God is the one who initiates healing and restoration in the victim, and it is with the victim that God begins. . . .
>
> Reconciliation seen from this perspective is about the possibility of a new creation. . . . It does believe that a new future is possible. Belief in the resurrection of the dead stands as the horizon for this belief— namely, that even the dead shall experience justice. *(Schreiter,* "Gobalization and Reconciliation," *Mission in the Third Millennium* [Maryknoll, N.Y.:Orbis Books, 2001], 139–41)

One of the defining commitments of the Pax Christi movement is reconciliation. Pax Christi was founded after World War II to promote reconciliation between the French and Germans. Over the years in small and not so small ways Pax Christi has participated in transitional justice and reconciliation processes in various countries, including South Africa, Guatemala, Sierra Leone, Liberia, Peru, El Salvador, Haiti, Colombia, and others. Every one of those truth and reconciliation processes—some of which were only small steps in a yet ongoing transition to lasting peace—confirms that the restoration of right relationships after decades of war and ongoing violence is always a monumental task and an important area of work for Catholic peace-building.

How, in the wake of war and/or terrible atrocities, can deep and lasting peace with justice be achieved?

John Ashworth, who has worked in South Sudan for decades, speaks about the price of peace, the fact that if a society wants to move toward peace, someone will have to pay a price. For example,

- in South Africa: the price was paid (perpetrators free and undisturbed) by the victims of apartheid to have a measure of peace and a chance at a future;

- in Uganda: people of Northern Uganda were willing to pay a big price for peace, even amnesty for the Lord's Resistance Army, or at least Ugandan justice rather than International Criminal Court (ICC) justice; the indictment of Joseph Kony by the ICC was extremely controversial;

- in Kenya and Zimbabwe: in both countries, the political opposition paid the price of the presidency that they probably had won in the elections in the hope of gaining an end to the chaos and violence through a unity government.

Pax Christi describes the challenge clearly:

> In modern practice, negative peace—or the absence of war—is often the only peace attainable. Peace negotiations, they say, often produce far from uplifting compromises in which war criminals go unpunished, the dead are forgotten, and surviving victims and next of kin are left to their own devices. In many cases there is only an *ugly peace* in which practical, attainable peace and the principles of law get in one another's way. (IKV Pax Christi)

Negative peace is in itself valuable, but even that is unlikely or seems impossible in Iraq, Afghanistan, or in the context of the so-called global war on terror. But *positive peace* should be the lasting goal: positive peace with a lasting order that has room for social justice and ecological integrity. It will require that we engage the full spectrum of peace work and recognize the interrelatedness of peace with social and economic justice and respect for the integrity of creation. Climate change-related displacement and conflict are making that clear, as is the reality of scarce basic and other natural resources on which "modern" life depends.

Spirituality of Mission as Peacemaking

Bob Schreiter's work highlights the rich resources of the Catholic Christian tradition for engaging the mission of peacemaking, peace building, and reconciliation: Scripture, our rituals, our sacramental life and obviously the sacrament of reconciliation, and especially the Eucharist, where the "broken, damaged, and abused bodies of individual victims and the broken body of the Church are taken up into the body of Christ. Christ's body has known torture; it has known shame. In his complete solidarity with victims, he has gone to the limit of violent death. And his body becomes a holy medicine to heal those broken bodies today"—in Sudan and Colombia, in Iraq and Yemen, in Burundi and Afghanistan, in Cambodia and Pakistan, in the United States and El Salvador, and in so many other places where war and violence have held sway.

The death of Jesus on the cross was, it seems to me, the ultimate witness for the peacemaking mission of the Church as he took on the horrific violence of his own time and overcame it with the fullness of life and resurrection. To imitate Christ now, to overcome, root out, and heal from the multifaceted and multilayered violences of this world is one of the most urgent challenges for the mission of the Church in the twenty-first century.

17

Mission in the Care of Creation

Ann Braudis, MM

This short presentation will explore creation as the context in which mission takes place. An assumption is that humanity has brought to Earth immense ecological devastation causing the breakdown of life-support systems, hardship for many peoples, and heartbreaking injustice.

The opening story of the Bible sets the background for these considerations: In this story our forebears did the best they could to account for the origins of life and for their place in the grand scheme of things. They addressed the questions:

- Who made us?

- Where did we come from?

- How did everything else get here?

- What do things mean?

- Where are we going?

And they did the very best they could to answer these questions with the knowledge available to them at the time.

Today we have exactly the same challenge. We must answer the same questions, to the best of our ability, with the knowledge available to us—which is vastly different from that of our ancestors.

- Who made us?

- Where did we come from?

- How did everything else get here?

- What do things mean?

- Where are we going?

It is only in establishing this foundation that we can envision the task of our generation.

It is well established now that we are part of a long evolutionary journey. This is the most fundamental knowledge that we have today, and it deeply influences how we know and understand God.

Our work today is not to look at the evolutionary story so much as to look at the main shaping patterns within the evolutionary story. We do this in order to understand our mission challenges and to better recognize the opportunities before us. I have chosen to use five ideas to shape the challenges and five Maryknoll projects to illustrate the opportunities. (The original presentation was accompanied by a slide presentation.—Ed.)

Main Shaping Patterns within the Evolutionary Story

1. *The Continuous Unfurling of the Universe and the Future.*

- The long unfolding of the Universe from the distant past established the pattern for how the Universe will go into the future, with an urgent pressing forward toward more complex life forms. (*Image of space*)

- There was a grand spiraling out from the origins into unimaginable forms. Who could have imagined the flowers when there was only the stony crust of Earth, before any form of life appeared? (*Image of spiral art*)

- Today we see the flower itself, capturing the planet's tendency to push beyond all odds, in this case, the late winter cold, the dead leaves, and the discarded trash. (*Image of flower*)

- The intelligent consciousness of today's child will contribute to shaping the actual evolutionary journey of the Earth tomorrow. (*Image of baby*)

2. *The Unfolding of Beauty and the Spiritual Dimension of Reality.*

- It would seem that the ultimate purpose of Creation is to bring forth beauty in increasingly intricate forms. (*Image of butterfly and flower*)

- Beyond beauty there is an inner spiritual quest that causes the human person to find expression through monuments signaling that there is more to life than what is seen. (*Image of pyramid*)

- Through mysticism, we learn the practice of inner silence and alignment of the breath. (*Image of Buddhist monks*)

- Through art, feminism today brings forth the image of the Holy Mother forever pregnant, forever giving birth to and nourishing Creation. *(Icon of Virgin)*

3. Creation as the Source of Moral and Ethical Guidance.

- The world renowned Indian physicist Vandana Shiva roots her monumental ethical work in behalf of the sustainability of Earth in the principle of harmony with nature. (*Image of Vandana Shiva*)

- Evo Morales, president of Bolivia, has brought before the United Nations breakthrough thinking regarding the rights of Earth. (*Image of Evo Morales*)

- Barbara Marx Hubbard is a futurist who convincingly imagines the role of humanity for the next two thousand years based on the past two thousand years. She richly describes the emerging universal human, who assumes personal responsibility for the well-being of the planet. (*Image of Barbara Marx Hubbard*)

4. The Centrality of Relationality.

- At the subatomic level of the Universe, not only do all things affect each other, but everything is the other. How does this apply on the human species level? (*Image of candles with mingled flames*)

- Charlene Spretnak wrestles with this question in her beautiful book *Relational Reality: New Discoveries of Interrelatedness That Are Transforming the Modern World*. (*Image of Charlene Spretnak*)

- Tevyn East is a performer whose work makes art of the nexus of faith, economy, and ecology. (*Image of Tevyn East*)

- All of us long to build bridges from one to another and from culture to culture. (*Image of hanging bridge*)

5. *Mission to the Entire Earth Community.*

♦ Humanity has unleashed toxic materials that all must do their best to render neutral for the sake of the whole community of life. (*Image of nuclear toxic spill site*)

♦ More and more individuals are taking on moral accountability for the state of the planet. Whether or not one is personally responsible for trashing the Earth, there is a movement toward responding as a species in assuming responsibility for cleaning it up. (*Image of citizens cleaning the trash from road*)

♦ All questions of justice are ultimately questions of who decides how the resources of the Earth are to be used, and who benefits. These insights need to be thoroughly investigated and effectively resisted. (*Image of protest against hunger*)

Maryknoll Projects for the Care of Creation
(*accompanied by slides of projects*)

Maryknoll Fathers and Brothers Pachamama Organic Farm, Maryknoll, New York. This project shows the relationships among all the life-sustaining natural processes, including the transformation of food into our bodies, minds, and brains through which the sacred is known.

Maryknoll Sisters Conservation Easement, Maryknoll, New York. This project highlights the moral obligation of preserving the forests and wetlands for future inhabitants of the Earth community. It preserves the beauty of the land for those who will succeed us.

The Maryknoll Office for Global Concerns Project for Sustainable Development at the United Nations. This work highlights the importance of working together as one human community to influence international policy about the moral and ethical considerations rooted in the nature of creation.

Maryknoll Cosmic Journey, Baguio, Philippines. In life-size Earth art this project shows humanity, culture, and the quest for spiritual depth emerging as part of the evolutionary journey.

Center for Human Rights and the Environment, Puno Region, Peru. This project uses all the force of law to bring about the restoration of Indigenous land following toxic spoilage from large-scale irresponsible mining for tungsten.

These projects hail from efforts to understand mission in the light of what we know today regarding the questions raised at the outset. We are part of the natural world, and at this point in our evolutionary journey it is becoming increasingly clear that we are responsible for how our planet will evolve in the future. It becomes more and more apparent that we stand at the threshold of our next evolutionary phase, a phase that will be characterized by the moral project of assuming personal responsibility for the health and well-being of the planet.

18

Women in Mission:
The Call from Scripture

Barbara E. Reid, OP

It is a great honor and privilege to be invited to share these reflections with you on the occasion of the Maryknoll Society's centennial. As a youngster, I was greatly attracted to the Maryknollers and wondered if I might have a missionary vocation. Only after becoming a Dominican did I discover that the Maryknoll Sisters are also Dominicans. I have been blessed to come to know you more closely through your students studying at the Catholic Theological Union and through the number of times Maryknoll has hosted me in Cochabamba, Bolivia, where I have learned from you and the women there what it means to be a woman in mission.

Mission Rooted in the Call to Discipleship

In the Gospels it is clear that mission is rooted in the call to discipleship. Linked with Jesus' invitation to Peter, Andrew, James, and John, to follow Jesus is the commission to be "fishers of people" (Mark 1:16–20). In the subsequent episode of the sending of the twelve, Jesus first "called to him those whom he wanted" and then sent them out "to preach and to have authority over demons" (Mark 3:13–19).

When we turn to the question of women in mission, it is clear that there were women disciples engaged in many forms of ministry from the earliest days of the Jesus movement. But there are not the equivalent stories of the call or sending of women as there are of the male disciples. Trying to retrieve the history of women in mission from the Scriptures is difficult because of the nature of the texts. The Scriptures were not written from women's perspectives. The Gospels, for the most part, do not tell the story of Jesus and his mission as a woman might.[1] Therefore what traces we do have of women in mission can be considered but the tip of the iceberg. It is important to realize, however, that women were not relegated to the periphery of the mission as adjuncts to the men. Women were at the heart and center of the Christian mission from the very start.

Traces of Call Stories of Women Disciples

While there are no call stories per se of women disciples in the Gospels, there are traces of such in two instances: the annunciation to Mary (Luke 1:26–36) and the healing of Simon's mother-in-law (Matt. 8:14–17). Most biblical scholars readily recognize that the annunciation to Mary follows the form of other annunciation of birth stories,[2] but it also has the same elements as a prophetic call story, as in the call of Moses (Exod. 3:1–12) and of Peter (Luke 5:1–11).

First, the person called encounters the Divine while going about that person's normal daily activities. Moses is tending his sheep; Peter is cleaning his nets; Mary is at home making wedding plans. There is an introductory word and then the commission. This is followed by an objection. For Moses, the impediment is his difficulty in speaking; for Peter, it is his sinfulness; for Mary, what God asks appears physically impossible. Then a reassurance and a sign are given. For Moses, the burning bush is not consumed and Aaron and Miriam will help him speak; for Peter, there is a miraculous catch of fish and a reassurance that from now on he will catch people. Mary is assured that nothing is impossible with God, as is evident in the pregnancy of Elizabeth. Mary can be seen as the paradigmatic disciple, who responds to God's call with utter fidelity even when the mission entrusted to her seems impossible.

One can also see traces of a call story in the Matthean version of the healing of Simon's mother-in-law. Australian biblical scholar Elaine Wainwright has noted the parallels between this story and the call of Matthew the tax collector (Matt. 9:9–13; contrast Luke 4:38–39).[3] In a healing story, the ill person or the ill person's friends approach Jesus. In a call story, Jesus takes the initiative, as when Jesus sees Matthew sitting at his toll booth and invites him to follow him (Matt. 9:9). Likewise, Jesus sees Simon's mother-in-law lying in bed with a fever and touches her (Matt. 8:14). In both these episodes, Jesus sees, *eiden*, the person called. The response of Matthew is to follow Jesus and then to host a dinner for him. Simon's mother-in-law, in response, "arose and waited on him (*diēkōnei autō*)" (Matt. 8:15). The verb *diakonein* is also translated as "served" or "ministered." It is the response of a disciple called to mission. It is also notable that in Matthew's version, the response is to Jesus alone (*autō*, "him," is in the singular, in contrast to "them," *autois*, Mark 1:31 and Luke 4:39).

It is possible that this was originally a call story that has blended with a healing story. In the final form, the latter has now overshadowed the former. The call story of Simon's mother-in-law, who was remembered for her ministry to and with Jesus, may have been preserved in circles of women disciples, much as the story of her son-in-law was preserved by Jesus' male followers.

Women Disciples: Following and Ministering

All the Gospels speak about women disciples of Jesus.[4] The Gospel of Mark recounts that at Jesus' crucifixion, there were "women looking on from a distance; among them were Mary Magdalene, and Mary the mother of James the younger and of Joses, and Salome. These used to follow (*ēkolouthoun*) him and provided for (*diēkonoun*) him when he was in Galilee; and there were many other women who had come up with him to Jerusalem" (Mark 15:40–41; see also Matt. 27:55–56). Just as the male disciples followed Jesus when called by him (*ēkolouthēsan*, Mark 1:18 and pars.), so did the Galilean women. Their ministry is described in the same terms as Jesus' mission, when he declared that he "came not to be served (*diakonēthēnai*) but to serve (*diakonēsai*) and to give his life as a ransom for many" (Mark 10:45). The Greek verbs used to describe the women's following and ministering are in the imperfect tense, indicating repeated or ongoing action in the past.

Among the evangelists, only Luke introduces Galilean women disciples before the crucifixion, and he alone spells out what kind of ministry the women were doing. In the midst of the Galilean mission, Jesus was going

> through cities and villages proclaiming and bringing the good news of the kingdom of God. The twelve were with him, as well as some women who had been cured of evil spirits and infirmities. Mary, called Magdalene, from whom seven demons had gone out, and Joanna, the wife of Herod's steward Chuza, and Susanna, and many others, who provided [*diēkonoun*] for them out of their resources [*hyparchontōn*]." (Luke 8:1–3)

The noun *hyparchontōn*, "resources," means "possessions, property, money, or goods."[5] The women are accompanying Jesus and financing his preaching mission. At the end of the Gospel, these same women minister to Jesus through their presence at his execution and then are entrusted with proclaiming the good news of the resurrection (Luke 24:1–12 and parallels).

Sent Forth on Mission

In the synoptic Gospels it is the Twelve who are sent out on mission (Mark 6:6b–13; Matt. 10:5–15; Luke 9:1–6), and for some this justifies the exclusion of women from certain ministries. However, "the Twelve" can be understood not as an exclusive group of men entrusted with the mission, but as a symbolic number that exemplifies the mission that is entrusted to all of the renewed Israel. Equally important is the commissioning of the women disciples at the empty tomb (Mark 16:1–8; Matt. 28:1–12; Luke 24:1–11; John 20:1–2, 11–18). Moreover, in the Gospel of Luke there is a second sending of seventy-two disciples (also symbolic for a full number) in pairs, possibly male and female (10:1–12). In the Gospel of John, there is no call or sending of the Twelve. The fruitful harvest of Samaritans who are brought to Jesus by the woman whom he encounters at the well (John 4:42) is the paradigm for mission.[6]

All Empowered by the Spirit

In the Acts of the Apostles, all are empowered for mission. Acts 1:14 explicitly tells us the women, including Jesus' mother and his siblings, were gathered with the disciples in the upper room, where they awaited the promised Spirit. On the day of Pentecost, Peter invokes Joel 3:1–5 to explain their experience of the Spirit being poured out on all, women and men, empowering all to prophesy (Acts 2:17–18).

Women in the Pauline Churches

There is a considerable number of women whom Paul names in his letters as coworkers: Mary, Tryphaena, Tryphosa, and Persis (Rom. 16:6, 12), Euodia and Syntyche (Phil. 4:2–4), and Prisca, who, along with her husband, Aquila, risked her life for him and led a house church (Rom. 16:3–5; 1 Cor. 16:19). Junia is said to be "notable among the apostles"

(Rom 16:7). Phoebe was deacon of the church at Cenchrea, whom Paul acknowledges as a leader of many, including himself (Rom. 16:1–2). Other women heads of house churches included Mary (Acts 12:12), Lydia (Acts 16:40), and Nympha (Col. 4:14).

Post-Pauline Attempts to Control, Silence, and Discount the Ministry of Women

In addition to the number of affirmative references to women disciples and ministers in the Gospels and Paul's letters, there is also ample evidence of persistent attempts to silence and discount the ministry of women. There are conflicts over women speaking in the assembly (1 Cor. 14:34–35), transgressing the bounds of patriarchal household arrangements (Col. 3:18; Eph 5:22); teaching men (1 Tim. 2:12), and being admitted to the ministry of widow and receiving payment from the church for it (1 Tim. 5:3–16).

In the Gospels there is also a silencing of women and a restriction of their ministries to supportive roles behind the scenes. In the Gospel of Luke and the Acts of the Apostles, for example, after the infancy narratives, women never speak except to be disbelieved or corrected. Only the male disciples are depicted as doing what Jesus did by healing, exorcising, resuscitating from the dead, forgiving, feeding, enduring persecution, and imparting the Spirit to others.[7]

We can also see two strands of tradition concerning who was first to see the risen Christ and to be entrusted with proclaiming him alive. In Matthew 28:1–10 and John 20:1–18, it is Mary Magdalene. In 1 Corinthians 15:3–11 and Luke 24:34, primacy of place is given to Peter. Struggles over women's proclamation of the Gospel, especially at Eucharist, continue to this day.

The Christian Mission in Female Language and Imagery

The Gospel of John stands out as one told in a different key. From the outset it paints Jesus in parallel terms to Woman Wisdom.[8] Strong women characters refract the story through female lenses. The Samaritan woman's proclamation to her townspeople is the paradigm for mission (4:4–42). The insight into Jesus' messiahship is pronounced by Martha (11:27), rather than Peter (Mark 8:29). Mary's anointing of Jesus' feet (12:1-12) mirrors Jesus' washing of the disciples' feet (13:1-20). There is no disbelieving or discrediting of Mary Magdalene's encounter with the risen Christ or her proclamation (20:1-18). Jesus' mother is a key character who initiates the birth of Jesus' public mission at Cana (2:1-12) and who witnesses its completion (19:25-27) and the birth of the renewed people of God to whom his mission is entrusted after his death.

The theme of birthing is woven through the whole of the Gospel of John and provides a key insight into understanding Jesus' life and mission. The Prologue tells that all things were birthed through the *Logos* (1:3-4) and that those who believe in his name are born as children of God (1:12-13). In his dialogue with Nicodemus, Jesus elaborates on the need to be born again/from above[9] and to be born of water and the Spirit (3:3-5). The image of water carries the symbolism forward in the next chapters, as Jesus promises the Samaritan woman living water (4:10), and as he speaks of "rivers of living water" that flow from his womb[10] and that of the believer (7:38).[11] In the Last Discourse, Jesus speaks to his disciples of his coming passion as like the labor pangs of a woman giving birth (16:20-21). The birthing image culminates at 19:34, where the side of the crucified Jesus is pierced, and from it flow blood and water, the two liquids that accompany the birthing process. The women witnesses at the cross (19:25) can be likened to midwives who help to draw forth the new life that is emerging. The final cry of Jesus, "It is finished!" (19:30) acclaims this birth as accomplished. The wrapping of his body in linen cloths (19:40) is evocative of the swaddling of a newborn, as in Luke 2:7. And when the risen Christ breathes on the disciples to impart the Spirit (20:22), it recalls the Creator breathing into the nostrils of the first human being, causing it to come to life (Gen. 2:7).[12]

This prevalent imagery of birthing, along with the prominence of women characters and the portrayal of Jesus as Woman Wisdom incarnate, gives us a glimpse of how the story of the Jesus movement can be told through women's lenses and with female symbols and imagery. Moreover, the structures of discipleship are circular and inclusive in this Gospel. There is no call or sending of the Twelve, and there is no inner circle of three (Peter, James, and John) in this Gospel. The Beloved Disciple, who embodies all that is ideal in abiding in Jesus and engaging in his mission, is never named, allowing any disciple to find herself or himself in that privileged space. There is no hierarchical ranking of Jesus' followers. In this Gospel, all are friends (15:15), where service to a friend, even willingness to lay down a friend's life, erases any status distinctions (13:1–20).

Maryknoll Women Missionaries

Maryknoll Sisters, I see in you the same bold embodiment of Jesus' mission in a distinctly feminine key. Like the first Galilean women disciples and the women who ministered in the Pauline churches, you have been pioneers in unexplored mission territories, both geographically and theologically. At the time of your founding, the prevailing culture would have had you cooking and caring for the men, not engaging directly in the overseas evangelizing mission. But your founder, Mary Rogers, "was opposed to the idea that Maryknoll Sisters should be relegated to domestic chores for the men."[13] Like the fourth evangelist, Mary Rogers came to understand Jesus' mother as a model for you, as the one who gave Christ directly to others.[14]

From your earliest days, you embraced a noninstitutional approach to mission and have been able to minister in ways that men could not. You have had a tremendous impact on women worldwide, empowering women and working for systemic change that moves us toward a fuller realization of the reign of God.[15] What you have birthed in these first hundred years has been extraordinary.[16] I wonder what will the next century of Christian missionary theology and praxis look like if the wisdom of women becomes central?

Notes

1. There is some speculation that the fourth Gospel may have been authored by a woman. See further chapter 15, "Because of the Woman's Testimony," in Sandra M. Schneiders, *Written That You May Believe: Encountering Jesus in the Fourth Gospel*, rev. ed. (New York: Crossroad, 2003), 233–54. Schneiders presents good reasons to think that the author may have been female. She notes, however, that the actual identity of the author has been permanently disguised and proposes that the Samaritan woman in John 4 functions as the textual alter ego of the evangelist.

2. See the annunciation of the birth of Ishmael (Gen. 16:1–16), Isaac (Gen. 18:1–16), Samson (Judg. 13:2–23), and John the Baptist (Luke 1:5–23), and the form analysis by Raymond E. Brown in *The Birth of the Messiah: A Commentary on the Infancy Narratives in the Gospels of Matthew and Luke* (New York: Doubleday, 1993).

3. Elaine M. Wainwright, *Towards a Feminist Critical Reading of the Gospel according to Matthew* (Berlin: de Gruyter, 1991), 177–91.

4. In addition, in Acts 9:36 Tabitha is introduced as a "disciple," *mathētria*, the only time in the New Testament that this title is attached to a single individual.

5. Luke 12:15, 33, 44; 14:33; 16:1; 19:8; Acts 4:32.

6. See Schneiders, *Written That You May Believe*, 126–48.

7. See further Barbara E. Reid, *Choosing the Better Part? Women in the Gospel of Luke* (Collegeville, Minn.: Liturgical Press, 1996), 21–54.

8. There are many parallels between John 1:1–18, John 7, and Job 28; Prov. 1–9; Bar. 3:9–4:4; Sir. 1, 4:11–19, 6:18–31, 14:20–15:10; and Wis. 6–10.

9. There is a word play, as the Greek word *anōthen* has both meanings.

10. The NRSV and NJB translate the word as "heart," the NAB "from within," KJV "belly," but the word *kolia* in Greek literally means "womb."

11. The possessive prounoun *autō* is ambiguous and could refer either to Jesus or the believer. I propose that this allows for both to be kept in view.

12. Many early Church Fathers, such as Clement of Alexandria and Ambrose, as well as medieval mystics like Julian of Norwich and Meister Eckhart also recognized this birthing imagery in the Johannine crucifixion scene. For further elaboration and other references, see chapter 5 in Barbara E. Reid, *Taking Up the Cross: New Testament Interpretations through Latina and Feminist Eyes* (Minneapolis: Fortress, 2007).

13. Susan E. Smith, *Women in Mission: From the New Testament to Today* (Maryknoll, N.Y.: Orbis Books, 2007), 143.

14. Dana L. Robert, *American Women in Mission: A Social History of Their Thought and Practice* (Macon, Ga.: Mercer University Press, 1996), 356.

15. See Angelyn Dries, OSF, "American Catholic 'Woman's Work for Woman' in the Twentieth Century," in *Gospel Bearers, Gender Barriers: Missionary Women in the Twentieth Century*, ed. Dana L. Robert (Maryknoll, N.Y.: Orbis Books, 2002), 127–42, especially 138–40.

16. For an inspiring portrait of the first seventy-five years of the history of the Maryknoll Sisters, see Penny Lernoux, *Hearts on Fire: The Story of the Maryknoll Sisters*, rev. ed. (Maryknoll, N.Y.: Orbis Books, 2012).

19

Mission and the Art of Parachuting

Michael C. Kirwen, MM

All persons come into human consciousness through one of the more than six thousand cultures worldwide. There is no other means to become a normal, functioning human being. Cultures, which are learned behavior, are the operative systems by which people interpret their experiences, generate their actions and reactions as their lives unfold, and create their artifacts. The learning process is so long and embedded that it is almost impossible to change foundational values, themes, and ideas. It takes up to twenty-five years for a person to become fully integrated into a particular cultural pattern. Thus, each and every person is fundamentally a person of only one culture. Within this cultural matrix there is always a spirituality, which is like a glue that keeps all the parts of the culture holistic and promotes its values, attitudes, and morality.

Given this human cultural reality, the messenger of change who enters into a foreign cultural arena has to learn as soon as possible the local cultural knowledge, especially its spirituality, if there is to be any hope of sustainable change or conversion. And this applies not only to missionaries but to all types of developers, whether medical, educational, or social. Without firsthand knowledge of the host cultures, foreign agents of change are figuratively parachuted into and crash-land on the cultures' institutions with their unique attitudes, values, and spirituality. Indeed, the spirituality of most non-Western cultures is so embedded within its cultural knowledge that everything human has a sacral/sacred dimension. Moreover, reality is personalized to the point that many of the local languages have no passive voice structures; there is always a personal actor carrying out a cultural activity.

By contrast, the Westernized agents of change arrive with a secular worldview in which reality is objectified and manipulated. So the landings in terms of the intellectual and spiritual situation of the messengers are always crash landings. However, in terms of the hospitality of the host cultures, the messengers may be misled to think that they are soft landings, which can lure them into thinking that there is mutual understanding. However, and most importantly, the foreign agents of change, the parachutists, are just as ethnocentric and resistant to change as the people they are attempting to influence.

Until recently, there was no way to learn systematically about the cultural knowledge of a host culture. The approach has been just to participate as much as possible in the society with the expectation that sooner or later one would absorb the cultural attitudes and knowledge. This has not worked for most people. Where there were language courses, the participants were able to become somewhat fluent in the spoken languages, but would continue to interact with the society from the mindset of their cultures of origin. As one missionary was told: "You speak our language well, but you don't know what you are saying," as he was interpreting everything via his Western, secular, impersonal, objectified worldview.

This participatory, discipleship approach to cultural learning is no longer the only way to connect with a culture. For eighteen years, the Maryknoll Institute of African Studies (MIAS), a postgraduate institute academically affiliated with St. Mary's University of Minnesota and Tangaza College in Nairobi, Kenya, has undertaken professional quality field research involving close to one thousand postgraduate students and field assistants and twenty-five university lecturers to discover the foundational structure of cultural knowledge that applies to all cultures worldwide. It was found that this structure is delineated into fifteen deep-seated values/themes/ideas/points-of-density that mirror the synaptic organization of the neocortex of the brain. Furthermore, the research discovered that the major cultural events and activities that unfold in a person's life from birth to death can be demarcated into thirty-five distinct happenings, rites of passage, attitudes, and activities that are called domains by the social scientists. The important issue here is that the meaning, interpretation, and the living out of all events in a person's life are determined by one's cultural knowledge. Therefore, any permanent behavioral change of an ethnic group is always preceded by a permanent change in its embedded cultural knowledge. This is the reason why most attempts to change people's behavior, whether religious, social, or political, falter and are ineffective, as there has been no change in the embedded and resilient cultural knowledge of the targeted group.

In brief, the fifteen universal foundational themes are (1) Creator God: nature of the transcendent; (2) ancestors: grandparents; (3) living dead: status of the elderly and recently deceased; (4) nominal reincarnation: ultimate fate of the dead whether resurrected or recycled; (5) lineage: family structures; (6) leadership: social, political, and religious; (7) adulthood and elderhood; (8) bridewealth: marriage gifts; (9) marriage structures and rituals; (10) polygyny: many wives or husbands; (11) herbalist: pharmacist, medical doctors; (12) diviners: priests and spiritual leaders; (13) witch: the problem of evil; (14) witchcraft: ways and means of causing evil; and (15) death: the exit from human existence.

This understanding of the structure of cultural knowledge has been published in a book titled *African Cultural Knowledge: Themes and Embedded Beliefs* (Nairobi: MIAS, 2005). Each of the fifteen chapters is organized as a learning module with contributions from both African and non-African participants. It is available on at *www.africancultures.org*. Regarding the thirty-five cultural events and activities that unfold in one's life, two of four books presenting this paradigm have been published. One is titled *African Cultural Domains: Life Cycle of an Individual* (Nairobi: MIAS, 2008), and the other is *African Cultural Domains: Cycle of Family and Interpersonal Relationship* (Nairobi: MIAS, 2008); both are available on the same website.

The value of this model of cultural knowledge is that any culture worldwide can be broken down into these fifteen themes, thereby enabling an outsider to learn and appropriate each of the foundational ideas, attitudes, and values in a systematic way. The result is that one can become fluent in the cultural realities of the local people in a relatively short time to the point that people will begin to say "You [really] understand us."

This kind of training is employed in language schools, where the sounds and grammar of a language are embedded through repetition to a point of fluency. Moreover, as is the case in language learning, students have to go out into the local societies and do professional-quality field research on every theme of the local cultural knowledge if there is to be any beginning wisdom regarding the culture, and some hope of it being a factor for development. Like in language learning, one has to "talk" to people about their cultural knowledge on site. This means that the training has to be done within the local cultural communities if it is to be effective. Schools of theology in the United States that are training missionaries cannot adequately prepare students to work outside of North America, as they are situated in and profoundly challenged and influenced by the theological and spiritual issues derived from the secular, impersonal cultural realities of the North American society.

Even if the seminaries and universities overseas are sometimes more Western and more Roman than the Romans in terms of the theological and social training they offer, the fact of living in the local society is the essential element as the students, at least informally, realize that they are in someone else's cultural world and that through a MIAS-type program, they can begin to learn and appropriate systematically the mindset and spirituality of the local people. One of the great values of systematically learning another's cultural knowledge is that one becomes aware of and articulate regarding one's own cultural knowledge—a profoundly challenging kind of intellectual conversion. Again, this learning process has to take place on site, as anyone trying to learn a foreign language off site knows.

Given the breakthrough of the MIAS program in delineating the nature of cultural knowledge, there is now a way of teaching cultural knowledge on site in a host community so that the parachutist's landing is no longer a crash landing, but a soft landing. The reason is that it is a nonjudgmental parachutist who arrives and is prepared to contextualize his or her own cultural knowledge and to appropriate the cultural reality of the host culture through serious professional study. This MIAS-type study combines professional quality field research facilitated by a trained local university graduate with classroom lectures and selected nonprejudicial readings publishable in fifteen-page papers interrelating the lecture material with the field data.

Crash landings of messengers of change should no longer be tolerated, as they not only frustrate the messengers and the host cultures, but they also leave a bad taste in the mouths of both as each side claims that the other is resistant to change and will not adapt, or has gone back to the traditional ways. At this point in time, no matter where one resides worldwide, there are local resource persons available in the universities and institutes of higher learning who would be happy to participate in the systematic training of "parachutists," holding the *African Cultural Knowledge* book in one hand as a guide, and with the other directing the students into the highways and byways of the local society on organized field research projects related to the fifteen themes. Programs designed with these guiding principles in mind are needed worldwide.

20

Mission in a Globalized Economy

Albino Barrera, OP

The "gift of mission" invites us to be creative and agile in adapting evangelization to changing times. This requires an understanding of how the terrain for preaching the Gospel is being transformed by the Information Revolution that we are currently witnessing. Contemporary globalization consists of the twin phenomena of global economic integration and the emergence of the knowledge economy. The whole world is increasingly functioning as a single workshop, making nations and peoples ever more interdependent. Furthermore, knowledge has replaced industrial capital as the engine of wealth and value creation, due largely to the microelectronics revolution that has provided more, better, and cheaper information. Global economic integration and the emerging knowledge economy mutually reinforce each other to produce epochal shifts in the way we live, work, consume, and relate to each other. The changes we are witnessing are as dramatic and transformative as the Industrial Revolution was for the modern era. These shifts present both hurdles and opportunities to mission and evangelization in the twenty-first century and beyond.

Greater Obligations for Mission and Evangelization

The globalized knowledge economy has created even greater obligations for mission and evangelization, for at least two reasons. First, religion and mission have a new role, that of correcting some of the harmful values spawned by the marketplace.

Economics matters enormously because it is what drives contemporary globalization. Global economic integration and cross-border trade in goods and services are responsible for many of the other facets of globalization: cultural globalization and the export of American pop culture, the globalization of crime, the globalization of politics, and immigration. All these transpire in a terrain shaped and defined by the marketplace. This is the phenomenon of "marketization" in which market rules and modes of operation are seeping into every facet of social life, including those that have been traditionally noneconomic.

For example, note commercial surrogacy and the outsourcing of some government functions, such as the management of school and prison systems or the provision of water and sanitation services. Indeed, the market has emerged as a powerful social institution. In fact, the 2010–12 euro debt crisis is an excellent example of the potency of the market in shaping global events. Financial markets singlehandedly forced nations in the southern rim of the euro zone (Portugal, Spain, Italy, and Greece) to curb their fiscal excesses. In many of these cases, the markets were instrumental in precipitating a change in government.

The power of the market goes beyond merely shaping monetary and fiscal policy. It can also shape public economic morality. Without an active social effort to shape the public's ethos, it is the market itself that will fill the void. The market can nurture good habits such as an excellent work ethic, collaborative work and private initiative. However, "marketization" can also bring in its wake injurious values, such as individualism, impersonalism, productionism, consumerism, materialism, and an egoistic utilitarianism. We find evidence of this in the erosion of the much-vaunted Asian morals in the face of the economic boom in East Asia in the last three decades. Confucian values, such as respect for the elderly and the family, the desire for children, and the premium attached to marriage and family life, have been upended in the race to succeed in the marketplace. (See, for example, the August 20, 2011, cover story of *The Economist* on the Asian flight from marriage.) As part of this emerging globalized knowledge economy, we see the spread of Western pop culture and the promotion of attitudes that are inimical to religious belief and personal growth, courtesy of the market.

The market is not merely an enabler of diverse ideas. It is itself a competitor for people's hearts and minds. Economics itself can and does change people's mindset. As Peter Phan noted in his plenary presentation at this symposium, secularism is not the most formidable rival to religion. Instead, it is the unfettered marketplace and some of the misplaced values that it spawns that are the more menacing competitors. Thus, mission and evangelization must address some of the aforesaid ill effects of a market-shaped morality. There is an even greater obligation on the part of religion to lead hearts and minds to morals that are genuinely human, ennobling, and enduring.

Unfortunately, the task of mission has become much more difficult because a globalized knowledge economy has greatly expanded people's opportunity set. Their time is ever more valuable because of the many other opportunities now open to them through the marketplace and the worldwide web. Mission and evangelization will now have to compete even more for people's time and attention.

A second reason for the greater obligations of mission and evangelization is the greater interdependence of nations and peoples. While globalization has led to greater cooperation, it has also created new sources and flashpoints of conflict, including religion. Localized incidents can easily turn into a global sectarian conflagration, as in the case of the Danish cartoons of the Prophet Mohammed that provoked worldwide violence and protest in Islamic nations. Such is the power of easy communication and travel. Globalization has put religions in ever closer proximity to each other.

Greater contact with other faiths, even if only virtual through the Internet, brings opportunities for conversation and cooperation, but it can also bring strife because of misunderstandings or the machinations of extremists. In other words, religion is a two-edged sword. It can be a polarizing force or a healing balm, or both. Mission in a globalized knowledge economy will have to be keenly aware of his.

An Even Stronger Link between Evangelization and Social Action, Especially Poverty Alleviation

Globalization has tightened even further the link between faith and good works. Mission has become even more inextricably tied to social justice work. We find a convergence between *Octogesima Adveniens* (work on behalf of justice is constitutive of the Gospel) and *Evangelii Nuntiandi* (the centrality of preaching the Good News). The cause for this tighter link is the intensification of our moral responsibilities for one another's well-being. After all, the globalized knowledge economy has brought about greater interdependence, better knowledge of the plight of others, a better understanding of the adverse ripple effects of our actions, and a better capacity to ameliorate suffering. We can no longer plead ignorance or a lack of resources as an excuse for doing nothing to help those who are suffering halfway across the globe. Moreover, globalization has given rise to better moral sensibilities through higher mutual expectations and better moral development and education.

The theological foundation for this is that faith and good works are complementary—two sides of the same coin. Mission and evangelization are sterile if they are limited to words alone. They must be backed by action and example. The most eloquent articulation of these weightier responsibilities engendered by globalization is found in the opening lines of *Gaudium et Spes,* in which the hopes and joys, the griefs and anxieties of the people of this age, especially of the poor, are also the hopes and joys, the griefs and anxieties of Jesus Christ. For nothing genuinely human can fail to raise an echo in the human heart. Globalization has brought us in ever closer proximity (virtual or physical) to others' hopes and joys, griefs and anxieties. This development must be reflected as well in the manner by which we engage in mission in the twenty-first century. Not only have we become keenly aware of one another's hopes and joys, griefs and anxieties, but we are in a much better position to do something about them in a spirit of mutual, familial love.

Need for a Forward-Leaning Approach to Mission

The Information Revolution has brought not only new opportunities, but it has also created fresh challenges. Even as information and communication technologies have expanded our capabilities, they have also unleashed an information overload. The hapless Internet user is deluged with a cornucopia of data and stimuli. Religion faces a fierce fight and an uphill battle to get heard and to stay relevant. It is an increasingly crowded public square of ideas in the new terrain for missions: the e-highway! Younger generations are increasingly dependent on social media for their information and interpersonal relationships. The next generations will most likely be even more reliant on this rapidly evolving medium.

This means that mission requires imagination, flexibility, and agility in communicating its message. There is need for organizational innovations and tech-savvy evangelists. There is need for a healthy and vibrant engagement with the world through this new highway; mission must not flee from it, as the e-highway has redefined the scope of mission and evangelization. Mission's scope in an earlier time was centered on the less-developed countries. Now it is the whole world because of the "death of distance." The whole world is a mission field—virtual and not merely geographic.

The e-highway has also redefined the target audience of mission and evangelization. It used to be primarily the populations of isolated poor countries. Now, it also includes the wealthy nations in dire need of reevangelization. In fact, the poor have much to teach the rich regarding simplicity and enduring values.

Conclusions

The Information Revolution presents mission with the challenge of preaching its message in the midst of a cacophony of competing voices. Faith and good works hold the key to overcoming the new hurdles to evangelization. Charity (friendship with God) convinces by the power of its own truth (although creativity in presentation helps). One word of caution: We should nevertheless not exaggerate the impact of the microelectronics revolution and the Web. In the final analysis, it is still personal contact, example, and friendship that are key to mission. Technology, while possibly a necessary condition, is not a sufficient condition for evangelization. An extreme or exclusive reliance on technology for evangelization can lead to an impersonal mission. After all, the gift of mission is, in fact, the opportunity of being able to give of oneself in friendship.

Part IV

The Mission of the U.S. Church

21

The U.S. Church and Mission *ad Gentes*

Francis Cardinal George, OMI

Allow me to thank Maryknoll for the invitation to be with you and to thank the Chicago Theological Union for hosting us. I regret that I was not here to listen to all of the reflections and discussions because it would undoubtedly have sharpened my own presentation. Maryknoll did send me questions to consider. They are all very good questions, and each one could have undergirded a lecture or a conference of its own.

We are in the midst of a conversation, and no one of us has the final answer to all the questions. The challenge is always to take the next step, even if we do not understand the entire context. The context we are talking about is the context of Maryknoll as a mission society, founded to participate in the Church's mission *ad gentes*. Because this mission or purpose is central to the Church's sense of who she is, Maryknoll is central to the U.S. Church's sense of who we are and what we have accomplished.

When we look at Maryknoll's beginnings, we see two very holy priests who understood that we could not be a self-sufficient Church without going out and doing elsewhere what had been done for us here over the years, from the time of the Spanish Franciscans to the French Jesuits, to all the later mission societies that came to help establish the Church on this continent before there was a United States of America. As an American bishop, I thank Maryknoll with all my heart for placing the U.S. Church in this long history of mission sending.

I am not sure there has ever been a formal dialogue between Maryknoll, which was founded to convert the world to Christ, beginning in China, and the Paulists, who are the other indigenous American religious institution, founded to convert America to the Catholic Church. Basically, there are two sorts of motives for turning to Christ and giving one's life to him. Some people turn to Christ and to the Church because they have a sense that their life is not complete. Things aren't bad, but something is missing—the meaning and the centrality of what it means to live, to pass time on this Earth, not knowing what will come next. People are looking for something more. That was Isaac Hecker's idea of presenting the Catholic Church in American guise to an America that was turning very materialistic and that had turned to the Transcendentalist movement in the mid-nineteenth century in order to contest materialism in American culture. Hecker felt that America could not be complete, could not be itself, until it became Catholic. He had confidence that the Holy Spirit works in cultures in order to bring about this completion.

The other reason why people turn to Christ is because things are falling apart. They are caught in the mystery of evil, and people and societies need to be healed. They need to be rescued from darkness: they need some sense of forgiveness, and of wholeness. This is a conversion, a real sense of rupture with their old ways because their old ways left them mired in evil.

Fathers Price and Walsh and the first Maryknollers were convinced that the Church was missioned to heal a broken world. This purpose of mission is well captured in a hymn that Maryknoll used to sing as missionaries departed. The rhetoric is a little baroque, but it captures this purpose of mission:

> Dear brothers, hasten then to save the heathen
> engulfed deep in death's dark, cold abyss.
> Without true God, without a hope to soothe him,
> he shall be forever a child of wrath.
> Brave soldiers, rise and destroy the throne of Satan.
> Deliver from his grasp the groveling slave.
> Bring souls the freedom which Christ was given
> and plant the cross in every land.

That is a hymn St. Augustine could have sung, and so could the Church throughout most of its history. It captures the purpose that sent missioners to an uncertain future out of love for sinners who would otherwise be lost, in this life and the next.

Why do people go out to proclaim Christ, whether in this country or anywhere else in the world? The mission is always the same. The mission of the Church is to introduce the world to its Savior until he returns in glory. Every generation must pick up that mission by reason of our baptism and do so in new contexts that are ever changing, using new means and methods adjusted to the times. As we talk about means and about changed contexts, it is good to remember the purpose. Mission is purpose; it is why we do what we're called to do.

Priests and others are very skilled at ministry. They are used to serving; this is what they are trained to do. But what happens when nobody wants your service? This brings a crisis of identity. This is why it is imperative to keep ministry and mission together, to keep service joined to the purpose for serving. Why do we have parishes, why do we have hospitals and schools, why do we support RCIA and Catholic Charities? The proper way out of a ministerial crisis is to remember why the Church exists. It exists for the mission: to introduce the world to its Savior. Everything else is relative.

What's the relationship between mission and Church and how did the early Church understand it? A classic example of mission *ad gentes* was that of St. Paul; as described in Acts 17, he journeyed to a people who were not Jews and therefore could not understand the historical and biblical context in which Christ was proclaimed as the fulfillment, the completion of the work of God's salvific action to rescue his people. Rather, Paul presented Christ as someone entirely new in nature, someone who had risen from the dead, to people who could not fit resurrection into their rationalist worldview.

Paul started where the people were by referring to Seneca's poetry and by telling them that they were well known everywhere for discussing important questions about an unknown God. Paul said, in effect, "Let me tell you who this unknown God is, let me complete your knowledge, complete your self-understanding by coming to know the God whom you already worship without knowing it." He got along fairly well until he told them that Jesus had risen from the dead. The Jews understood what that meant, although some of them, the Sadducees, didn't believe in it. But as soon as Paul mentioned resurrection to the Athenians, they turned away, some of them laughing, with only a few, including Dionysius, converting. The memory of Paul's rejection has haunted mission *ad gentes* ever since. When do you present the fundamental belief of the apostolic faith, Christ's resurrection from the dead, and where do you start?

You start where people are. Where you go and how you get there is a psychological and pastoral problem that we all wrestle with. When do you say what you have to say and when do you prudently wait for a while, hoping that the Holy Spirit will work quietly and silently in people's hearts and minds so that they might understand and be converted.

The motives for this proclamation can vary. The classic scriptural reference is Matthew 28, the great commission. It is an extrinsic command that initiates action broadly motivated by the conviction on the believer's part that all people need to know their Savior and hand their lives over to him.

There is also an internal command for mission. When the U.S. bishops have spoken about missions they have sometimes started with St. John and not with Matthew's great commission. This begins from the ecclesiology of communion of Vatican II. In John 6, for example, the evangelist speaks about sharing Christ's great gift of his body and blood, the holy Eucharist. The reception of the body of the Risen Lord, the seed of immortality in our still mortal bodies, moves us to share this gift as widely as possible. The purpose of mission is to share the gifts of Christ, because that is how the Church is formed: by sharing the gifts of Christ. Once received, spiritual gifts have to be shared with others or they will be lost.

The invisible gifts of faith and the other infused virtues of the life of grace are protected by the visible gifts: the proclamation of the Gospel, apostolic governance, and the celebration of the seven sacraments of the apostolic Churches. When you share a gift, you create a relationship. If somebody gives you a gift, a new and stronger relationship comes to be. If you refuse a gift, you break off the relationship. "I don't want the socks you knitted for me, Grandma," signals the end of your relationship with your grandmother. Sharing the gifts of Christ creates the foundation for the relationships that constitute ecclesial communion.

Mission and Vatican II

The theology of ecclesial communion of the Second Vatican Council infuses the approach to mission with an inner impulse to be generous with Christ's gifts as he has been generous with us. This approach respects the missionary purpose of the Second Vatican Council and also expresses the new ecclesial self-consciousness that arose from the Council. This new ecclesial self-consciousness was necessary because the old self-consciousness of the Church as a primarily juridical reality was no longer adequate to motivate the conversion of the world. Pope John XXIII worried about the Church's effectiveness in introducing the world to its Savior. The Church had become, at times, an obstacle to helping people understand who Christ is. So the Church itself had to be purified, first of all, by returning to worship in forms that were more persuasive (*Sacrosanctum Concilium*). Worship is always central to religion; after all, religion is about God, not first of all about Church or morals or ourselves.

Starting with worship, the Council moved on to the sources of what we know about God from divine self-revelation (*Dei Verbum*) and then taught how the Church is formed in receiving the gift of revelation and in receiving the gift of the Eucharist and the other sacraments (*Lumen Gentium*). The last great conciliar constitution related the Church, aware of itself in renewed fashion, to the contemporary world (*Gaudium et Spes*). We were a premodern Church that tried to navigate the shoals of modernity, in which Protestants were much more at home. Nonetheless, all of us now live in a postmodern world that is rapidly secularizing in the West. How should we position the Church vis-à-vis a world that, whether it knows it or not, has been redeemed? Because the introduction to the world's Savior is problematic if the Church gets in the way, the Church had to change in order to change the world. The Council was called in order to convert and unite a divided world.

Pope John XXIII's letter convoking the Second Vatican Council rehearsed his reasons for calling a council. It was to complete the work on divine revelation and the Constitution of the Church of the First Vatican Council, but it was also called because recent world history had made it clear that the world needed to be told that all human beings constitute a single human family. John XXIII had experienced two world wars, the Russian revolution, communism and Nazism, the destruction of the Jews of Europe, extreme nationalism, and the racism that permeated societies everywhere, along with unjust economic structures that had created class conflict. Saintly man that he was, Pope John XXIII asked, "Who will tell the human race that we

are all brothers and sisters?" Who else but the Catholic Church? The Church is to be, as the Second Vatican Council in *Lumen Gentium* calls it, "the sacrament of the unity of the human race" (*Lumen Gentium* 1). How do you unite the human race? By introducing it to its Savior and by sharing his gifts so that the relationships among ourselves can be one of friendship and even brotherhood and sisterhood instead of enmity.

The Council, as you know, wasn't sure at first, in light of the theology of communion, that it really had to say something directly about mission *ad gentes*. At the insistence of a number of bishops, especially from mission areas, they wrote *Ad Gentes*. It started with a missiological problem that was academic in origin but important in its consequences. Something of a crisis of conscience had been created for missioners who were wondering what they should concentrate on first. The classical missionary approach was what the first Maryknollers evidently chose: convert individuals to Jesus Christ and that will establish the Church and transform society. This was the Münster School of missiology's approach. By contrast, the Louvain School of Missiology said that the purpose of mission is, of course, to bring people to Christ, but that is the work of invisible grace. Therefore, the Church's first responsibility is to plant the Church so that the means of grace are visibly available. Of course, if the new Church is not self-sufficient, then Propaganda Fide helps to govern its area; when the Church is self-sufficient, it becomes pastoral territory under the regular Code of Canon Law.

However, planting the Church and creating the network of visible relationships that shape it are the primary objects of missionary activity. The discussion, as you are aware, was not only academic. It influenced the way people decided how they were going to approach mission *ad gentes*. The Council document finessed the discussion by combining the two approaches. Paragraph 6 of the Second Vatican Council's document says,

> The special undertakings in which preachers of the Gospel, sent by the Church, and going into the whole world, carry out the work of preaching the Gospel and implanting the Church among people who do not yet believe in Christ, are generally called "missions." Such undertakings are accomplished by missionary activity and are,

for the most part, carried out in defined territories recognized by the Holy See. The special end of this missionary activity is the evangelization and the implanting of the Church among peoples or groups in which it has not yet taken root. (*Ad Gentes* 6)

With that being said, the Council went on to mention other dimensions of the missionary enterprise, topics that were addressed more completely by *Evangelii Nuntiandi* in 1975. In that Post-Synodal Apostolic Exhortation, Pope Paul VI wanted to bring mission into focus in the light of the Council's redefinition of the Church-world relationship. If the Church was not a defensive fortress but rather a network of relationships open to the world in order to convert the world, its approach to converting should be primarily dialogical. Paul VI therefore said that a missionary must listen respectfully to the world, although even within dialogue the truth about who Christ is must be expressed. Proclamation remains at the heart of Pope Paul VI's understanding of evangelization, which became the privileged term for speaking about the missionary activities of the Church.

Pope John Paul II felt that "mission" was still a useful term and one that was not completely summed up in "evangelization." In *Redemptoris Missio* (1990), John Paul II acknowledged the activity of evangelizing while restoring an attention to place. He spoke of a new *areopagus*. Where today do we find St. Paul's *areopagus*? We find it in the new communications media. To proclaim and dialogue, one must be where the centers of communication are. In order to introduce the Lord, one must be where people talk. There was some discussion after the Council, given the fact that mission is universal, whether Propaganda Fide's role in Church government was otiose! But there are particular problems of the Churches in lands where the community can't yet be self-sufficient, and Propaganda Fide is the instrument for sharing gifts among local Churches, especially with young Churches.

The Church is universal, because she wants to share the gifts of Christ with everyone Christ saved, yet the Council recognized the obvious fact that there are vast differences among local Churches. To explain how the Church is everywhere missionary and everywhere visibly gathered into local Churches, we must address the question of the context of mission.

The Social and Cultural Context of Mission

Everywhere Jesus Christ is the context of mission as well as the content of missionary proclamation. After the Council, the question of the relation of the Kingdom of God to the Church of Christ became problematic. What becomes clear from reflecting on the Gospel itself is that the Kingdom is not a place, nor a set of values as such. The Kingdom is a person. It is Jesus Christ whose life and values transform the world. One does not start with the missionary or with the people addressed in missionary activity when focusing on the Church's mission. At times, starting with something other than Christ himself might be a precondition necessary for the mission, but the Kingdom is Jesus Christ. The proclamation of who Christ is, whether by direct proclamation or in the midst of dialogue, is the heart of mission. The Church proposes, without imposing, the Gospel given by Christ and handed on through the apostles and later missionaries. Values are intrinsic to the message, but they have to be defined in the context of Christ's Gospel, not as society defines them. The content and context of mission is always Jesus Christ crucified and risen from the dead. The cultural context, however, changed as the distinction between mission lands and pastoral Churches also became more problematic.

After the Second World War, France began to recognize that, despite its great history as a mission-sending society, France was itself a mission territory. The recognition that the Gospel had to be proclaimed in France to those who did not know Christ meant that the distinction between primary evangelization (going out and proclaiming who Christ is in lands that have never heard of him before) and secondary evangelization (recalling believers to the moral demands of their faith) was not adequate. Secondary evangelization in pastoral lands was the work of parish missions. Their purpose was not to preach who Christ is: catechesis was assumed. Instead, the commandments of God and the Church became the main content of secondary evangelization. The parish mission called people to moral conversion. The believers in the parishes knew who Christ is, but they had fallen away from following him because of their sinfulness. The parish missioner proclaimed the moral law and brought people to personal confession of their sins. At the end of three days or a week in a parish, if the mission preachers were successful in bringing a good number of people to confession, the parish mission was a success. The distinction between the doctrinal priority of primary evangelization and the moral preaching of secondary evangelization was brought into question by the recognition that, even in France, not everybody knows who Christ is.

It was John Paul II, who, with his philosophical anthropologist's sensitivity to culture and using the dialogue between faith and culture of *Gaudium et Spes* as background, most clearly expanded the goal of conversion to extend to cultures, entire ways of life. People act from nature and from grace within the normative systems of culture and of faith. Culture as second nature was introduced into ecclesial conversation as John Paul II built on Paul VI's *Evangelii Nuntiandi*. He drew the Church's attention to whole cultures, once shaped in conversation with the Church, with the faith, and with Christ—whether Protestant in our case or Catholic in the cases of Poland and Mexico—where belief in Christ is now countercultural. Not only do people not know who Christ is in adequate fashion; they have rejected him. Christianity is now superseded by contemporary postmodern pluralism and secularism.

Paul VI had said that we have to look at societal structures, but John Paul II went one step farther: faith and culture are both normative systems and, since tensions are inevitable, the missionary has to convert not just individuals but entire cultures. "Faith becomes culture," he often said. Faith is not just an invisible reality. It expresses itself first of all in language and then in other cultural forms as well. Working to bring a culture back to Christ is a lot harder than introducing people to Christ for the first time. The missionary has to do it in such a way that it is not a return to a past that cannot be recaptured. It must be a return to principle. The goal is to help reconvert, to convert ethnic cultures so that it makes sense for individuals in a given social order to accept and love the risen Lord.

I received a letter a couple of days ago from a woman who was quite angry. One of the lines she wrote was, "Nobody tells Americans what to do!" Part of her response is cultural; it indicates the difficulty in calling people to conversion of mind and heart in our society so often marked by self-righteousness. If not even God can tell us what to do, we have an obstacle to evangelization!

The Ecclesial Context of Mission

The ecclesial context for Catholic missionaries is a Church that claims to speak and govern in Christ's name. When the Second Vatican Council was interpreted as a conflict between liberals and conservatives, the Church herself became a distraction to the Council's implementation and to the evangelization the Council called for. Liberals and conservatives define themselves vis-à-vis authority, but the Gospel is neither liberal nor conservative. The Gospel is about true and false. If one is unable to think or analyze beyond political terminology, then politics remains the final and highest human conversation. If that occurs, Catholicism is just one more ideology, one more pressure group trying to find its way in a society based upon will and power. If you don't go beyond that dynamic to the truth question—what is true and what is false—the Church will always be conservative doctrinally and liberal socially. But that does not express the truth about Jesus Christ in an integrated way. New Testament prophets point first to Christ. Church structures need to be reformed and changed, but the criterion for change is Christ himself, who is judge of the living and the dead.

Paul VI

Since the Council, the popes have implemented its teachings in light of their own skills and concerns. Paul VI was an expert in Church governance. He reformed the curia, being faithful to the Council's call to internationalize it. He created the Synod of Bishops, and he established the pontifical councils for justice and peace, for health care, for the laity, for immigration—all those pontifical councils that have no jurisdiction but expand the breadth of the Church's concerns from within the curia itself. These concerns are often institutionalized now in diocesan curias as well. A diocese is a local Church and not just a collection of parishes, and the bishop is pastor in the fullest sense of the term.

We ordain bishops now rather than consecrating them, because the bishop receives the fullness of Holy Orders, not just additional jurisdictional power. He has authority over the sacramental body of Christ because he has authority from Christ to govern the mystical body of Christ. That understanding of the theology of Orders, within the theology of ecclesial communion, takes the concerns of a local Church beyond parochial-based ministries. It expands the missionary outreach of the Church in ecumenical dialogue, interfaith communication, and action for social justice in order to create the unity and cohesiveness that will bring the world to believe in Christ from within his body, the Church.

John Paul II

For Pope John Paul II, the ecclesial context was not just the Roman curia. He came to the papacy as a residential bishop from a country that had lost its freedom. He preached a Christ who sets us free. He helped free Poland by delegitimizing the Communist regime. On his first visit back to Poland after his election as bishop of Rome, he stood in Victory Square in Warsaw and declared that no one can understand the history of Poland without reference to Jesus Christ. The crowd started chanting, "We want God! We want God!" Other people and events certainly contributed to radical social and political change in Poland, but Pope John Paul had the courage to preach the truth about who Christ is. Then all the ideological contortions of the Marxist regime were suddenly exposed for what they were—false consciousness.

As a philosopher, he expressed the ancient faith in modern language, using phenomenology and anthropology, and a vocabulary that complemented scholastic philosophy and theology. But he returned always to one critical insight: in order to understand who we really are, we have to understand who Christ is. He preached this truth everywhere in multiple languages and was a great missionary pope, proclaiming the truth in love, bringing freedom as a gift from Christ to be universally shared.

Benedict XVI

With Pope Benedict XVI, the ecclesial context is all of Church history and eternity itself. He speaks as often about God as he does of Christ, because he is concerned about cultures closing themselves off to the transcendent. He talks first about God, because the search for the truth about God will lead to Jesus Christ and to experiencing the power of the Spirit. Benedict demonstrates from history that an ideological system, an economic system, or a political system that doesn't permit the

God question to be publicly addressed organizes itself as if God did not exist. Such a system will turn in on itself and become a closed system. It is God who saves us from closing in on ourselves, from living in prisons of our own making. It is God who opens us to eternity, because God is always more. No one can capture God. If a missionary is proclaiming the true God, he or she is saving the world from itself and opening the world to its truest possibilities.

Pope Benedict believes that the secularist society of the West has turned in on itself in ways that prevent our renewing ourselves as peoples. He keeps together truth and freedom along with love, and he is particularly concerned about conscience as the voice of truth. He was pleased to beatify Cardinal Newman because Newman is a great teacher about the nature and formation of conscience, whose freedom was emphasized in the Council. Benedict is also concerned about worship because that is where we meet God as God wants to be met. True worship brings us to meet Christ in the Eucharist. In that concern, the pope is implementing what the Council taught. It started with God and our worship of God; in that context everything else falls into its proper place. The Council changed much about the Church and developed doctrine in key areas, but in the end it is the eternal verities that we proclaim. We proclaim them in the liturgy when we come together because Christ is Lord, and we say that most clearly to the world when we worship God in spirit and truth.

The U.S. Context for Mission

A last point is the question of the U.S. context for mission. Maryknoll was not created to convert the United States, as were the Paulists, but nonetheless it was created as an American mission society. Missionaries change the Church that sends them as well as the Church that receives them. We know that missionaries inevitably bring their own culture along with the Gospel. When I went around visiting the Oblates in many countries, one of the questions in the common rooms at night was: Are we bringing our own culture inappropriately as we proclaim who Christ is to people of very different cultures? How do we sort it out so that missionaries are not imposing their own culture on other people in the name of the Gospel? Paul was a Jew and, in making pagan Greeks into Christians, he

Judaized them to a certain extent. He certainly brought the Old Testament with him. The Gospel is never "culture free." You know that if you go to a mission station and the missioners are Italians, they will usually have a really nice chapel. If you go to a missionary land and the missionaries are French, they will always have a generator for a refrigerator so they can have cheese. If you go to the mission and the first missionaries were Americans, you will always find showers. Inevitably, missioners bring themselves with the Gospel and usually not inappropriately so.

Missionary spirituality is based on the ascesis of giving up much of oneself and trying to identify with a new people, even though the missioner is never totally one with them. The people know that, but they are grateful for the missionary's presence. Then the missionary returns home and is never totally one with the land that had been left. That's missionary ascesis. It's a journey to holiness. Because there's no "pure" faith unrelated to any culture, and there's no culture that doesn't have some belief system underneath, the question always remains whether such a journey is explicitly religious or not.

What are we now facing in our country? Greg Darr, an organizer of this symposium, posed excellent questions to me, and one was about trends or factors that are unique in U.S. society, global trends and factors that have a unique impact on our society and on the Church here. One characteristic of Catholics in this country that is truly distinctive is that while we are Catholic in faith, we have Protestant sensibilities, and that can be helpful in some ways. We can bring sensibilities honed here into the network of Catholic communion, expressing from within Catholicism attitudes and directions from other sources.

Remaining totally Catholic in faith but with certain Protestant sensibilities gives us a different vision of Church governance. Luther dismissed the visible government structure of the Church as a human invention; Catholics believe ecclesial structures are in their fundamental form the will of Christ. Thus we cannot change certain central structures any more than we can change the nature of the apostolic sacraments. We cannot celebrate the Eucharist with Coke and pizza no matter what some of our young people might like us to do. Likewise, we are bound to certain forms of pastoral governance because this is the will of the Lord until he comes again.

However, with the freedom from certain external structures that is part of the Protestant tradition comes a sensitivity to issues of accountability and transparency. This is good, but not if we are more influenced by our American culture than we are by our Catholic faith. I received a letter ten years ago from someone who was very upset, feeling that Pope John Paul II didn't understand our country's mission in wanting to bring freedom to Iraq. He was sixty-five years old when he wrote, and he enclosed his baptismal certificate. He said he was ashamed of being a Catholic. He was most sincere, but his letter showed how the American sense of national mission can make of the country itself an ersatz church.

America is a classically Protestant project, and we have never existed as a people apart from democratic institutions. We have more than just a democratic form of government; we have a democratic society and a democratic culture, which gives us certain inclinations that other peoples do not have. We are a product of choice, not a product of linguistic uniformity or of blood or race. Our society is based upon choice that is expressed in an eighteenth-century social contract. Therefore, law and culture cannot be separated in this country as in other countries. The legal system is the most important social instrument we have in common, and it is marked by our culture more than in other countries. Here, how you stand before the law is how you stand as a human being. That is at the root of the political imbroglio that is the immigration problem. An "outlaw" is less than human.

We should recognize the downside of any culture, including ours. A missionary does not just react against culture but rather tries to plumb it for its true worth and use it to preach the Gospel. We are not a privileged people, we are not an "almost chosen people," as Lincoln called us. Nonetheless we are a people who have done a lot to advance the course of political freedom. Freedom is a Gospel value, provided that it is not reduced to individual choice.

In this country, before the Second World War Catholics were often considered interlopers. One of the reasons that the thirteen colonies felt free to break their oath of loyalty to King George III was because he had broken his coronation oath. Against English law, he permitted the worship practices of the Catholic Church—the Mass—to be celebrated publicly in conquered French Canada. That freed the English colonists in the thirteen colonies from their oath of loyalty to a monarch who had made himself a threat to the Protestant religion.

By the time the Second World War ended, almost everybody had become American. The country was no longer just Protestant; it was Protestant, Catholic, and Jewish. We were home at last when John F. Kennedy was elected president. Today it is not just Protestant, Catholic, and Jewish; it is Protestant, Catholic, Jewish, and Muslim. It is multicultural, multireligious, and multiethnic, with people trying to figure out if religion of any sort is important to the American project. The dominant culture continues to be a Protestanized secularism or a secularized Protestantism. It is good to be aware of this history with its limits and its richness. Without critical intelligence, the culture simply controls our thought and action.

Additional Mission Questions

One source of tension in the U.S. Church is the contrast between the way we understand who we are as a people and the self-understanding of recent immigrants. The immigrants from Catholic cultures have brought us back to Catholic customs that we had forgotten. In the Archdiocese of Chicago, at least, after the Second Vatican Council, public devotion was largely forgotten or discouraged; devotion was undertaken in private. The only public religious exercise was the liturgy. The Mexicans tell us: No, there's public veneration of the Blessed Virgin Mary; the Poles tell us: No, there's public worship of the Blessed Sacrament, even in the streets on Corpus Christi. In exchanging gifts based on faith in their different cultural expressions, we receive a reconstituted sense of Church. Forty percent of the 2.3 million Catholics in this geographically quite limited archdiocese were not born in this country. A new internal dialogue is taking place.

After the First World War and the closing of our borders to immigrants, Cardinal Mundelein realized that our mission was to create an American Catholic Church. He belonged to the second wave of Americanizers in the Catholic hierarchy and helped to create an American Catholic Church that worked extremely well for three generations. Now we are in a multicultural world shaped again by immigrants to this country; if the South is the future, the South is here with the immigrants. For three, four, five, or six generations, we assimilated foreigners into an American Catholic Church, helping them to assimilate also to American society. That assimilation is more cautiously approached now. Missionaries, it seems to me, acquire a pastoral perspective that relativizes any single cultural expression of the faith, including their own. They have a particular ability to keep different cultural sensitivities alive in a supposedly multicultural society that is in fact quite controlled in what it will allow people to think, what it will demand that they do, how it will permit them to worship. Missionaries' ability to be self-controlled in the life of discipleship is a great blessing for the Church and for the society in which they live as strangers in a strange land, which is sometimes even the land of their birth.

Looking to the field afar, what distinguishes U.S. efforts in mission from the efforts of local Churches elsewhere in the world? How do these distinguishing characteristics of our culture enhance or inhibit the U.S. Church's mission *ad gentes*? As I traveled around the world I found out that while people knew who I was as a Catholic priest, they were often distrustful of me as an American citizen. Is that changing now? Much anti-Americanism was the result of Marxist propaganda, which painted the United States and the Church herself in a very bad light, but suspicion was also rooted in the experience of others that "nobody tells Americans what to do." I had to listen and listen and listen before others would listen to me. That's a good missionary approach, but it is not always easy, especially when you really do know what is right!

This is a leaderless world right now. China does not want to step in, nor does India; it seems that the United States is the only one who can still lead, but we seem uncertain. After the Second World War, we re-created the world economically and politically. The world now has shifted. Our financial power is relatively diminished, although our military prowess remains great. Internally, we seem to be politically deadlocked. The challenge for us as members of a global Church, a universal Church, is to try to help our own people into the future, a future where the universal Church is already at home. Catholics might be able to help moderate the American transition from being the only or the dominant superpower to being one of many. A leaderless world does not have to descend into anarchy; instead, it can become a more cooperative world. Catholics could be the leaven in the transition, because we know this country is not a church and that this country is not the total context of our self-understanding.

When we talk about the future of the Church and the world, one of the challenges for American Catholics, particularly those with a dialogical sense of mission, is to think about how we can help our own country into thinking about itself in a different way that will permit us to be part of a global society that may or may not be better than American hegemony. These last fifty years of American hegemony were better than many periods for the human race, and we do not know what will happen next. The challenge is to be ourselves in a genuinely open way so that the world's cultures will be seen not as obstacles to unity but as gifts to be shared. We do this in the Church, especially in multi-cultural parishes. If permitted, we can be helpful on a societal stage.

Globalization is a welcome challenge for missionaries because, for the first time in modern times, Catholics can really be at home in the world. When Paul VI went to the United Nations, the first pope ever to address the only secular analogue to his own position, he said, "I come among you as an expert in humanity," the representative of "the sacrament of the unity of the human race." Political representatives are not very good at uniting the human race, but the Church can be an agent of global unity.

The last point was brought up by Pope Benedict in his recent address in Germany before the Bundestag, when he talked about ecological consciousness. He was not talking about the Green Party but about the enlarged scope of our consciousness. The Holy Spirit is the soul of the Church, active throughout the world, even outside the structures of the Church. We know that spiritually we can rely on the virtues of the saints because they are ours in the family of God, and we know also that anyone's sinfulness weakens everybody else spiritually. We see the social consequences of sin in the sexual abuse crisis; actions done furtively have had enormous consequences for the whole body of Christ. In the communion of saints we understand ecological consciousness. We do not translate the theology of communion into biological or physical or cosmological terms, but we know what it is to say that everything is interrelated. It is all communion. Therefore in his encyclical *Caritas in Veritate* Pope Benedict presents a still unfinished, very rudimentary model of a political and an economic order based upon the sharing of gifts.

The Church is a communion based upon the sharing of the gifts of Christ. If one could invent a political or an economic order that would be based upon the sharing of gifts, the social environment would be a better context for the Church's life and service. If gifts in a corporate budget do not come as philanthropy after the bottom line is figured, if the gifts are before the bottom line, the economic system would look more like a secular analogue of ecclesial communion. Pope John Paul II talked about the secular analogue of ecclesial communion as solidarity, and Pope Benedict has taken it one step further and explained that solidarity is not based only upon a shared project, but upon the sharing of gifts. Gift is at the heart of everything. Life is a gift, as is new life in Christ. Being is itself a gift from an infinite God who loves us. It is all gift, and it all holds together. Our mission as Catholics here and everywhere is to hold everything together in Christ's name, for Christ is Lord.

22

The U.S. Church:
Serving Mission *ad Gentes*

Madge Karecki, SSJ-TOSF

I feel very privileged to share in this conversation. When I came to the Mission Office of the Archdiocese of Chicago in 2008, after twenty-one years in South Africa, some of my very first visitors were from Maryknoll. Greg Darr came with Fr. Bill Donnelly and Fr. Jerry McCrane. That meeting has blossomed into a wonderful and enriching friendship that has brought abundant blessings to me and my staff.

In what is more a complement than a response to Cardinal George's presentation, I add my own voice to the missiological discourse enriched by the variety of our experience and research.

In an article published in *America* about the beginnings of the Maryknoll community, there is an excerpt from *A Field Afar* in which Fr. Walsh invited young men who were willing to go afar to "toil for the souls of heathen people . . . with no hope of earthly recompense" to write to him about their willingness to commit themselves to such a mission. This is not exactly what we find today in a typical vocation brochure! Nevertheless, at the time it was enough to motivate young men to respond to the call to mission as it was articulated by Fr. Walsh. The invitation obviously worked, and so I asked myself what would it take to captivate young Americans to respond to the call of mission *ad gentes* today?

First we have to come to a deeper understanding of young Catholics today, how they think and what is important to them. In John L. Allen, Jr.'s column about those participating in World Youth Day in Madrid (*National Catholic Reporter*, August 19, 2011), he described the youth gathered for that celebration of faith. I think his description could be helpful in reaching out in terms of mission to what he calls "Evangelical Catholics." He said that these are young Catholics who defy the usual political labels of "conservative" or "liberal." Instead, he says, three things characterize their "Catholic worldview":

183

- A strong defense of traditional Catholic identity, meaning attachment to classic markers of Catholic thought (doctrinal orthodoxy) and Catholic practice (liturgical tradition, devotional life, and authority).

- Robust public proclamation of Catholic teaching, with the accent on Catholicism's mission *ad extra*, transforming the culture in light of the Gospel, rather than *ad intra*, on internal church reform.

- Faith seen as a matter of personal choice rather than cultural inheritance, which among other things implies that in a highly secular culture, Catholic identity can never be taken for granted. It always has to be proven, defended, and made manifest.

Allen continues,

> We're talking about that inner core of actively practicing young Catholics who are most likely to discern a vocation to the priesthood or religious life, most likely to enroll in graduate programs of theology, and most likely to pursue a career in the church as a lay person—youth ministers, parish life coordinators, liturgical ministers, diocesan officials, and so on. In that sub-segment of today's younger Catholic population, there's an Evangelical energy so thick you can cut it with a knife. Needless to say, the groups I've just described constitute the church's future leadership.

I think Allen's insights are valuable. We need to tap into the generosity of spirit that lives within young people and make them aware that commitment to the Church means commitment to mission.

For our part, those of us fifty-five and older, who might be still reacting to the pre–Vatican II fortress mentality to the Church, might instead make thoughtful and informed responses to help shape the Catholic identity of young people to enable them to respond to the call of mission. In other words, if the Church in the United States is going to continue to respond generously to the call to mission *ad gentes*, then we need to engage young people at the deeper level of faith where a missionary spirit is enkindled.

Second, we need to share the best of our Catholic faith tradition with young people so as to feed their Catholic imagination. Andrew Greeley argues that the Catholic imagination is shaped by rituals and symbols and biblical texts that are "in their origins and in their primal power, tenacious and durable narrative symbols that take possession of the imagination early in the socialization process and provide patterns which shape the rest of life." "These patterns," Greeley continues, "are encoded in different stories of God's relationships with the world and with humankind" (*The Catholic Imagination* [Berkeley: University of California Press, 2001], 133). Our God wants to be in relationship with humanity and to engage us at the level of self-revelation that nurtures union and communion and that brings out the best in the human person.

Fr. Walsh, Fr. Price, Bro. McCann, and Mollie Rogers grasped the legitimacy of this perspective. They knew that the imagination of Catholics, shaped by a rich liturgical tradition and augmented with stories of missionaries serving in distant land, would be "the good ground" where mission vocations would flourish.

We also have to take seriously the Trinitarian theology of mission found in the often quoted text from the *Decree on the Missionary Activity of the Church*: "The pilgrim Church is missionary by her very nature, since it is from the mission of the Son and the mission of the Holy Spirit that she draws her origin, in accordance with the decree of God the Father" (par. 2). If this is indeed what we believe, then mission formation, education, and preparation programs need to take this passage very seriously. We need, I think, to talk less about missionary "activity" and speak more about missionary "identity," less about mission as a task and more about mission as a way of life. We need to act with conviction on our own baptismal and missionary identity founded on John 20:21: "As the Father sent me, I also send you." In the double movement of being called and sent, our identity as missionary disciples is born and sustained. We need to cultivate this sense of our identity so that the quality of our witness is strengthened.

If our witness is going to attract others to Christ, then we need to respond with contemplation to the invitation to intimacy with the Lord. As we grow in intimacy with Christ we do whatever is necessary to make this relationship the primary one of our lives. Slowly we find that we are able to make choices that better reflect God's love for the world. Contemplation is never an escape from reality.

In the contemplative experience of union with Christ one is called out of one's self in progressive stages of growth in love. In the Lord's embrace we become empowered by the Spirit with a love that we are taught by the One who is love. A spirituality shaped and sustained by union with the Trinity does not lead us away from people or disengage us from reality, but instead opens us to union with others, especially poor people and those suffering any form of oppression.

Contemplation also leads to a desire to live out a deep sense of communion with others whether here at home or abroad. The individualism, materialism, economic wealth, and competitiveness that often characterize American culture cannot find a place in mission praxis today if mission *ad gentes* is taken seriously.

In *Ecclesiam Suam* (1964) Paul VI described what is needed to live in solidarity with people and with profound respect for their cultures and traditions:

> Since the world cannot be saved from the outside, we must first of all identify ourselves with those to whom we would bring the Christian message—like the Word of God who Himself became man. Next we must forego all privilege and the use of unintelligible language, and adopt the way of life of ordinary people in all that is human and honorable. Indeed we must adopt the way of life of the most humble people, if we wish to be listened to and understood. Then, before speaking, we must take great care to listen not only to what people say, but more especially to what they have in the hearts to say. (87)

Concretely this means that our own lifestyles have to reflect a "downward mobility" that renders us capable of living as prophetic witnesses in every culture. Ours must be a kenotic presence when we stand with people, aware in awe of how the Spirit of God is at work in their lives. Then we will be able to act with "bold humility" among people and proclaim with them the riches of Christ by our words and by our life. To both young and adult Catholics we need to give a clear witness to faith and give evidence of the difference Christ makes in our lives so that they will join us as companions on the journey of conversion and mission. All people are then respected; no one is ever forced, and Christ is always proclaimed not in words, but in deeds of charity, friendship, companionship, advocacy, justice, and peace.

We need to challenge all Catholics and make them aware that they are responsible for continuing the mission of God in the world. We cannot be timid about this. Pope Benedict XVI said it so well in his Post-Synodal Apostolic Exhortation *Verbum Domini*: "It is not a matter of preaching a word of consolation, but rather a word which disrupts, which calls to conversion, and which opens the way to an encounter with the one through whom a new humanity flowers" (93).

We are called to invite people to be attentive to the transcendent dimension where God is found. In this way they can, if they are open, experience life in the Trinity as a sending community and live out their deepest identity as those sent to bring good news to the poor, proclaim liberty to captives, give new sight to the blind, set the downtrodden free, and proclaim that indeed our God is God-with-us and that our God bids us to share in his mission in the world.

If we are going to be serious about living out the missionary identity of the Church, then at every level of Church life we will need to allow our thinking to be shaped by mission theology. We will need to take mission as a starting point in our theological reflection and discussions. Mission will need to be the lens through which we view the whole of Catholic life.

Seminaries and institutes of higher education will need to give missiology pride of place in shaping curricula. Parishes will need to shape parish life so that mission is reflected in catechesis, adult faith formation, sacramental preparation, liturgical celebrations, and outreach beyond parish boundaries. High schools, colleges, and parishes that sponsor service trips need to demonstrate how these are outward expressions of our missionary vocation rooted in our baptism and not just humanitarian projects.

Diocesan mission offices will need to focus on mission education and formation. We need to educate Catholics so that all of us hold together a sense that all of us are called to mission and some are called to mission in other countries. Nonetheless, mission is always a sharing in God's mission, the *missio Dei*. I might add here that plans are underway at the National Office of the Pontifical Mission Societies to see if an online missiology course can be developed.

I am convinced that we do not need more documents. The encyclicals of Paul VI, John Paul II, and Benedict XVI are clear about our call to mission as are the documents of the Second Vatican Council. The American bishops' 1986 pastoral statement on World Mission, *To the Ends of the Earth, Called to Global Solidarity: International Challenges for US Parishes* (1997) and *Teaching in the Spirit of Mission ad*

Gentes: Continuing Pentecost Today published in 2005 for World Mission Sunday have helped to concretize mission theology and praxis in the American missionary praxis. We have only to put love in action and set out in hope to make God known and loved.

The legacy of the American Missionary Movement, so typified in Fr. Walsh, Fr. Price, Mother Mary Joseph Rogers, and Bro. Thomas McCann, and the mission theology that finds expression in Church documents deserves nothing less.

23

U.S. Hispanic Values and Challenges in Mission *ad Gentes*

Ana María Pineda, RSM

In Cuzco, Peru, for the Feast of Corpus Christi, crowds gather in the main plaza. From every outlying direction patron saints are carried over cobblestone streets into the ancient city to converge and enter the cathedral with the doors closing behind them and the faithful outside. According to tradition, the *santos* within are required to stand before Jesus and give an accounting—*la cuenta*—of their duties of the past year in caring for their particular peasant community.

The occasion of the Maryknoll centennial is a similar moment for *la cuenta*. It is an opportunity to pause and reflect on the nature and future of the Church as "missionary."

A historical framework provides a perspective to understand the place of U.S. Hispanics in the mission of the U.S. Catholic Church. Although many of us who have been involved in Hispanic ministry have lived this history, it is worthwhile to present an overview of its salient moments.

The U.S. Hispanic reality began painfully with the "first stage" of conquest. The voyage of Christopher Columbus in 1492 forever changed the world on both sides of the Atlantic. Unfortunately the violent conquest of the Americas was forged with the missionary efforts of Spain.

Besides the genocide of indigenous people, it led to the intermingling of Indian, Spanish, and African blood—creating the *mestizo* peoples of today. But the birth of this new people came at great cost. Despite the best intentions of the missionaries, the oppressed indigenous peoples found it essentially difficult to reconcile the brutality of the *conquistadores* with the preaching of a loving God by the missionaries. Thus the initial experience of conquest reflected a profound disconnect between word and action.

189

The arrival of the Pilgrim fathers and mothers at Plymouth Rock marked the second stage of conquest in the growth of a new nation that was essentially white, Anglo-Saxon, and Protestant. With the absorption of Spanish and Mexican lands into the expanding new nation, the "Second Conquest" impoverished the indigenous/Spanish/*mestizo* people, who lost not only their land, culture, and identity, but also their sense of belonging.

For decades, Latinos in the United States felt like strangers in what had once been their own land. Nor did the Catholic Church make them feel at "home," leading them to sometimes question whether in fact they had any place in the Church. The early 1960s, however, opened the door to a new moment in the life of the Church that would have positive consequences for Latinos/as in the United States.

The Civil Rights Movement

It is impossible to ignore the Civil Rights movement of the 1960s that initiated a dynamic that specifically demanded equality for African Americans, a quest and search embodied in the committed life of Martin Luther King Jr. The movement, however, also exposed the lack of dignity and justice for other marginalized members of society. It revealed the disparity in pay and the inhumane treatment of the farm workers who labored for long hours to provide food for the American home. In the fields a nonviolent struggle for justice began, led by Cesar Chavez. In Los Angeles, protesting their poor educational treatment, hundreds of Latino/a students marched out of their classrooms.

Within the Church, serious Mexican-American priests stood up for the social rights of U.S. Hispanic communities, demanding pastoral attention for Hispanics and leading to the national organization of Priests Associated for Religious, Educational, and Social Rights (PADRES).

Latina women members of religious communities also found reason to protest, as they often found themselves denied education and an opportunity to work with Hispanic communities. This protest gave birth to the organization known as Las Hermanas, giving special attention to the injustices Latinas were subjected to not only by civil society, but also within the Catholic Church.

The Second Vatican Council

Convoking the Second Vatican Council in the 1960s, Pope John XXIII called the Church to assess itself, to give an accounting of itself—*una cuenta*—in relation to the modern world. According to *Gaudium et Spes*, the Church was to pay particular attention to the poor, emphasizing the right and responsibility of all faithful, laity as well as religious, to engage actively in the life of the Church and in the proclamation of the "Good News." With an active new role, the Hispanic laity introduced a fresh dynamic into the process of evangelization.

The prophetic spirit of the Second Vatican Council flowed into the convocation of the Latin American Conference of Bishops in Medellín, Colombia, in 1968. The conference stirred a new hope in U.S. Latino/a Hispanic communities by offering a new vision for what it might mean to be recognized as plenary members of the Catholic Church. In the United States, pastoral centers were established for Hispanic Catholics to learn more about their faith. The Mexican-American Cultural Center in San Antonio, Texas, became a preeminent model of these centers.

U.S. Hispanic Catholics

With an ever growing Latino/a population, clergy often found themselves at a loss for how to address the pastoral needs of Hispanic communities. In the early 1970s, Fr. Robert Stern, director of the Spanish-speaking apostolate of the Archdiocese of New York, invited Fr. Edgard Beltrán from Colombia to initiate a process of pastoral planning for Hispanic Catholics.

From that process developed in 1972, the First Encuentro Nacional Hispano de Pastoral began an assessment of needed pastoral care for U.S. Hispanic Catholics. The gathering of bishops, priests, and laity included the only Hispanic bishop (Patricio Flores, son of a migrant family), a few Hispanic lay leaders, and very few women. Even without Hispanic leadership in the Encuentro, the Church began to move from a policy of assimilation to one of pluralism.

The Encuentros of 1977 and 1985 marked the infancy stage of Hispanic ministry, shifting the pastoral perspective from a passive position to a more active one, a new moment in the proclamation of God's

Word. The Encuentros encouraged Hispanics to assume the role as lay ministers as properly theirs.

The II Encuentro (1977), invoking the theme "Pueblo de Dios en Marcha—People of God on the March," acknowledged the importance of Hispanic faith, culture, and language as well as diversity among Latino communities. In this context, for Hispanics the obligation inherent in *ad gentes* meant to seek out the underserved and marginalized among them. Referencing the rights and obligations of the baptized, the convocation encouraged leadership in Hispanic ministry, a focus eagerly embraced by the Hispanic Catholic laity.

In 1983, the U.S. Bishops' Pastoral Letter, *The Hispanic Presence: Challenge and Commitment*, affirmed that Hispanic people, through the rich cultural and religious values of their communities, were God's blessing to the Church and nation.

The III Encuentro (1985) stated: "The Church, after the Second Vatican Council, is not content to look within herself. She also looks out at the world in its totality to realize there the presence of God, which denounces sin and announces a new set of values." The Hispanic option was directed toward the poor, youth, women, the undocumented, farm workers, and any of those marginalized in society. Hispanic Catholics also voiced the expectation that language and cultural and religious traditions demanded respect.

On many fronts, the contributions of Hispanics to the Church's understanding of mission continued to grow. But during the process of the Encuentros, Hispanic Catholics began to theologize from their own experience, a dynamic that uncovered the paucity of prepared U.S. Hispanic theologians.

Academy of Catholic Hispanic Theologians of the United States

In the mid-1980s Allan Figueroa Deck, S.J., and Arturo Bañuelas, two priests engaged in doctoral studies in Rome, discussed the near nonexistence of Hispanic/Latino theologians. In 1989, they began to envision the creation of the Academy of Catholic Hispanic Theologians of the United States (ACHTUS). Its mission statement accentuates the importance of paying close attention to the presence of the Spirit in the lives of U.S. Hispanic communities, and it privileges the people's faith as a locus for doing theology.

Since its inception, ACHTUS has developed a theology operating from the context of U.S. Hispanic realities. In addition, it goes beyond its own interests to dialogue with theologians not only from Latin America but also from the many diverse cultural groups within the United States, such as Asian Americans, African Americans, and Afro Caribbeans, thus reinforcing the overall quest for justice.

Through the Encuentros, the U.S. Hispanic leadership learned the value of moving away from a centralized, clerical approach to evangelization to the involvement of laity in missionary activities. Hispanics extended an invitation to move beyond those who had heard the Word of God to those who as yet had not.

In the United States today multicultural parishes are a reality. Again, often without realizing it, Hispanic Catholics have nourished the spirituality of others by sharing devotions, popular expressions of faith, and celebrations. While many Catholic churches emptied their sanctuaries of statues and images—tangible expressions of the faith— Hispanic Catholics continued to nourish the sacred imagination of others in the celebrations of Good Friday, Las Posadas, and feasts of Mary, and the saints.

A fourth national Encuentro, "Encuentro 2000: Many Faces in God's House," recognized and affirmed cultural diversity as integral to the Church's mission. In May 2010, a gathering convened by the National Conference of Catholic Bishops and hosted at the University of Notre Dame with the theme of "Catholic Cultural Diversity Network Convocation" focused on the multicultural reality of the U.S. Church. Six cultural families participated in this event: Native American, Hispanic/Latino, European American, African American, Asian and Pacific Islanders, and Migrants, Refugees, and Travelers.

Traditionally, *ad gentes* was understood as a call to venture out to evangelize. But what if the peoples we are to evangelize are in our very midst, having left their home countries in pursuit of a better future? Surprisingly, the new dynamic focuses on the United States itself as a locus for missionary activity. In this new configuration of mission, Hispanic Catholics are the evangelizers, challenging us to think of *ad gentes* in fresh ways.

Returning to consider the Corpus Christi celebration in Cuzco, Peru, it might be interesting to reimagine that plaza in Cuzco as the U.S./Mexican border and other borders. In this new vision, a crowd of U.S. Hispanic Catholics steps up to *la cuenta* to give an accounting before Our Lady of Guadalupe. Perhaps, on this occasion of Maryknoll's centennial, the Church is at another Pentecost moment in which everything must be reconsidered, turned upside down, in order to discover the reality of missionary evangelization in the light of yet another new flame.

24

A Theology of U.S. Mission *ad Gentes*

Kevin J. Hanlon, MM

Since this symposium centers on Maryknoll's hundredth anniversary of its founding, my focus will be somewhat "Maryknoll-centric." But as much of mission thought in the United States in the twentieth century went hand in hand with Maryknoll's growth and development, I hope that this presentation will also speak to those outside the "Maryknoll world."

The Historical Background of U.S. Mission *ad Gentes*

When we speak of a theology of U.S. *ad gentes* mission, it has to be grounded in the reality from which it grew. For practical reasons, I will limit myself to the last century, when the Church in this country ceased being considered a "mission territory." That momentous change, made by Rome in 1908, enabled us to think of ourselves not just as a "missionary-receiving" Church, but also as a "missionary-sending" Church.

There were many principal players in this mission effort, but certainly Bishop James Anthony Walsh, cofounder of Maryknoll, has to be placed near the top. Much of our U.S. mission consciousness comes from his tremendous promotional and educational efforts. James Anthony (another famous Bishop Walsh, James Edward Walsh, spent twelve years in a Communist prison, so we distinguish between them by using just their first and middle names) was born in Cambridge, Massachusetts, in 1867. His father dealt in real estate and was an owner of what New Englanders call a "package store," a respectable profession before prohibition. The family lived a comfortable middle-class life. From his early years James seemed to be destined for the priesthood. Such was the dream of most Irish families of the time, to have a child who would dedicate himself or herself to God. He was an intelligent and serious child with a quick wit, and even at a young age he had good musical and oratorical abilities. His idyllic life was shattered, though, at the age of eleven when his mother contracted pneumonia and died.

After high school, he entered Boston College, which at that time was considered a school for those entering the seminary. He helped start *The Stylus of Boston College*, which today is one of the oldest collegiate art and literature journals in existence. While in college, his father's fortunes took a downward turn, and James felt himself a burden on his father's finances. He may also have become a little unsure of his path. For whatever reason, he left Boston College and transferred to Harvard for a semester, close to the family home. Although he did well at Harvard, he came to realize with even more conviction that he was destined for the priesthood. He was accepted and entered St. John's Seminary. The rector of St. John's, a Sulpician, Abbé Hogan, became a great influence on James Anthony and spoke to the seminarians often about the heroic French missionaries in Indochina. James Anthony Walsh was ordained in 1892.

He was assigned to St. Patrick's, the "mother church" of Roxbury, and began a very busy life as a curate. He came to be known in his years there as the priest who paid special attention to the sick. It was because of his devotion to the sick that we have come to know of his great love for the Holy Eucharist (which eventually would be at the center of his mission thought).

One time he was visiting a dying woman who had a great devotion to the Christ in the Host. As Daniel Sargent, Walsh's principal biographer, describes, "It came over him as he attended her that she, growing blind, was on the point of at last seeing, and it made him feel, in comparison with her, in darkness." It was no original thought, but the power with which it took hold of him was unusual. Although the experience was ineffable, something of it could be told. It became a poem, called "Only a Veil," which ran thus:

> Only a veil between me and Thee,
> Jesus, my Lord!
> A veil of bread it appears to me,
> Yet seemeth such, that I may not see
> Jesus, my God.
>
> Lift not the veil between me and Thee,
> Jesus, my Lord!

These eyes of earth can never see
The glory of Thy Divinity,
Jesus, my God.

Keep then the veil between me and Thee,
Jesus, my Lord!
Some day 'twill fall when my soul is free
To gaze on Thee for eternity,
Jesus, my God.[1]

This poem demonstrates Fr. Walsh's Eucharistic spirituality and how Christ "touched" him as he attended to the dying woman. Fr. Walsh saw the need for the sick and dying to have Christ accompany them ("When I was sick you cared for me," Matt. 25:36). He also saw Christ "through the veil," and it changed him forever. It undoubtedly increased his desire to help those who suffer from not knowing Christ at all.

Fr. Walsh did what he could to promote the missions, and this mission spirit was rewarded in 1903 when he was made the archdiocesan director of the Society for the Propagation of the Faith. Knowing that a better informed Catholic would be more willing to support the missions, he began a mission magazine titled *The Field Afar*. He worked tirelessly throughout the diocese to raise awareness and funds, enlisting the preaching help of other priests, and making use of lay volunteers for the work. In his short seven years as head of the office, he doubled the amount of donations for the missions. As other bishops took notice, he traveled to other archdioceses to help them improve their own mission offices. Much of the success of the diocesan mission offices in the United States finds its origins in the pioneering work of James Anthony.

In 1904, Fr. Walsh went to Washington to address the Catholic Missionary Union, a group devoted to mission works within U.S. boundaries. It was there that he met for the first time the North Carolinian home missionary Fr. Thomas Fredrick Price, who together with him would found Maryknoll. The talk Fr. Walsh gave that day demonstrates how Father Walsh's spirituality of mission had grown. In "Only a Veil" we see his personal love and devotion for Christ and his presence in the Holy Eucharist. In this talk to the Missionary Union, though, he made a connection between the Holy Sacrifice of the Mass and the mission of the priest to the whole world. Allow me to quote it here at length:

> While conscious of the need of priests in most parts of our country, I believe that to send some of our young men and women to more remote districts would stimulate the vocations for home needs, and especially for the more remote missions of the United States.
>
> The true priest lives his short life for the salvation of his fellow creatures. Every sincere Christian longs for the day when the Kingdom of the Savior shall rule all men's hearts. What we priests and laymen can do by effort and prayer to win the world to Christ, this we should do, so that the altars may be more numerous on the earth than the stars in the heavens; that multitudes in every land may be nourished with the Bread of Life—the Body of Christ; that this earth may be deluged in the Precious Blood of the Lamb—a ruby earth glistening like a radiant jewel under the sunlight of the glorious Cross of Him who died on it, *not for you or me alone, but for every child of man.*

Walsh's understanding of mission centered on Christ, and especially on the Christ of the altar. He envisioned people everywhere being nourished by Christ, that the world would become a "radiant jewel" reflecting the Paschal Mystery ("the glorious Cross"). His theological focus for mission is thus both Eucharistic and paschal.

The Why of Mission: Gospel Missionary Mandates

This fundamental vision of mission of James Anthony finds resonance in what other U.S. thinkers of mission propose today. The Gospel has various themes that could be suggested as underpinning missionary efforts. Let us first consider the foremost "missionary mandate" of the Gospel of Matthew.

The Mandate to Carry Out ad Gentes Mission

Enshrined over the entrance to Maryknoll's main building are the words, *Euntes Docete Omnes Gentes*. These words represent what we usually mean when we refer to the "missionary mandate," that is, "Go and teach all the nations" (Matt. 28:19ff). When James Anthony chose these words to permanently consecrate the major seminary, he would have recognized them as the primary justification for the endeavor that he and Fr. Price were beginning: Christ commanded; we obey and go on mission. The complete command is a beautiful one:

> Then Jesus approached and said to them, "All power in heaven and on earth has been given to me. Go, therefore, and make disciples of all nations, baptizing them in the name of the Father, and of the Son, and of the Holy Spirit, teaching them to observe all that I have commanded you. And behold, I am with you always, until the end of the age." (Matt. 28:18–29)

While this is the preeminent mandate for mission and one that is specifically sacramental ("baptize them"), there are other passages in Gospels that powerfully suggest a call to mission.

The Mandate to Gather All to the Banquet

Roger Schroeder, an SVD missionary and professor of missiology at the Chicago Theological Union, proposes several Gospel ideas as foundational calls to mission in his book *What Is the Mission of the Church?* (Orbis Books, 2008). A principal one is found in Luke 14:15–24. In the parable of the banquet, we see the Lord giving the great invitation:

> One of his fellow guests on hearing this said to him, "Blessed is the one who will dine in the kingdom of God." He replied to him, "A man gave a great dinner to which he invited many. When the time for the dinner came, he dispatched his servant to say to those invited, 'Come, everything is now ready.' But one by one, they all began to excuse themselves. The first said to him, 'I have purchased a field and must go to examine it; I ask you, consider me excused.' And another said, 'I have purchased five yoke of oxen and am on my way to evaluate them; I ask you, consider me excused.' And another said, 'I have just married a woman, and therefore I cannot come.' The servant went and reported this to his master. Then the master of the house in a rage commanded his servant, 'Go out quickly into the streets and alleys of the town and bring in here the poor and the crippled, the blind and the lame.' The servant reported, 'Sir, your orders have been carried out and still there is room.' The master then ordered the servant, 'Go out to the highways and hedgerows and make people come in that my home may be filled. For, I tell you, none of those men who were invited will taste my dinner.'"

Thus, we are called to "teach all nations" and to "invite all people to the banquet." As has been noted by Robert Schreiter, this was a principal "mission mandate" before the modern age.

Schroeder sees this "invitation to the banquet" also reflected in Jesus' feeding of the five thousand in Luke: Jesus blesses the bread and distributes it to the multitudes, a prophetic sign of what he will do through the apostles in the future.

Surely there is a strong correlation between what these two modern thinkers of mission propose and what James Anthony said in his theological vision of mission: "that multitudes in every land may be nourished with the Bread of Life." It is good to see this "banquet" idea of mission present in both early and later twentieth-century thought regarding *ad gentes* mission. It should also be mentioned that both Schroeder (in his book) and Cardinal George (during his address to this symposium) focused on "Bread of Life" discourses in John 6 as fundamental images of the future missionary Church.

The Mandate to Be Sent as Jesus Was (John 20:19–23)

In the twentieth chapter of John, the evangelist presents Jesus giving the apostolic mandate in a more intimate way than we see in Luke-Acts. The Holy Spirit descends upon them through the very breath of Jesus:

> On the evening of that first day of the week, when the doors were locked, where the disciples were, for fear of the Jews, Jesus came and stood in their midst and said to them, "Peace be with you." When he had said this, he showed them his hands and his side. The disciples rejoiced when they saw the Lord. Jesus said to them again, "Peace be with you. As the Father has sent me, so I send you." And when he had said this, he breathed on them and said to them, "Receive the Holy Spirit. Whose sins you forgive are forgiven them, and whose sins you retain are retained."

Here we see Christ making them new creatures, for just as God breathed his Spirit into the clay of Adam to give him life, Jesus breathes the Spirit into his disciples to make them apostles. He changes their role from those who simply receive the message as disciples to those who are sent out with the message, in other words, apostles ("those sent," *apostolos* in Greek).

This Johannine missionary mandate has elements that in two ways both complement and complete the other mandates mentioned above. In the first place, the mandate is *obediential*. Christ commands, and he assumes the compliance of the disciples. But the Johannine mandate has a deeper level of obedience contained within it since it directs the new apostles to the way Christ was sent, out of obedience to the Father's will (see Phil. 2:8). As such, the apostles participate in the saving action of Christ not only by proclaiming, but also by the simple act of being obedient to his command.

Second, this Johannine mandate is *paschal*. The words "As the Father has sent me" encompass both the manner and the reason the Word was sent: in the womb of the Virgin, the Son would take on our flesh, and on the cross he would fulfill his paschal mission to forgive our sins. He then sends his apostles in the same way: they are born from Christ and his mission and are to go out with Christ's Spirit to forgive sins. For the most part, they themselves also would give their lives by the shedding of their blood. They not only preach the Gospel; they also witness (in Greek *martys*, from which "martyr" is derived) to its veracity by the shedding of their blood.

A Theology of U.S. Mission *ad Gentes:* Then and Now

If we take James Anthony's theology mentioned in the first section as representative of early twentieth-century mission thought, we would have to say that things have greatly changed by the second half of the century. I will use Pope Paul VI's words to express, in a general and poetic way, the theological and ecclesiological changes that came upon the Church:

> We thought that after the Council a day of sunshine would have dawned for the history of the Church. What dawned, instead, was a day of clouds and storms, of darkness, of searching and uncertainties. (Sermon during the Mass for Sts. Peter and Paul in St. Peter's Basilica, on the occasion of the ninth anniversary of his coronation, June 29, 1972)

One of Paul VI's words, "searching," is a potent one for describing post–Vatican II mission thought in the United States and elsewhere.

While James Anthony proposes a mission vision with great confidence in its goodness, there was a search after the Council to make mission more relevant to the world. Many of these searches brought good results: much of the best work we have had on interreligious dialogue, inculturation, working in common for social progress, and the like, have been a result of this search; they are summarized and expressed well by John Paul II's successor in *Redemptoris Missio*.

But along with the progress, there has been "darkness." James Anthony wished simply that Christ be proclaimed in a world that thirsted for him so that people might be saved. Though the Council wished no diminishment in missionary fervor, the statements that people can be saved without becoming explicitly Christian (*Lumen Gentium* 16) gave rise to the postconciliar question of why the Gospel *must* be proclaimed. Given these questions and doubts a later generation has asked if there is any truth that can be believed with conviction, creating a milieu that Pope Benedict XVI described at the beginning of the 2005 conclave as a "dictatorship of relativism."

To make mission more relevant and more rational, we have paired evangelization with other practices such as "mission and human development," or "mission and human liberation," "mission and dialogue," and so on. However, all these more tangible or rational ends have their logical endpoint. For example, when a country has moved from an oppressive dictatorship to a more or less representational democracy, partly because of the efforts of the Church for social justice and liberation, is there any more need for the Church? For missionary evangelization? (My answer would be, only if the proclaimers understood of what true liberation consists.) Or, in opposition to our "mission *and* x, y, or z," we might consider the success of many Evangelical or Pentecostal Protestant groups who focus exclusively on proclamation. They have a primarily eschatological and spiritual Christianity and have succeeded in both non-Christian and "Catholic" lands alike. What were these non-Christians longing for? And what were Catholics longing for that they did not find in their own homes?

It is to be hoped that questions and challenges such as these are teaching us to draw from our roots. James Anthony Walsh and the earlier missionaries of the twentieth century went out with great confidence in the value of the message alone, in the need for humility on the part of the messenger, and with hope for the communities that would spring up when the seeds were planted. These times of doubt call us to have more confidence in the Gospel and in our apostolic task. We already know that not all seed will fall on fertile soil. But it will spring up from the fertile soil only if we have the confidence to sow it.

Notes

1. Daniel Sargent, *All the Day Long* (New York: Longmans, 1941). Most of the biographical information used here comes from Sargent's work.

25

Interculturality:
A Foundation for U.S. Mission

Joanne (Jaruko) Doi, MM

The participants of the workshop "Interculturality: A Foundation for U.S. Mission" experienced a process of rich sharing and mutual learning. I will highlight some important points from the discussion and then refer the reader to the endnotes for further reflection.

I was nurtured in culture and faith through the unique experience of the gift of mission in the context of the Maryknoll Japanese Catholic community in Los Angeles. Subsequently I experienced the gift of mission among the Aymara people in the southern Andes of Peru. The crossing over of barriers in friendship is the common gift of mission in both settings, shedding light through time on the dynamics of interculturality. Interculturality is a faith experience and gift of global mission that goes far beyond the binary of the mission in the United States and foreign mission.

This reflection is dedicated to the memory of my father, Vincent Doi (1913–2011), who found home at Maryknoll throughout his life, whether in Los Angeles, Manzanar, or Chicago. Ultimately returning to California, together with my mother, Agnes, he raised five children as part of the St. Francis Xavier parish and Maryknoll grammar school, together known simply as "Maryknoll" and located in the Little Tokyo area in downtown Los Angeles. In 2012, "Maryknoll" of Little Tokyo also celebrates its centennial anniversary. The Japanese mission in Los Angeles was one of only two missions established by Maryknoll in the continental United States before World War II.[1]

My father would want to remember and honor many Maryknollers and thank them for their steadfast friendship through difficult and joyous times. For example, Sisters Bernadette Yoshimochi and Susana Hayashi had the option of returning to Maryknoll, New York, after Executive Order 9066 (February 19, 1942) set in motion the detention of 120,000 Japanese and Japanese Americans living on the West Coast

204

during World War II. Instead they chose to go with their people to Manzanar, one of ten concentration camps.[2] Brother Theophane Walsh accompanied and assisted with the leave clearance process. He and my father met with the bishop in Chicago to ask for assistance in setting up a resettlement house on La Salle Street, a place for those arriving from the various "camps" to find support and community. (On a personal note, Brother Theophane also introduced my parents to each other, and they were married six months later on a wintry February day in Chicago!) Fr. Hugh Lavery stood by the Japanese pre-, during, and post–World War II, welcoming them back and reopening the school and parish in 1948. My father had Fr. Hugh's name inscribed at the Japanese American National Museum in Los Angeles (when usually you have your family name or your grandchildren's names inscribed) to bear witness to this true friend of the Issei and Nisei.[3]

While the diversity of cultures has always been present within the U.S. Church, the Civil Rights movement and post-1965 immigration legislation shed light on increased intercultural interactions within church and society today. The peopling of the United States during the colonial period from the 1400s to the 1700s also involved black slavery and Native American genocide. Primarily Anglocentric until the 1800s, the first and second waves of European migrations caused by population growth and industrialization resulted in a Eurocentric focus by the early 1900s.[4] Since 1965 the U.S. population has taken on a global complexion, with new immigrants from Asia, the Pacific Islands, Latin America, the Caribbean, Africa, and a continuing flow from Europe.

Our full names illustrate the inherent interculturality and different webs of relationships to which we belong. While the various "centrisms" of history cast shadows that may cause us to overlook meaningful roots and the narratives that pertain to them, the process of sharing about our names often reveals hidden meanings as we dialogue with others. Most notably, rather than differences separating us, the sharing of narratives and questions deepens our connections with one another.[5] As H. Richard Niebuhr writes, one becomes conscious of collective memory and the contemplative sense of time:

> What is past is not gone; it abides in us as our memory; what is future is not non-existent but present in us as our potentiality. . . . Time in our history is not another dimension of the external space world

in which we live, but a dimension of our life and of our community's being. We are not in this time, but it is in us.

The revelatory moment is one which makes our past intelligible. Through it we understand what we remember, remember what we have forgotten and appropriate as our own past much that seemed alien to us.[6]

Maryknoll strived to offset the two main strands of anti-Japanese hostility: (1) the exclusion of Japanese from American life since they were considered inassimilable or (2) the inclusion of Japanese on the condition that they conform to Anglo ways. Maryknoll's dedication of friendship, service, and cultural sensitivity helped to create an intercultural space that reversed both of these tendencies. This intercultural space formed a community of faith that sought to include the Japanese in American life in a way that integrated their cultural heritage. This intercultural space was also an interreligious space as Maryknoll in Los Angeles did not minister exclusively to Catholics but to all the Japanese people. Cultural, national, and religious borders do not have to be obstacles to friendship.

When I began mission work in Peru, I expected a barrenness caused by difference as my greatest challenge in entering the "unknown world" of the Aymara people.[7] Yet instead of an estrangement due to our differences, I experienced a deep connection with the Aymara in our mutual vulnerability, solidarity, and friendship. Instead of "otherness," they recognized and embraced me as another.[8] They taught me how to live with the Earth and each other, how to be afraid and fearless at the same time, how to feel hurt and anger, how to heal and forgive, how to create and empower life itself in the midst of suffering, how to celebrate and dance, how to embody joy and trust in each other, and how to embrace those who have labeled you "the other." This freed me to reconnect to the memory of suffering and hope in the "unknown world" of my parents and grandparents as they moved from immigration through detention to redress and beyond. I felt reconnected to our hidden history and our historicity.

Popular religious practice among the Aymara and other indigenous peoples relates profoundly with the Earth. Land holds memory and is embedded with spiritual resonance through regular pilgrimages, prayers, and rituals. This understanding helped me reconnect with the Manzanar Pilgrimage and the experiences of other Japanese Americans interned in concentration camps.

Such postcolonial pilgrimages revisit sacred traces of suffering and hope. The cemetery obelisk at Manzanar incorporates the message, "This is the place of consolation for all of humanity."[9] It is about reconnection with each other, with our ancestors, and with the mystery and the depth of life. It is not the escape of tourism but a returning to the center of pivotal events that have marked us and embedded narratives in the land itself.

The postcolonial pilgrim's journey seeks a restoration of wholeness by a recentering, reentering, and recovery of history. It is a rediscovery that we are part of a living and vital collective memory. We remember in order to heal, to recover memory, to decolonize ourselves, to restore our deeper souls. Pilgrimage is a collective experience, a practice of resistance through remembering, as healing through memory, and as an emotional catharsis through compassionate action. As we journey together, we experience together more than we could alone.[10] Through our dialogue and discussion here, we become part of this ongoing pilgrimage as we cross over barriers and widen the circle of friendship in the gift of mission.

Notes

1. Please refer to Joanne Doi, MM, "Dance of a Thousand Cranes: A Legacy of Suffering and Hope from the Maryknoll Japanese American Catholic Community" (M.A. Thesis, Pacific School of Religion, 1997).

2. During the World War II detention period of Japanese Americans, the terms "assembly center," "internment camps," "relocation centers," and "concentration camps" were used as well as the popularized "camps." Concentration camp—a place to which persons are sent because of race or ethnicity, not due to crimes or legal status—is the most accurate term, while the others were employed as euphemisms. See Roger Daniels, "Words Do Matter: A Note on Inappropriate Terminology and the Incarceration of the Japanese Americans" in *Nikkei in the Pacific Northwest: Japanese American and Japanese Canadians in the Twentieth Century*, ed. Louis Fiset and Gail Nomura (Seattle: University of Washington Press, 2005), 183–207.

3. *Issei* are the first generation of Japanese to migrate and live in the United States. The first legal contract laborers arrived in Hawaii in 1885. *Nisei* are U.S.-born and the second generation to live in the United States. *Sansei, Yonsei*, and *Gosei* are the third, fourth, and fifth generations of Japanese Americans, respectively. *Kibei* are U.S.-born of Japanese ancestry (usually Nisei) who went to Japan at a young age for schooling and subsequently returned to the United States. *Nikkei* are people of Japa-

nese ancestry born outside of Japan, regardless of generation or country (for example, there are generations of Nikkei in North, Central, and South America).

4. The first wave, which ends around 1815, includes the Dutch, German, Irish, and Scandinavian peoples. The second wave, which ends around 1914, includes the Italian, Greek, Polish, Russian, Czech, Hungarian, Slovakian, and Jewish peoples.

5. This reverses the general tendency that "difference is not appreciated or embraced in this [U.S.] culture. Difference breeds at best a competitiveness that has to end in someone's losing. And at its worst, difference breeds a destructive contempt commonly defined as racism and ethnic prejudice. . . . This destructive contempt, which results in oppression, depends on domination and works by subjugating, exploiting, and repressing" (Ada María Isasi-Diaz, *En La Lucha—In the Struggle* [Minneapolis: Fortress Press, 1993]), 188.

6. H. Richard Niebuhr, *The Meaning of Revelation* (New York: Macmillan. 1941), 69, 110.

7. Melinda Roper, MM, former president of the Maryknoll Sisters, wrote in 1983: "Very simply, mission is being called and being sent beyond the confines of our 'known world' in order to proclaim as did Jesus. When I speak of our 'known world' I mean all those dimensions of our lives with which we are familiar, our own society and culture, our own attitudes and values, our own sense of security and identity, our own family and friends, and ultimately our very selves."

8. "How can I come to know *another* and the world in which they dwell in a way that not only transforms us as individuals but enables us together to transform the world?" (Susan B. Thistlethwaite, *Beyond Theological Tourism* [Maryknoll, N.Y.: Orbis Books, 1994], 6).

9. Mr. Ryozo Kado, a stonemason for the Archdiocese of Los Angeles and a Maryknoll parishioner, created and supervised the work. Later he and his family would be given leave clearance upon the invitation of Mother Mary Joseph to work on the Maryknoll, New York, grounds, where he created the Lourdes grotto and the indoor/outdoor river bed design in the Rogers Library, among other works.

10. The film *Pilgrimage* by Tadashi H. Nakamura (2006) about the Manzanar Pilgrimage was shown. See also Joanne Doi, MM, "Bridge to Compassion: Theological Pilgrimage to Tule Lake and Manzanar," Ph.D. dissertation, 2007, Graduate Theological Union, Berkeley, Calif.

26

The Mission of U.S. Dioceses

John J. Wall

As Maryknoll joyfully celebrates its centenary, Catholic Extension has reached its 107th anniversary. Both were born at the moment of a seismic shift in the history of the American Catholic Church. In the first decade of the twentieth century, the United States ceased to be considered a mission country by the Universal Church and Propagation of the Faith. It was a "coming of age" moment when we were called not only to take care of ourselves as American Catholics, but to reach out beyond our shores and take up the challenge of evangelization by going out to "the whole world!" Thus was born Maryknoll and its global mission.

But there was also a huge challenge to be faced here in the United States. While the Church was growing and flourishing in large urban dioceses of the Northeast, it was facing daunting obstacles in the large swath of territory that was the rest of our country. Facing prejudice and hostility in the Bible Belt, confronted by the vastness and remoteness of the western frontier, and dealing with the endemic poverty of much of rural America, the Catholic Church was not prepared to respond effectively to the call to evangelize and establish the Church in over two-thirds of our country's land mass. It was estimated that over four million Catholics ceased to be Catholic in the first two decades of the twentieth century simply because there was no established presence of the Church in countless "priest-less" counties.

It took the creative genius and spiritual passion of Fr. Francis Clement Kelley to rise up to the challenge. In 1905, he founded the Catholic Church Extension Society and, for over a hundred years, it has labored to build up and strengthen the Catholic Church in underresourced regions throughout the United States. Based in Chicago, and presently serving 90 of our 196 dioceses that are home to 11 million of the 64 million Catholics located in thirty-six of the fifty states, Catholic Extension has been the primary agent to support missionary activity within our own domestic mission dioceses. These are dioceses that cannot sustain themselves without support beyond their own people.

Catholic Extension serves as the conduit for American Catholics to bond together generously and help build and strengthen these emerging faith communities in our country's poorest regions. Hundreds of millions of dollars have been raised and invested. In this year alone, almost $22 million has been directed toward supporting a thousand separate grants. Our goal is to build faith, inspire hope, and ignite change in each of these ninety mission dioceses. Our strategy is to invest in the people, the ministries, and the critical infrastructures that give witness to the transformative power of faith and that encourage excellence in church life and ministry no matter what the external circumstances.

Catholic Extension invests in people. Our funding helps support priests, religious, and lay leaders who simply would not be able to be present among the poor of our country without providing salaries for their subsistence. Equally important is the substantive funding we provide to train the future ordained, religious, and lay leadership of these ninety dioceses through tuition support and through joint ventures with Catholic universities and ministry training centers.

Catholic Extension invests in ministries. Catholic Extension makes the ministries that are essential to a vibrant Church life possible throughout our home mission dioceses. We place a special emphasis on developing the young Church where the future of the Church is taking shape and form in youth, campus, and young adult ministry.

Catholic Extension invests in infrastructure. We build churches—twelve thousand of them in a hundred years! We also help bring technology to the work of evangelization in areas where "long distance learning" is essential to catechetical and formational training. "If you build it, they will come!"

Our founder, Francis Clement Kelley, had as his rallying cry, "Raise up the Mission Spirit in America!" Catholic Extension takes this moment to congratulate Maryknoll for all you have accomplished in raising up that Mission Spirit and taking it beyond our shores in the last hundred years. Together, may Maryknoll and Catholic Extension continue to be driven by that Mission Spirit both in our own land and across the globe.

27

Diocesan Mission Animation

Rosanne Elizabeth Fischer

The Maryknoll Centennial Symposium has set out to "address the nature and future of the Catholic Church as a 'missionary' Church," exploring the factors that have influenced and shaped the activities of the Church over the past century. As part of the effort to understand how missionary activity has influenced people and formed the Church, the last day of the symposium was dedicated to the role of the U.S. Church in mission.

Symposium speaker Fr. Robert Schreiter outlined four models of mission for the future: (1) *ad extra*, animating the faithful to reach outward from their familiar places to new cultures, cultivating self-emptying and catholicity; (2) *ad altera*, providing opportunities for connecting with others who are different, those within one's own community; (3) *in altum*, utilizing new technologies to build connectedness and understanding and share the Good News in new social spaces; and (4) *ad vulnera*, walking with others where there is woundedness, bridging the gaps between peoples and with all of creation. Sister Nonie Gutzler added a fifth model, mission *inter gentes*, among the nations, to describe partnerships whose members recognize that they do not have the fullness of what is to be preached and taught so they place importance on both proclamation and dialogue. This model emphasizes not so much "*to*," but "*with whom.*" All of these models are currently operative within the work of the diocesan mission office.

The mission office carries the primary responsibility for the global outreach of the diocese by serving as a conduit between the faithful in its own diocese and members of our global family of faith. It serves as a reminder to each diocesan church that its gifts are not for itself alone. We develop and nurture our own growth, faith, and vitality in order to contribute to the building up of the entire people of God throughout the world. The mission office creates opportunities for mutual sharing of gifts and active solidarity, and each local diocesan community is both a giver and receiver of gifts within our one body of Christ.

Using the concrete example of the St. Cloud Mission Office in Minnesota, we have examined how the Pontifical Mission Societies (PMS), Catholic Relief Services (CRS), the Missionary Cooperation Plan (MCP), and diocesan mission animation and partnerships intersect and complement each other within the St. Cloud Mission Office in Minnesota. Mission animation includes prayer, celebration, mission education, global solidarity, relationships and partnerships, communication and outreach, and receiving and sending missioners. Collaboration with other diocesan offices such as Catholic Education, Worship, Social Concerns, Multicultural Relations, and Communications is an important aspect of diocesan mission animation. Relationship-building with diverse members within one's own diocese such as immigrants, international students and professors, and people of other faiths, is an important component of mission. Collaborative events with other Christian denominations, such as the World Day of Prayer, a Crop Walk, and participation in ministerial associations, build community and are life giving for all.

Ideally, the diocesan mission office provides multiple and diverse ways for people of all ages and backgrounds to enter into the *missio Dei* both locally and abroad. First and foremost, the staff of the office views its work as a ministry and begins each day in shared prayer, recognizing that they are led by the Spirit. Prayer is also an integral part of every activity planned and executed by the office.

The St. Cloud Diocese has close to two hundred parish mission groups. Many of these groups are made up of women who have prayed and acted on their missionary spirit for decades. Some attend to places of woundedness within their own communities; others sew quilts, curtains, and clothing, which are shared with faith partners around the world; some organize hospitality and fellowship in their parishes with diocesan partners when they visit from Kenya, Venezuela, or other places; yet others, often including younger people of both genders, sell fair trade items, or guide their parish's relationship with a sister parish in another part of the country or the world. All of these activities increase awareness of our unity with others. The relational aspects in particular serve as a vehicle to make concrete

our catholicity and connectedness with others, creating transformative friendships and opening hearts and minds outward toward our
larger family around the world. With sister parishes, care is taken that
a relationship not become exclusive and inward, which may diminish
its purpose and dynamism. Every eighteen months the mission office
offers a day-long formation workshop for all parishes involved in sister
parish relationships.

In addition to these particular relationships, collections are taken
to support the ministries of the Pontifical Mission Societies and Catholic Relief Services, which connect us with all our brothers and sisters
around the world, even those we do not know. PMS and CRS draw us
to the more wounded places within our body of Christ, to dioceses
struggling to develop and maintain infrastructure and leadership in
the church, joining us in prayer and mutual support. PMS also provides outreach to children through the Holy Childhood Association
educational materials and the World Mission Rosary. In St. Cloud, the
World Mission Rosary is a way for elders and youth to connect, one
teaching the other how to make rosaries, followed by joint prayer for
the peoples of each region. On Holy Childhood day, the first Friday
in October, major events are sponsored in the schools and Churches
that focus on prayer for our global family of faith using the World Mission Rosary and other forms of prayer with varied cultural expressions.
Mass intentions are another way of being in communion through
prayer by offering funds to assist parishes all over the world, who then
remember in their liturgies the faithful deceased of St. Cloud.

The CRS Rice Bowl ministry provides an opportunity for youth and
adults alike to learn about cultures and cuisine from around the world
while sharing something of themselves with others. It raises awareness
that our missionary call is to be lived out both near and far, since 25
percent of funds raised go toward hunger elimination programs within
the local diocese and 75 percent go toward reducing hunger around
the globe. CRS provides educational material and advocacy advice for
actions that benefit peoples the world over by impacting legislation
and social policies. CRS also helps dioceses develop global partnerships so they can form friendships with those who are "other," which
ground us in our Catholic teachings and prayers of oneness. Living out
our unity with a specific community that is different from ourselves

helps us to match our deeds to our creeds and broadens our perspective and understanding of our catholicity.

Diocesan partnerships are long term and provide opportunities for those who have been relating longer to assist those at the initial stages of intercultural relating. They are effective when the partnership committees in each diocese represent a broad cross-section of the populations within the diocese and when membership on the leadership committees and the short-term mission delegations rotates, always inviting in new participants. They are also most effective when there is shared power, shared accountability, and open and honest communication between the partners, and when prayer is an integral part of the exchange experiences. St. Cloud has strong global relationships with the dioceses of Maracay, Venezuela, and Homa Bay, Kenya. These partnerships have brought new life to the church in St. Cloud, Maracay, and Homa Bay. Because of points of difference, it is not always easy to relate, but as deceased Kenyan priest Valentine Miyoma once stated, "Blood may be thicker than water, but love is stronger than both."

Missioners from St. Cloud who serve elsewhere and missioners from elsewhere who live and minister in St. Cloud provide bridges of global relationship and connection. Our Missionary Cooperation Plan provides another point of connection and collaboration with our global family of faith. Through this plan, long-term missioners who minister around the world come to share their stories and receive support for the building up of the Church. It is helpful if those who come to speak at Sunday liturgies through the MCP program also connect with students in the schools and faith formation programs.

The Speakers Bureau maintained by the St. Cloud Mission Office allows both short- and long-term missioners to share the richness of their stories and journeys with people across the diocese. Social media also open up spaces for the expansion of stories through blog spots and websites that complement the traditional quarterly newsletter and special mission edition of the diocesan paper in October.

The mission office raises awareness of our call as missionary disciples of Christ to participate in God's mission in the world. The shape of our response to God's call changes and evolves along with changes in society and the world. A major task for mission in the Church today is to connect the resources and wisdom that long-term mission organizations have gained over the past century with diocesan mission offices, campus ministry departments, and other faithful groups who are carrying on God's mission in new and innovative ways. Through practices of dialogue and reconciliation with peoples both within the Church and outside of it, and by openness to the Spirit who moves us all toward communion, we will contribute to the reign of God in our world.

Part V

Rewards and Challenges
of Mission

28

The Gift of Mission: A Synthesis

James H. Kroeger, MM
Carmen Nanko-Fernández
Stephen B. Bevans, SVD

James H. Kroeger, MM

When participants in the Maryknoll Centennial Symposium arrived two days ago, they received a small bag that had the centennial logo printed on it along with the words: "The Gift of Mission: The Maryknoll Journey." This logo has been widely used throughout the centennial year for all the Maryknoll publications, letters, and promotional material. My short reflections this afternoon will be focused on this theme of the gift of mission.

Indeed, mission is a unique gift, an extraordinary gift. Throughout these three days we have explored the diverse ways in which this gift has been given and received for the past century (1911–2011)—as well as in the present and into the future. Mission is always a "two-way street," accomplished in reciprocity and mutuality; one experiences the giving and sharing as well as the receiving and accepting.

The centennial logo (see the back cover) contains some rich theology. In the very center one finds the *chi-rho*, the traditional representation of Christ, a symbol that Maryknoll has been using for decades. Yes, Christ is at the center of the Maryknoll mission century from 1911 to 2011. With another look one perceives a pathway, which can creatively be interpreted as a path that both leads to Christ and originates from Christ. The logo is filled with creativity and symbolism; it engages one's imagination and reflection.

Many presenters have evoked the theme of mission as gift. During Steve Judd's opening keynote address the first evening we heard the narrative about the Maryknoll presence in the Japanese internment camps during the Second World War. Realizing a special need and opportunity, Maryknollers, especially those who knew Japanese, voluntarily entered the camps to serve the diverse needs of those interred. It seemed the "natural" and human thing to do. Maryknollers, through their persons and presence, became freely given gifts. It is true that the gift of self is the most precious of gifts.

Steve narrated several other inspirational stories from the margins. He asserted that missioners by nature love to tell stories; at heart they are story brokers and tellers of tall tales. Throughout these days we all have been hearing and telling our stories of faith and service. This reminds me of the incident in the Gospel where Jesus tells the healed demoniac who wished to follow him: "Go home to your people and tell them all that the Lord in his mercy has done for you" (Mark 5:19). One might say that we have been creatively engaged in "narrative missiology" these past days.

Sister Janice McLaughlin spoke about mission as making people feel needed and loved, and she noted that this dynamic happens only with the gift of self. Her inspiring talk helped us appreciate how she and the Maryknoll Sisters envision and live out their assertion that mission is "making God's love visible." Janice told how an African orphan boy was transformed by the loving gift of a Maryknoll Sister, who made him feel "needed and loved." Indeed, love becomes concrete and incarnate through the uniqueness of each missioner, in the person through which the gift is given. Janice further enabled us to appreciate the rich "Maryknoll mosaic," how the wide variety of gifts have been shared through the century by hundreds of Maryknoll missioners, all unique in their persons and personalities.

On that same first evening Brother Wayne Fitzpatrick spoke of the special gift that the Maryknoll Brothers bring to mission and how this gift was first proffered through Brother Thomas McCann. Merwyn DeMello spoke of the generous gift of the scores of lay missioners. Of course, one could add the affiliates, associate members, sponsors, members' families, and dedicated employees to the list of "gifts of self" in mission.

All appreciated the presentation of Robert Schreiter on the morning of the second day on how the gift of mission has been freely shared over twenty centuries. Different eras, varied contexts, diverse peoples, and rich theologies have all transmitted, even though in often divergent ways, the love of God, particularly the most precious gift of the Son. Bob and others spoke of various "models" of being in mission, employing Latin phrases: *ad extra, ad altera, in altum, ad vulnera, inter gentes,* and *cum gentibus.* Whatever your proficiency in Latin may be, mission as gift integrates them all.

Sister Antoinette Gutzler creatively elaborated on the giftedness of the agents of mission, the older and younger, the women and men, those overseas and those at home. Nonie emphasized that mission is best realized in personal, face-to-face engagement. Necessarily, mission is more than only some kind of virtual contact through Twitter or Facebook. It is always personal gifts that have the deepest, long-lasting effect on people's lives. Nonie challenged everyone: Are you a happy missioner? Are you peace-filled? Do you seek and treasure the "mystical moments" of your mission journey? Do you give your gift from a "profound interiority"? Are you an attractive "gift-package" that appeals to people? Nonie and I are both Asian missioners, and we constantly hear the Asian Church challenging us to transmit the gift of faith through Christlike deeds of service.

Beginning on Friday, the middle day of the symposium, a total of seventeen "break-out" sessions were offered to participants. Resource persons unwrapped the gifts from Africa, Asia, Latin America, and China. Some gifts came in thematic packages: Islam, migration, proclamation and dialogue, peacemaking, care of creation, Scripture, inculturation, globalized economy, Hispanic values, interculturality, diocesan initiatives, animation, and mission theology. A rich banquet was available—to everyone's delight.

Peter Phan piqued our imaginations as he spoke about how the gift of faith is offered in countries that experience limited religious freedom, using China, Vietnam, and other Socialist-dominated countries as specific examples. Peter spoke convincingly, drawing upon his own direct experience of mission within severely circumscribed situations. Difficult contexts demand much creativity in mission.

Dana Robert focused on mission as relationships across borders and emphasized the centrality of hospitality and the importance of friendship in communicating the faith-gift missioners desire to transmit. As she spoke I recalled that the first book that the famous missioner Matteo Ricci translated into Chinese was Cicero's *De Amicitia,*

On Friendship. I remembered that Chrys McVey, a Dominican priest working in Pakistan, has a creatively written a piece entitled: "Befriending: The Heart of Mission." Authentic friendship imitates Jesus' barrier-breaking ministry, often moving across social, religious, cultural, and societal boundaries; his table fellowship was radically inclusive.

The final day of the symposium brought us two special speakers on the topic of the involvement of the U.S. Church in *ad gentes* mission. Within a broad panorama of insights, Cardinal George of Chicago noted that when one shares a gift, one develops a new relationship, a new friendship. The Church is to be a community of shared gifts, visible and invisible, material and spiritual, freely offered to all peoples.

Sister Madge Karecki captured everyone's attention as she spoke about the gifts of contemplation and spirituality in mission. One of the greatest gifts a missioner brings is the personal sharing of one's in-depth experience of God. And in the exchange of gifts, the God experience of people, even of diverse cultures and religions, fosters mutual enrichment.

We have experienced three days of exchanging gifts. We have accomplished the 3 "R"s of gift-giving: we have *recognized* the beautiful gifts in our midst; we have *received* them with grateful hearts; and we seek to *reciprocate* them in all our encounters. I believe that we all have become "richly transformed gifts" through this Maryknoll Centennial Symposium. In closing, allow me a simple word of profound gratitude: sincere thanks to everyone for generously sharing in these days of gift-giving. All mission is gift, a gift *par excellence! Deo gratias!*

Carmen Nanko-Fernández

Good afternoon; *buenas tardes. Felicidades y* happy centennial anniversary to the Maryknoll Fathers and Brothers, and happy ninety-ninth to the much younger Maryknoll Sisters. Maryknoll is a community worthy of two years of ongoing celebration, in the tradition of fiesta, a "celebration of life and hope amid struggle."[1]

I must confess I have a profound admiration for a society that, in the words of your own Joseph Veneroso, "has always done its best mission work at the margins."[2] My relationship with Maryknoll is situated at three primary points of intersection. First, a Maryknoll missioner taught on the religion faculty of my high school. While I'm not quite sure how a bunch of kids from the Bronx, New York, merited the outreach of the Catholic Foreign Mission Society, but Fr. Matthew Kelleher, MM, touched countless lives at both Cardinal Spellman and Cardinal Hayes High Schools.

Second, Maryknoll's publishing arm, Orbis Books, is regarded with high esteem among theologians; further, for those of us theologians from underrepresented racial, ethnic, and two-thirds world communities, Orbis has faithfully provided a space in the academic *areopagus*. From its founding in 1970 with the groundbreaking *Theology of Liberation* by Gustavo Gutiérrez to the 2011 ebook release of Nuyorican biblical scholar Jean-Pierre Ruiz's *Reading from the Edges: The Bible and People on the Move*, Orbis has actively cultivated relationships that promote the agency and scholarship of theologians arising from within the heart of the margins.

My third point of intersection comes from here at the Catholic Theological Union, where I have the privilege of accompanying the future of Maryknoll through their studies. From my experience of Maryknoll in this context of mutual teaching and learning I can only look forward with confidence to your next hundred years.

In my understanding, the purpose of a wrap-up session such as this is to function as a forum to identify threads, follow hypertexts, propose connections, and attend to those areas that were missing and perhaps are needed as the immediate and long-term future is strategically considered. These perceptions come from the particularities of our respective locations, and in my case the lenses I bring to bear are specifically related to my slice of the universal Church as a U.S. Hispanic lay theologian.

The Need for Acts of Decolonization

In listening across the rich sessions, I humbly bring two areas to your attention. The first is the recognition that a postcolonial world requires acts of decolonization. This symposium has demonstrated that the past of so-called foreign missions has been intimately connected—explicitly and/or implicitly—with imperial and colonizing forces. Evangelization cannot easily shake the implications of these complicated networks with their power dimensions that cross generations. For a mission society born and bred in the context of the twentieth-century

United States, what critical reexamination does a hundred years of experience bring to bear for the twenty-first century?

The imperial project is part of our missional and national past, and some would suggest our present and even future. The gun and the Bible participated in the colonizing efforts of the U.S. invasion of Mexican lands in the 1850s and of the seizure of Hawaiian, Caribbean, and Pacific islands at the turn of the last century. For all our U.S. talk about the separation of church and state, this nation too readily ascribes to a certain set of narrowly defined Christian values, values that ironically would have excluded Catholics at the time of Maryknoll's founding. U.S. interventions continue today in lands where we find our Church's missions, and sadly our national illiteracy when it comes to the world's religions, especially Islam, too often fuels unsubstantiated fears and even violence. We would be remiss not to remember that yesterday (October 7) marked the tenth anniversary of the Afghan war.

How does a U.S. Catholic mission society with a global reach attend to the necessary work of decolonization in an era that attests a postcoloniality that certain lived realities challenge? Culture studies scholar Juan Flores elaborates: "For the purpose of identifying the conditions faced by Puerto Rican, Mexican American, Dominican, and other Latino peoples in the United States, and the economic and political domination of their home countries, the term 'postcolonial' seems to be jumping the gun at best."[3] How do religious communities from the United States participate in a national and global reimagining of identity that would dismantle American exceptionalism while socioeconomic and political forces shake the "super" out of the superpower?

Acts of decolonization are also acts of resistance that arise from those too easily dismissed and disenfranchised. One need only look at the global phenomenon of migrations to appreciate that the colonial diaspora has not only struck back; it has talked back, bitten back, written back, and moved in, with or without the acceptable documentation. The growth of the simultaneously ancient yet new Latino/a presence in the U.S. Church challenges and complicates ecclesial narratives about an immigrant Church and one-sided paradigms of mission and its recipients. Consider the story of Cuban Catholic priest Félix Varela. He arrived in New York in 1823 and ministered among the immigrants of New York City, the Irish immigrants. His advocacy for human rights and social reform in both his Cuban home and in his U.S. exilic land is evident today in the parish he pastored in lower Manhattan that now is home to Chinese immigrants and their pastor, Maryknoll missioner Raymond Nobiletti.

Recognition of the Forgotten Option: con la Gente Joven

The preferential option for the poor has long been integrated into Maryknoll's self-understanding of mission at all levels of its outreach. This advocacy articulated first in the lived experience of Latin America crosses borders through the ministries of missioners, the publications of Orbis, and the journeys of migrants, and takes flight via Alitalia in Pope John Paul II's visits and encyclicals.

Curiously marginalized is a second area, the other option also proclaimed at Puebla, the preferential option for the young. In terms of the Church's history, Maryknoll is itself young, and in some ways to make such an option is to make a commitment to insure your own collective future. The questions posed to you (questions on the tables at the wrap-up session) are more than fodder for personal reflection; they represent the voices of Maryknoll's young emerging from your global communities of accountability. They raise issues worth considering about alterity and hybridity. One question, for example, comes from Africa: "How do foreign missioners cope with the new ethnicity in the region?" From Latin America a new turn on who should be "assimilated": "How is the USA Church influenced by the theologies, liturgies, pastoral practices, and religiosity of Latin Americans?"

These questions from your young highlight dimensions of power that cannot easily be glossed over, especially when one's home base is the United States. From China, "Are missionaries serving the needs of their own sending communities more than the local people to whom they are sent?" From Africa and Latin America, "What does mission mean in an age of the emerging role of the laity?"

Related to this preferential option is a critical openness to the possibilities of digital technologies in the hands of the young and the not so young. Social networking got the word out when communications ground to a crawl in earthquake-stricken Japan and Haiti; social networks had a role in mobilizing the Arab Spring and Occupy Wall

Street. Social networking supports postcolonial theologies, allows for cross-generational mentoring among Latino/a theologians, and is at the heart of the grassroots, student-led fight for the DREAM Act, which would allow alternately documented immigrant young people to live without the shadow of *la migra*. To paraphrase the sentiments of one pastoral agent engaged in ministry with youth, for our young virtual reality is not virtual, it's *realidad!*[4]

In listening across the sessions these past few days, I have noted the variety of biblical passages informing the reflections of symposium presenters. From Matthew's great commission (28:16–20) to John's Gospel of love with its discourse on friendship, the New Testament in particular has played an integral role in articulating the past, present, and future of mission. I was struck by what was not cited in these reflections, namely, the book of Revelation and its vision of "a new heaven and a new earth" (21:1) with the accompanying call to "Behold, God's dwelling is with the human race" (21:3). This vision references Isaiah 65:17, which, with the Apocalypse, informed Christopher Columbus's (Cristóbal Colón) presentation of his mission enterprise. Perhaps then this is a most appropriate time to reflect on mission, this weekend before Columbus Day, known to Latino/as and many Latin Americans as el Día de la Raza and remembered by some of the native peoples of the Americas as the Day of Indigenous Resistance. After a hundred years it is a good time to retrieve the past, rehabilitate the present, and dream new dreams. It is a good time to re-imagine founding visions—*con las gentes*.

Happy anniversary, Maryknoll. From one privileged to witness your community's journey, for all you have done and for all you do—*mil gracias!*

Stephen B. Bevans, SVD

As so many speakers have said, I am grateful to the Maryknoll Society for all the work for mission that it has undertaken in the last hundred years. I am particularly grateful to Orbis Books for the inspiration it has given me over the years and, of course, for publishing several of my own works. This has been a great conference, and I am honored to be here. Jim Kroeger has reflected on the word "gift." I'd like to reflect with you on the phrase "hope for the future."

I had the privilege of attending the centennial celebration at Maryknoll last June 29, and in his homily Maryknoll's superior general, Fr. Edward Dougherty, spoke of the importance not only of gratitude for the past, but of hope for the future. At this conference, he mentioned in his opening remarks that about 25 percent of the sentiment at Maryknoll was for remembering the past and about 75 percent was about hope for the future.

This conference, as I understand it, is to explore some new ways of thinking about mission in that future. As we explored some of these new ways of mission I have realized that if we are to hope for the future we have to really embrace that first point of Sister Antoinette Gutzler, that we are living in a time of a "qualitative leap." The time of the missioner as the "marine" of the Catholic Church (we were told that SVDs were that as well) and the "Westchester Cowboy" is past. The time of *ad gentes* mission as we have known it in the sixteenth to nineteenth centuries, and in its form in the late nineteenth and twentieth centuries, is also past. I think Bob Schreiter alluded to this as well as Nonie Gutzler and Peter Phan.

We have experienced a qualitative leap as the people of the foreign missions have come to us here in the United States. As Cardinal George noted, "If the South is the future, the South is here." As the missioners of today are increasingly people from the so-called mission lands—think of Frs. Stephen and Rodrigo, who were ordained Maryknoll priests in recent years, and Daniel Kim, among others, who are students here at the Catholic Theological Union. Another example is the missioners from Korea and Nigeria who are pouring into the United States to minister to us, and in some cases convert us, as Dana Robert told us this morning.

We have, as Bob Schreiter noted, moved away from a *geographical* understanding of mission to one that is much more complex. In his address on Mission Sunday 2006, Benedict XVI said,

> The area of *"missio ad gentes"* appears to have been considerably extended and cannot be defined safely as the basis for geographical or juridical consideration: indeed the missionary activity of the People of God is not only intended for non-Christian peoples and distant lands, but above all for social and cultural contexts and hearts.

In light of this "qualitative leap" I wonder if I might skate on the edge of what for Maryknollers might be a kind of heresy, and I say this with a bit of fear and trembling, and I hope—to echo David Bosch—with "bold humility": I wonder if the time has not come to rethink the idea of a *foreign* mission society. Not that Maryknoll would stop going abroad. Foreign mission is still valid! Not, perhaps, that the foreign missions would not still have a kind of priority, but that in order to stay the same—to keep up hope for the future—Maryknoll might embrace the "qualitative leap" we are undergoing and be as creative in this new time as Fathers Walsh and Price, Brother Tom McCann, and Sister Mollie Rogers were in theirs. This means, I suggest, rethinking mission in a time when the *gentes* have arrived in the United States, and when all the challenges of crossing cultures and engaging in interreligious dialogue exist not only across oceans and borders, but in the streets of our cities and the roads of our rural counties.

It is interesting that Steve Judd focused on the solidarity of Maryknollers with Japanese detainees—a natural and creative response to the context. It is also interesting that one of the great works, as I see it, of Maryknoll today is its sponsorship of young Chinese women and men here in the United States. Such work among the *gentes* here "at home" is not at all unprecedented.

Several years ago the Scalabrini Missionaries reinvented themselves. They were founded to take care of Italian refugees going to North and South America and Australia in the nineteenth century. But when there ceased to be a need for this kind of work, they committed themselves to work with migrants all over the world. I wonder if Maryknoll—and all foreign mission societies—might need to reinvent themselves in the same creative way.

I think this is what Bob Schreiter, Nonie Gutzler, Dana Robert, and Peter Phan were all saying: Bob's *ad extra, ad altera, ad altum,* and *ad vulnera* have been interpreted by Nonie—and I'm sure Bob agrees—more accurately as *inter altera,* and so on. Peter interpreted them as *cum alteris, cum vulneribus.* This is a new field—a field afar perhaps not in geography but certainly in many peoples' experience, and it is truly a new way of doing mission.

It is in this context, too, I think, that contemplation will play such an important role—mentioned by so many of the speakers: Steve Judd,

Wayne Fitzpatrick, and Sister Madge Karecki. Contemplation gives us the space to see where the *gentes* are and how to respond to them.

There is, I think, great hope for the future, but the future *is* the future, and we need to face it knowing that the Lord is with us in this future, and to the end of time. As we prayed yesterday and today in John Walsh's prayer, "Give us the courage to dream new dreams, think new thoughts, and go forward into the future with the Spirit."

Notes

1. United States Catholic Conference, *The Hispanic Presence: Challenge and Commitment* (Washington, D.C.: United States Catholic Conference, 1983).

2. Joseph R. Veneroso, MM, *Mirrors of Grace: The Spirit and Spiritualities of the Maryknoll Fathers and Brothers* (Maryknoll, N.Y.: Orbis Books, 2011), 45.

3. Juan Flores, *From Bomba to Hip-Hop: Puerto Rican Culture and Latino Identity* (New York: Columbia University Press, 2000), 214.

4. Thanks to my colleague, Stephen Bevans, SVD, for sharing this insight from a *Catholics on Call* gathering. A program of the Bernardin Center at Catholic Theological Union, *Catholics on Call* is a national vocation discovery program for young adult men and women considering a life of service in the Church as a lay minister, religious sister or brother, or priest. *See* http://www.catholicsoncall.org/.

5. *See* Jean-Pierre Ruiz, *Readings from the Edges: The Bible and People on the Move* (Maryknoll, N.Y.: Orbis Books, 2011), 129. Ruiz cites Columbus's explanation from a letter to Doña Juana de la Torre, "God made me the messenger of the new heaven and the new earth of which he spoke through Saint John in the Apocalypse, after having spoken of it through Isaiah, and he showed me to that location" (from Consuelo Varela, ed., *Cristóbal Colón: Textos y documentos completos* [Madrid: Alianza Editorial, 1982], 243; translation from Djelal Kadir, *Columbus and the Ends of the Earth: Europe's Prophetic Rhetoric as Conquering Ideology* [Berkeley: University of California Press, 1992], 153).

29

Missiological Reflections on the Maryknoll Centenary

John F. Gorski, MM
Kevin J. Hanlon, MM
James H. Kroeger, MM
William J. LaRousse, MM

This year Maryknoll celebrates its founding as the Catholic Foreign Mission Society of America. In the early 1900s, the idea of founding a mission seminary in the United States circulated among the members of the Catholic Missionary Union. Archbishop John Farley of New York had suggested the establishment of such a seminary and also tried to entice the Paris Foreign Mission Society to open an American branch. Finally, two diocesan priests, Fathers James Anthony Walsh and Thomas Frederick Price, having gained a mandate to create a mission seminary from the archbishops of the United States, traveled to Rome and received Pope Pius X's permission to do so. The date was June 29, 1911, the Feast of Saints Peter and Paul. In the years since, well over a thousand Maryknoll priests and Brothers have gone on mission to dozens of countries throughout the world. Many died young in difficult missions, and not a few have shed their blood for Christ. This is a time to celebrate the glory given by Christ to this relatively young Society.

The main purpose of this event, though, is not to glory in our past. We celebrate principally to fulfill the burning desire of our founders, in words enshrined over the main entrance of the Seminary building, *Euntes Docete Omnes Gentes*, "Go and teach all nations" (Matt. 28:19). Nearly twenty centuries after Christ gave this command, the Church, during the Second Vatican Council, again defined this as the fundamental purpose of mission, being "sent out by the Church and going forth into the whole world, to carry out the task of preaching the Gospel and planting the Church among peoples or groups who do not yet believe in Christ" (*Ad Gentes* 6).

In our Maryknoll century of mission, the Church grew further in its understanding of its evangelical work. In 1965, the Council declared that the Church is missionary "by her very nature" (AG 2). Mission is not just one characteristic of the Church; it forms its fundamental identity. Nor is it something relegated to professional, lifetime missionaries; it is the responsibility of every member of the Church.

In retrospect, the Council proclaimed this at a time when the Church in the United States had reached a pinnacle in its missionary efforts: a great multitude of its sons and daughters were on lifetime mission in foreign lands. In 1965, Maryknoll had passed its fiftieth anniversary, and its membership was at a peak from which it would decline to where it is today, a little over a third of what it was then. Thus, we Maryknollers are not as numerous as before. In fact, there are only ten permanent members under the age of fifty. While we are still nearly two hundred active members "in the field," that number will decline steeply over the next two decades. In twenty years, depending on new vocations, we may have less than fifty active members on mission. We cannot deny this reality and act and live as if we were still hundreds more. We need to ask, "Where will we focus our missionary activity, and what will we let go of?" We have to help younger members among us plan for a more practical missionary future.

But we have hope in this smaller Society of the future. We were relatively few when we first went into China and pioneered some new mission strategies. The same holds true for many of the new missions we worked in and developed throughout the world.

In order to plan well for the future, it would be good to recognize some important developments in mission and the Church that have shaped our Maryknoll work over the past hundred years. Maryknoll has never been an island set apart, but a Missionary Society of Apostolic Life integrated with the greater world Church. At this critical juncture, in this year when we celebrate our foundation, we propose four foundational elements to reflect upon. They are (1) Maryknoll's unique history, (2) the local Church, (3) proclamation and dialogue, and (4) mission and the Paschal Mystery.

Maryknoll's Unique History and Role in Mission

Inspired by the Paris Foreign Mission Society, our founders sought, together with the bishops, to create something new within the U.S. Church: a vehicle for training and sending priests (and soon after, Brothers) to missionary fields abroad. Distinct from a religious order or congregation, they envisioned that diocesan priests, seminarians, and Brothers would come from their dioceses, through Maryknoll, and go forth to the missions. This required a special relationship with the U.S. bishops, which both cofounders fostered and nurtured. But Bishop James A. Walsh also wished Maryknollers to be humble about this unique status, often mentioning that there were other missionaries from the United States who had been on mission longer than those of the young Society. Bishop Walsh is remembered as a man who always approached both high and low within the U.S. Church with gratitude and humility, ever anxious to maintain and grow Maryknoll's connection to it.

We were eventually obliged to take on a firmer canonical structure, and, in some ways, we began to resemble the religious orders and congregations around us. Yet this special history of ours, as a Missionary Society of Apostolic Life formed by the U.S. bishops, is a gift that may enable us to be of greater service in the promotion of mission within the U.S. Church.

Fulfilling this goal depends upon our relationship with the bishops and the faithful. While we still have good relations with much of the hierarchy, clergy, religious, and laity within the U.S. Church, there is a growing ignorance about Maryknoll, especially among the younger clergy, religious, and laity. In addition, most of the numerous foreign clergy and religious working in the United States do not know us. Also, we must admit that there are others in the U.S. Church who have a less than positive opinion of us. A centennial presents us with an opportunity in this regard. The ancient Israelites would have "jubilee" years, when debts were forgiven and things were made right. Our present superior general, Fr. Edward Dougherty, has said that the centennial should be a jubilee, that along with the rejoicing, it should initiate a process of asking forgiveness for our past mistakes and for having alienated portions of the U.S. Church. This is the time to mend fences and rebuild bridges that were broken by our own arrogance.

These are foundational characteristics of our history: that we have a unique relationship to the U.S. Church; that we are not "religious" but "secular" (diocesan) priests and Brothers; that our founders wished us to promote vocations coming straight from the dioceses; that we exist totally for world mission and only for world mission. These are all elements we should rely upon as we revitalize ourselves for the future.

Developments in Ecclesiology:
The Mission Identity of the Local Church

Because of the Vatican Council, we have come to a new awareness of what is most essential about the Church, since she has her origin "from the mission of the Son and the mission of the Holy Spirit . . . in accordance with the decree of God the Father" (AG 2). We believe that the Church is born from the mission of the Holy Trinity and that the Church lives to proclaim Christ. This missionary nature of the Church should be part of the faith that all Catholics live: "[Since] the People of God lives in communities, especially in dioceses and parishes, and becomes somehow visible in them, it is also up to these to witness Christ before the nations" (AG 37). Years earlier, Fr. Price himself observed, "The matter of mission lies at the very essence of Catholicity."

It is up to each local Church to participate in mission, with the bishop as the leader in this effort. "All bishops, as members of the body of bishops succeeding to the College of Apostles, are consecrated not just for some one diocese, but for the salvation of the entire world. The mandate of Christ to preach the Gospel to every creature (Mark 16:15) primarily and immediately concerns them, with Peter and under Peter." Each bishop is called upon to make "the mission spirit and zeal of the People of God present and as it were visible, so that the whole diocese becomes missionary" (AG 38).

In practical ways, this growing sense of all local Churches being missionary has affected our Maryknoll work. At the time of our founding, the Church organized its foreign mission work by a set of principles set up in the 1600s known as the *jus commissionis*, meaning that certain mission territories would be entrusted to particular religious groups. To this end, James Anthony Walsh went to the Far East to search for territories that could be entrusted to Maryknoll so that we might become missionaries. The Church largely abandoned this system in 1969, making the local Church, and not missionary orders, responsible for evangelization. Thus, we can say from that time onward, Maryknoll began to think of itself less as developing a certain mission territory, and more as working in service to local Churches throughout the world.

This change, that all local Churches must be missionary, has become an important part of our identity as *ad gentes, ad vitam* ("to the nations, for life") missionaries. We are able to speak with authority from our own experience about mission to both the local Church from which we originate and to the local Churches to which we are sent. In fact, this could be one description of our "new" specific mission after the Council: enabling local Churches to assume and live their missionary identity. "In order that this missionary zeal may flourish among those in their own homeland, it is very fitting that the young Churches should participate as soon as possible in the universal missionary work of the Church" (AG 20).

This development is seen in local Churches that are young and growing. For example, the Federation of Asian Bishops' Conferences (FABC) reflected this thinking when it said: "The renewal of our sense of mission will mean . . . that the acting subject of mission is the local church living and acting in communion with the universal Church" (FABC V, 3.3.1). The fact that all local Churches are by nature *missionary* makes us ask the question: How can local Churches today find newer ways to structure their response to the vast needs for worldwide evangelization?

The Proclamation of Jesus Christ, Interreligious Dialogue, and Authentic Human Development

The Council opened the windows of the Church to see other faiths in a more positive light. While missionaries had been taught to accept local customs that do not directly conflict with faith and morals, the Holy Spirit inspired the Council to move even further toward an appreciation of other faiths and cultures.

Developing positive relations with other religions, or "interreligious dialogue," has become a significant part of our overall work and outlook. Blessed John Paul II explained that this dialogue should proceed not from tactical concerns or self-interest, but from a "deep respect for everything that has been brought about in human beings by the Spirit who blows where he wills" (*Redemptoris Missio* 56). In dialogue, the "seeds of the Word" are encountered within the faiths of others. John Paul II was aware that dialogue is not the work of dreamy idealists and that it has its challenges:

> Other religions constitute a positive challenge for the Church: they stimulate her both to discover and acknowledge the signs of Christ's presence and of the working of the Spirit, as well as to examine more deeply her own identity and to bear witness to the fullness of Revelation which she has received for the good of all." (RM 56)

Although this has all been enriching, it has not been the easiest shift for missionaries. We wonder: Is dialogue a substitute for proclamation? Is proclamation itself still valid? Is evangelization in the hopes of conversion a worthy activity? In answer to questions such as these, the Church has issued further clarifications. John Paul II himself quotes Paul VI, who said that "salvation comes from Christ and that dialogue does not dispense from evangelization" (RM 55). In addition, the Pontifical Council on Interreligious Dialogue explained that "Proclamation and dialogue are . . . both viewed, each in its own place, as component elements and authentic forms of the one evangelizing mission of the Church. They are both oriented towards the communication of salvific truth" (*Dialogue and Proclamation* 2).

In practical ways, these clarifications on dialogue could just as easily be addressed to Maryknollers involved in the social apostolate: all missionaries, whatever their everyday work, cannot avoid the fact that they are called to proclaim Christ. We work to better the lives of people in places where there is a need for action for integral development and liberation from all forms of oppression. In this, our work of evangelization and development does not begin and end on a strictly human level. The Gospel of Christ always sees human persons in both their finite and infinite ends. John Paul challenges missionaries to always attend to both:

> Through the gospel message, the Church offers a force for liberation which promotes development precisely because it leads to conversion of heart and of ways of thinking, fosters the recognition of each person's dignity, encourages solidarity, commitment and service of

one's neighbor, and gives everyone a place in God's plan, which is the building of his kingdom of peace and justice, beginning already in this life. Human development derives from God and must lead back to God. That is why there is a close connection between the proclamation of the Gospel and human promotion. (RM 58–59)

Wherever we work, we Maryknollers need to continue to ask ourselves, according to varying circumstances, how we are participating in the work of proclaiming Christ, and how we are fostering a missionary Church.

Mission and Participation in the Paschal Mystery

Why do we go on mission? Sometimes asking the simplest question brings the most fruit. One of John Paul II's answers to this question has a deep, spiritual appeal: "The ultimate purpose of mission is to enable people to share in the communion which exists between the Father and the Son" (RM 23).

God made human in Christ unites God with humanity. Christ, in the Paschal Mystery, took upon himself our sin and through the cross redeemed us, making it possible for us to be one with God. *Gaudium et Spes* states how this grace of redemption is communicated to us Christians by the Holy Spirit. But, surprisingly, it adds:

> All this holds true not only for Christians, but for all persons of good will in whose hearts grace works in an unseen way. For, since Christ died for all, and since the ultimate vocation of humanity is in fact one and divine, we ought to believe that the Holy Spirit in a manner known to God offers to every person the possibility of being associated with this paschal mystery. (GS 22)

We might define mission, then, as promoting a full, conscious participation in this Paschal Mystery, which the Holy Spirit has already begun in cultures not yet touched by the Gospel. People "of good will" will find the explicit and full understanding of what God has begun in them by their hearing of the Gospel. Beyond just the *understanding* of this mystery, they will come to participate more fully in it. "Evangelization is everything [the Church] does to promote the people's *participation* in the mystery of Christ" (from the *Instrumentum Laboris* for the 1974 Synod of Bishops; emphasis ours).

Mission promotes people's participation in the Paschal Mystery in many ways. There are the normal human encounters of the missioner with the unevangelized or of the newly baptized with the larger culture. There are shared projects among religious and secular groups for the development of peoples. But the pinnacle of our efforts to promote people's participation in the Paschal Mystery is found in the sacred liturgy. In the Mass, we encounter the Christ who has died for our sins, and "the victory and triumph of his death are again made present" (*Sancrosanctum Concilium* 6). The Church desires that the people participate in

> the sacred action conscious of what they are doing, with devotion and full collaboration. . . . They should give thanks to God; by offering the Immaculate Victim, not only through the hands of the priest, but also with him, they should learn also to offer themselves; through Christ the Mediator, they should be drawn day by day into ever more perfect union with God and with each other, so that finally God may be all in all." (SC 48)

The Council later expanded on the missionary nature of this liturgical participation, stating,

> The Most Blessed Eucharist contains the entire spiritual boon of the Church, that is, Christ himself, our Pasch and Living Bread, by the action of the Holy Spirit through his very flesh vital and vitalizing, giving life to all who are thus invited and encouraged to offer themselves, their labors and all created things, together with him. In this light, *the Eucharist shows itself as the source and the apex of the whole work of preaching the Gospel.* (*Presbyterorum Ordinis* 5, emphasis ours)

It is said that both the cofounders of Maryknoll took great care in the offering of the Sacred Mysteries and taught their spiritual sons to have the same devotion. They anticipated in their own way these later words of the Council, that the Eucharist is "the source and apex" of the work of evangelization. Bishop James Anthony Walsh expressed this thought in a similar way in an address he gave to the Catholic Missionary Union before the formation of Maryknoll:

> The true priest lives his short life for the salvation of his fellow creatures. Every sincere Christian longs for the day when the Kingdom

of the Savior shall rule all men's hearts. What we priests and laymen can do by effort and prayer to win the world to Christ, this we should do, so that the altars may be more numerous on the earth than the stars in the heavens; that multitudes in every land may be nourished with the Bread of Life—the Body of Christ; that this earth may be deluged in the Precious Blood of the Lamb—a ruby earth glistening like a radiant jewel under the sunlight of the glorious Cross of Him who died on it, not for you or me alone, but for every child of man.

From its beginning, then, Maryknoll has had a deep Eucharistic, paschal, and missionary foundation. We might ask ourselves in this time of Jubilee how we can best renew our sense and our practice of what James Anthony Walsh expressed above. We have been graced to see the growth of people's participation in the Paschal Mystery in dozens of countries over a number of generations. We can continue to ask ourselves how we find the Paschal Mystery already present in the cultures to which we are sent. Doing so, we become more able to proclaim Christ as the "Alpha and Omega" of this mystery, especially in our missionary Eucharistic actions.

As a final note to this section, we must add that Maryknollers participate in the work of proclaiming the Gospel even when we are no longer able to go on mission. Many of our elder members, suffering with debilitating illnesses, are now united more intimately to the paschal sufferings of Christ. Their mission has become one of prayer and of bearing their own infirmities for the sake of Christ's mission and his Church. In the words of St. Paul: "Now I rejoice in my sufferings for your sake, and in my flesh I am filling up what is lacking in the afflictions of Christ on behalf of his body, which is the Church" (Col. 1:24). Like the Church, the members of Maryknoll form one body, where the efforts, prayers, and sufferings of all work together for our one mission. "We know that all things work for good for those who love God, who are called according to his purpose" (Rom. 8:28).

Conclusion

In our centenary, while we think about our past, we also envision our future. We ask, "What do we hope the Society will become in the service of mission?"

In a recent encyclical centered on the meaning of hope, Pope Benedict XVI states: "The one who has hope lives differently; the one who hopes has been granted the gift of new life" (*Spe Salvi* 2). The Holy Father draws from Romans 8:24–25: "For in hope we were saved. Now hope that sees for itself is not hope. For who hopes for what one sees? But if we hope for what we do not see, we wait with endurance."

Given our present reality, what do we hope for? While we will be significantly more limited by numbers, we can also reflect upon the unique gifts we have to build upon. Two principal ones come to mind.

First, we are the only society of permanent members created by the U.S. bishops for the purpose of *ad gentes* ("to the nations"), *ad extra* ("beyond our borders"), and *ad vitam* ("for life") mission. In discussions with the Bishops' Advisory Board to Maryknoll over the past years, the bishops have been unanimous in encouraging us to retain this unique identity of being a U.S. Church response to world mission needs: they recognize that we are "their" mission Society. We can draw more upon this unique relationship. We can also increase our own identification of being a part of the Church in the United States, and we can encourage all the bishops to fulfill their missionary duty in new ways. We can look to recruitment, formation, and support as areas for further collaboration (see AG 38).

Second, we have vast mission experience to draw upon, both from the lives of the men who went before us, but also from the many of us who are still fully active in *ad gentes* mission. It would be hard to find a group more versed in the types and varieties of missions in which we have been involved. This experience should help us plan well for our future. Where do we realistically hope to work in the near future with our smaller numbers?

Keeping in mind the Holy Father's words above, we can approach these questions with hope. Although we may soon have to limit ourselves to a smaller number of missions, is it not possible that this will also create opportunities for us to become better evangelizers? Our situation may help us focus more deeply upon the foundations of mission mentioned above and upon many other questions as well. We may find that while we still involve ourselves with basic mission work with those who do not know Christ, we may devote more effort to helping many other local Churches themselves become *ad gentes* missionaries.

Finally, we remember that our primary hope is not in ourselves, but rather in the Lord, in whom our cofounders and earliest members trusted so completely. With Bishop James Anthony Walsh and Father Thomas Frederick Price, we ask again that Our Lady, Queen of Apostles, whose name our Society bears, intercede for us with her Son, that the Holy Spirit be sent upon us anew to shepherd our Society into a bright future.

30

A Tribute to Maryknoll

Gustavo Gutiérrez, OP

I am happy to have this wonderful occasion to express my gratitude, my very deep gratitude, to Maryknoll's priests, brothers, and sisters. My country of Peru owes a great debt to them. They arrived in Peru relatively early in the middle of the last century, and their contribution was very, very important for the Peruvian Church, but also for my country.

Because we are speaking at this symposium on the subject of mission, I would like to emphasize how I see the witness of Maryknoll in my country. It has been and is a witness of friendship. We can also speak about intercultural dialogue, which is certainly important as well, but nothing can equal support by friendship. We can recall this expression present in the Gospel of John, "I don't call you servants, but friends." Friendship supports equality, and to acknowledge that while you are different you are equal has been the witness of Maryknoll. This is true not only in Peru, but in the witness of Maryknollers to many, many, many people around the world.

Being genuine friends with people is the foundation of all mission efforts. It supports, for example, learning the language of the indigenous people in my country. Maryknollers not only speak the language very well, they also understand the mentality. In my opinion, one of the best theological statements to come from the Second Vatican Council was written by Fr. Yves Congar, who stated that mission is the task of the Church. Also emphasized was the need to remain "close" to the people.

To conclude, I would like to mention the conference of the Latin American bishops at Aparecida. A key idea explicated at the conference was that it is not possible to have a genuine commitment to the poor without friendship. We need to be close to them; this is the meaning of the preferential option for the poor. For its witness and friendship, many, many thanks to Maryknoll. Thank you!

31

In Honor of Maryknoll's Mission

Maryknoll Centennial Mass
Homily, October 7, 2011

Bishop Ricardo Ramírez, CSB

I was invited many years ago by one of your Maryknollers, Fr. Walter Winrich, to assist him at his mission in Merida, Yucatan. This was before I was a bishop and while I was working as a missioner at our Basilian Fathers Missions in Mexico. I was used to the pleasant cool climate of Central Mexico, and the humidity and heat of Yucatan was unbearable. The nights were the worst. I had a choice of sleeping in a hammock or in a bed. Neither worked; the bed was full of bedbugs, and in the hammock, I simply could not get the right curl of my body to get comfortable. I was glad to get back to the comfort of my bed back at the Basilian mission in Puebla. That was the extent of my sharing Maryknoll missionary life. I couldn't cut it!

Among the richest pearls in the treasure chest of the Church are its missionaries. "How beautiful upon the mountains are the feet of him who brings glad tidings, announcing peace, bearing good news, announcing salvation, and saying to Zion, 'Your God is King!'" (Isa. 52:7).

The hundred years of Maryknoll are a cause for the entire U.S. Church to rejoice and be glad. Your history and legacy are a tribute to the faith of the Catholics of this country. Today I join the immense number who salute the Maryknoll Fathers and Brothers, and I am proud to be a member of the United States Conference of Catholic Bishops, although the bishops went by a different name a hundred years ago when they gave their *beneplacitum* to the Society. The bishops recognized that the founders of Maryknoll, those noble, holy, visionary, and heroic men, were gripped by the desire to evangelize and who wanted nothing more than to be sent to proclaim the mystery of Jesus.

The call of missionaries, their privileged function in the Church and in the world, is rooted in the very identity of the Church and the reason for its existence: to announce to all the world the love of God. The missionary activity of the Church is what gives the Church its very identity.

All of us here owe our presence to the evangelizing mission, and we can trace our faith back to the preaching of the apostles—indeed back to the appearance in the world of the person of Jesus Christ himself. He is the first missionary, the first of the many who have been sent to invite us to be part of his Kingdom, exemplified by the image of the heavenly banquet. I learned long ago that God is a perfect gentleman: he always invites and gives us the freedom to open the doors of our hearts.

"As the Father has sent me so I send you. [Jesus] said to them again, 'Peace be with you. As the Father has sent me, so I send you'" (John 20:21). The Father sent him to bring us the invitation to eat with God. Isn't this the beautiful image in today's readings? "I invite you to come and eat."

> On this mountain the LORD of hosts
>   will provide for all peoples
> A feast of rich food and choice wines,
>   juicy, rich food and pure, choice wines.
> On this mountain he will destroy
>   the veil that veils all peoples,
> The web that is woven over all nations;
>   he will destroy death forever.
> The LORD God will wipe away
>   the tears from all faces;
> The reproach of his people he will remove
>   from the whole earth; for the LORD has spoken.
> On that day it will be said:
>   "Behold our God, to whom we looked to save us!
>   This is the LORD for whom we looked;
>   let us rejoice and be glad that he has saved us!" (Isa. 25:6–9)

Yes, we can now behold the God, "to whom we looked to save us!"

And would you believe that he was looking for us from all eternity? Salvation is nothing less than the blessed encounter between the God who searches for us and those who search for him and long to see his face. And the encounter is at a great sumptuous feast!

Everyone can grasp the image of the festive meal in the prophet Isaiah and in the Gospel. I remember when I was a child and my grandfather brought into grandma's kitchen lots of vegetables from his garden, and then my grandmother cooked a big dinner with the vegetables and a bit of meat. As we gathered around the table to eat that nice meal, my grandfather exclaimed, *"Hijos, estamos en la Gloria!"* ("Children, we are in heaven!")

In Las Cruces I befriended a family with small children. I knew they were going to a pizza place to celebrate the birthday of one of the kids. I wanted to treat them with dessert at my home. On the way out of the pizza parlor, their dad told them, "Now we're going to the bishop's for strawberry shortcake." The youngest of the children shouted, "That's my kind of bishop!" When the world hears the Good News of Jesus and the promised fiesta in heaven hopefully they will proclaim: "That's my kind of God!"

Missioners invite others to the banquet of love, the banquet of forgiveness, the banquet of justice and peace, mainly through their witness. And there is supposed to be excitement in the way we invite; we do it with or without words. Pope Paul VI wrote in the Apostolic Exhortation *Evangelii Nuntiandi*: "Christians stir up irresistible questions in the hearts of those who see how they live: Why are they like this? Why do they live in this way? What or who is it that inspires them? Why are they in our midst?"

This is the witness of the missioner. These are the questions they provoke in the remote places where they are sent. There is power and something compelling in their presence, in their sharing, and in their witness of solidarity.

Whether by this witness or by the explicit proclamation of the Gospel, the evangelizer invites people to hope in the promises made by God and through the preaching of God's love for us, and of our love for God made manifest in our love for others. The preaching and living out of the message of love necessarily leads people to the reality of the Eucharist and the promise it brings.

True missionaries join those who struggle to overcome everything that condemns them to remain on the margins of life and in the shadows of death: famine, chronic disease, illiteracy, poverty, and injustices of every kind. As we proclaim the Gospel, we encourage one another to do good and to commit ourselves to justice, reconciliation, and peace.

Pope Benedict XVI, in his Apostolic Exhortation *Verbum Domini*, writes that "God's word inspires men and women to build relationships based on rectitude and justice, and testifies to the great value in God's eyes of every effort to create a more just and more liveable world." He reminds us that a commitment to justice and to changing our world is an essential element of evangelization.

No one associated with Maryknoll can forget Mary. It's in your name! In the *Magnificat* Mary sings the praises of the Lord. Here we see how completely at home Mary is with the Word of God. With ease she moves in and out of it. She speaks and thinks with the Word of God, and the Word of God becomes her word, and her word issues from the Word of God. Here we see how her thoughts are attuned to the thoughts of God, how her will is one with the will of God.

For a hundred years Maryknollers have taught all of us how to act as a people "sent" to proclaim the Good News. Because of our baptism we are all called, as the Sixth General Conference of Latin American Bishops says, to be not only disciples, but also missionaries. Pope Benedict XVI's Apostolic Exhortation, *Verbum Domini*, repeats this teaching:

> No believer in Christ can feel dispensed from this responsibility which comes from belonging to the Body of Christ. A consciousness of this must be revived in every family, parish, community, association, and ecclesial movement. The Church, as a mystery of communion, is thus entirely missionary, and everyone, according to his or her proper state in life, is called to give an incisive contribution to the proclamation of Christ.

Today we most fittingly celebrate you of Maryknoll and what you have given. We also celebrate what you have received, your own faith, which has been strengthened and deepened by those to whom you have been sent. This is, after all, the dynamic of evangelization: it is the Christ that I bring meeting the Christ the people bring, and through this encounter, our relationship with Christ is deepened.

May God continue to bless you people of Maryknoll and may we all meet together at the banquet on the mountain where we will meet the generous God of Jesus Christ. That's my kind of God!

Contributors

Dr. Scott Alexander is associate professor of Islam and director of Catholic-Muslim Studies at the Catholic Theological Union in Chicago. His teaching and research interests include medieval Muslim sectarianism, the mystical traditions of Muslim spirituality, Quranic studies, and the history and future of Muslim-Christian relations.

Rev. Albino Barrera, OP, is professor of economics and theology at Providence College, Rhode Island. His books include *Market Complicity and Christian Ethics, God and the Evil of Scarcity: Moral Foundations of Economic Agency,* and *Modern Catholic Social Documents and Political Economy.*

Rev. Stephen B. Bevans, SVD, served as a missionary to the Philippines from 1972 to 1981 and is currently the Louis J. Luzbetak, SVD, Professor of Mission and Culture at the Catholic Theological Union. He is the author of *Models of Contextual Theology, An Introduction to Theology in Global Perspective*, and, with Roger Schroeder, *Constants in Context, Prophetic Dialogue*, and *Mission and Culture: The Louis J. Luzbetak Lectures.*

Sr. Ann Braudis, MM, founded the Maryknoll Sisters Center for Justice, Peace and the Integrity of Creation. She currently serves as the main representative of the Maryknoll Sisters' Non-Governmental Organization in consultative status to the Economic and Social Council at the United Nations and is co-chair of the NGO Committee on Sustainable Development. Her current work emphasizes the reform of international governance for a sustainable future based on social and environmental justice.

Merwyn De Mello has ministered in Japan, Tanzania, and Zimbabwe, where he has worked to create bridges between peacebuilding organizations. Currently he works in the Mission Services Department at the Maryknoll Lay Missioners.

Marie Dennis is co-president of Pax Christi International and also serves on the national boards of JustFaith and the Jubilee USA Network. She is on the steering committee of the Catholic Peacebuilding Network and is a contributing editor to *Soujourners*. She is the author of several books, including most recently *The Diversity of Vocations.*

Sr. Joanne (Jaruko) Doi, MM, served in Peru and the southern Andes mountains doing pastoral work and economic development projects among indigenous people. After completing her Ph.D. in interdisciplinary studies, she has been teaching as an adjunct professor. Her research interests have focused on the experience of Japanese Americans interned in relocation camps during World War II, includes her father and grandfather.

Rosanne Elizabeth Fischer worked for twelve years in the Mission Office for the Diocese of St. Cloud, Minnesota, and is now completing graduate studies in systematic theology at St. John's School of Theology Seminary in Collegeville. She has worked on a partnering program with Nicaragua and also directed the Yakima Interfaith Coalition in Yakima, Washington, connecting peoples of varying cultural, economic, and religious backgrounds.

Rev. Raymond J. Finch, MM, served in Peru for twenty-three years, most of that time with the Aymara of the southern Andean highlands. A former superior general of the Maryknoll Society, he is currently in Cochabamba, Bolivia, where he serves as the director of the Maryknoll Center for Mission in Latin America.

Br. Wayne J. Fitzpatrick, MM, the first Brother ever elected to Maryknoll's General Council, has been an active participant in the promotion of the Brotherhood vocation in the United States. He is presently director of life-long formation and continuing education for the Maryknoll Fathers and Brothers and serves as the assistant regional superior for the Society in the United States.

His Eminence Francis Cardinal George, OMI, was named the eighth archbishop of Chicago in 1997 by Pope John Paul II. In 1998 he was elevated to the Sacred College of Cardinals and in 2007 was elected president of the United States Conference of Catholic Bishops. He is the author of *The Difference God Makes* and, most recently, *God in Action: How Faith in God Can Address the Challenges of the World.*

Rev. John F. Gorski, MM, has served as a Maryknoll Missioner in Bolivia since his ordination to the priesthood in 1963. He has a doctorate in missiology from the Pontifical Gregorian University in Rome. From 1985 to 1989 he served as national director of the Pontifical Mission Societies in Bolivia, and since 1989 he has been professor of missiology and ecumenical theology at the Catholic University of Bolivia in Cochabamba. In 2000, he was elected the first president of the newly founded International Association of Catholic Missiologists and served in that post until October 2004.

Rev. Daniel G. Groody, CSC, is a scholar, teacher, and award-winning author and film producer, who lectures worldwide. He is currently an associate professor of theology and the director of the Center for Latino Spirituality and Culture at the Institute for Latino Studies at the University of Notre Dame.

His books include *Border of Death, Valley of Life: An Immigrant Journey of Heart and Spirit, Globalization, Spirituality, and Justice: Navigating the Path to Peace,* and, most recently, *Gustavo Gutiérrez: Spiritual Writings.*

Rev. Gustavo Gutiérrez, OP, is the John Cardinal O'Hara Professor of Theology at the University of Notre Dame. His many publications include his foundational work in Latin American liberation theology, *A Theology of Liberation: History, Politics, and Salvation.* Gutiérrez has been a principal professor at the Pontifical University of Peru and a visiting professor at many major universities in North America and Europe. In 1993 he was awarded the Legion of Honor by the French government for his tireless work for human dignity and life and against oppression in the Third World. He is currently working on a book exploring the historical background and continuing theological relevance of the preferential option for the poor.

Sr. Antoinette (Nonie) Gutzler, MM, has served in Tanzania and in Taiwan, where she is currently associate professor of theology at Fu Jen University's Faculty of Theology. She is a consultant to the Ecclesia of Women in Asia (EWA) and a standing committee member of the Association of Major Religious Superiors in Taiwan. Her recent publications include *"Lex Orandi, Lex Credendi:* 'Women Matters' as an Asian Theological Concern," and "'Am I My Sister's Keeper?': The 'Internalization' and 'Globalization' of Women's Homelessness: A Taiwan Perspective."

Rev. Kevin J. Hanlon, MM, was in mission in Japan before completing a doctorate in mission studies at the Gregorian University in Rome. He then returned to Japan and taught sacred scripture at Notre Dame Women's College in Kyoto. He is the author of *Popular Catholicism in Japan* and currently works in the United States as a missiologist, mission educator and promoter. He has also served as an advisor to the USCCB Committee on World Mission.

Rev. Stephen P. Judd, MM, worked for twelve years in Peru in various mission apostolates. After serving on the General Council of the Maryknoll Society, he returned to Peru and served as director of the Office of Campus Ministry at the National University of the Altiplano in Puno. He later became director of the Maryknoll Language Institute in Cochabamba, Bolivia, where he now serves as coordinator of the Office of Promotion and Leadership. He lectures frequently on topics related to mission theology in Latin America and the relationship between religions and society.

Sr. Madge Karecki, SSJ-TOSF, spent twenty-one years in South Africa, where she taught missiology at the University of South Africa. She is currently the director of the Office for Mission Education and Animation in the Archdiocese of Chicago. She also serves as an adjunct faculty member of the University of St. Mary of the Lake, Mundelein, Illinois.

Rev. Michael C. Kirwen, MM, has been a resident of East Africa for over forty-eight years, combining pastoral work among the Luo people with writing, field research, and teaching. He is the founder of the Maryknoll Institute of African Studies (MIAS), a graduate institute affiliated with St. Mary's University and with Tangaza College, Nairobi, Kenya, where he has served as professor of interdisciplinary studies and director and dean of studies. His books include *African Cultural Domains: Cycle of Family and Interpersonal Relationships, African Cultural Domains: Life Cycle of an Individual,* and *The Missionary and the Diviner.*

Rev. James H. Kroeger, MM, is a professor in the Ecclesiastical Faculty of Theology at the Loyola School of Theology in Manila, the Philippines. He has authored or contributed to over thirty books and numerous articles in various Western and Asian languages. Fr. Kroeger has served on the General Council of the Maryknoll Society and currently serves with the Office of Evangelization of the Federation of Asian Bishops' Conferences and is president of the Philippines Association of Catholic Missiologists. His books include *Living Mission* and *Once Upon a Time in Asia.*

Rev. William LaRousse, MM, is a professor at St. Francis Xavier Regional Major Seminary in Davao City, Philippines. He is the episcopal vicar for religious in the Archdiocese of Davao. He is also the executive secretary of the Office of Ecumenical and Interreligious Affairs of the Federation of Asian Bishops' Conferences.

Sr. Janice McLaughlin, MM, has worked in East Africa for more than thirty years, including an assignment as communications coordinator for the Catholic Church in Kenya from 1969 to 1977. After serving as communications coordinator for the Maryknoll Sisters, she returned to Zimbabwe as the training coordinator for Silveira House, a leadership training and development education center. She currently serves as president of the Maryknoll Sisters. Her books include *Ostriches, Dung Beetles and Other Spiritual Masters.*

Dr. Carmen Nanko-Fernández is associate professor of pastoral ministry at the Catholic Theological Union, where she also directs the ecumenical doctor of ministry program. A former president of the Academy of Catholic Hispanic Theologians of the United States (ACHTUS), she has published a number of scholarly articles and is the author of *Campus Ministry: Identity and Praxis* and *Theologizing in Espanglish: Context, Community and Ministry.*

Rev. Peter C. Phan is a priest of the Diocese of Dallas, Texas. He is currently the Ignacio Ellacuría Professor of Theology at Georgetown University. The 2010 recipient of the John Courtney Murray Award of the Catholic Theological Society of America, he is the author of many books, including *The Asian Synod, Christianity with an Asian Face,* and *Being Religious Interreligiously.* He is the general editor of the "Theology in Global Perspective" series from Orbis Books and the "Pastoral Spirituality" series from Paulist Press.

Sr. Ana María Pineda, RSM, is an associate professor of religious studies at Santa Clara University in Santa Clara, California, where she teaches courses in Latino/Hispanic theology. She has served on the boards of the Louisville Institute, the Academy of Catholic Hispanic Theologians of the United States (ACHTUS), and the U.S. Conference of Catholic Bishops. She is a founding member of the Hispanic Theological Initiative, which provides scholarships and mentoring for Latino doctoral students in theology. She is the co-editor of *Dialogue Rejoined: Theology and Ministry in the United States Hispanic Reality.*

Bishop Ricardo Ramírez, CSB, became in 1982 the first bishop of the Diocese of Las Cruces, New Mexico. He is a member of the USCCB Committees on International Justice and on Peace and Domestic Social Development, and is the episcopal advisor to the Institute for Hispanic Liturgy.

Sr. Barbara E. Reid, OP, is vice president and academic dean at the Catholic Theological Union in Chicago. She is the author of many books, including *Taking Up the Cross: New Testament Interpretations through Latina and Feminist Eyes* and *The Gospel according to Matthew.* She is the general editor of a new sixty-volume feminist commentary on the Bible. Sr. Barbara also writes a weekly column, "The Word," for *America* magazine.

Prof. Dana L. Robert is the Truman Collins Professor of World Christianity and History of Mission at Boston University's School of Theology. A leading historian of Christian mission, she is the author of a number of books, including *Christian Mission: How Christianity Became a World Religion,* and *American Women in Mission: A Social History of Their Thought and Practice.* With her husband, M. L. Daneel, an expert on African-initiated churches in southern Africa, Robert directs the Center for Global Christianity and Mission at the Boston University School of Theology.

Rev. Robert Schreiter, CPPS, holds the Vatican Council II Professorship of Theology at the Catholic Theological Union in Chicago. He has taught at CTU since 1974 and served as its dean for nine years. He lectures and writes in the areas of religion and culture, the mission of the Church, and international peacebuilding and reconciliation. He is a past president of the American

Society of Missiology and the Catholic Theological Society of America. His many books include *Constructing Local Theologies, The New Catholicity*, and *Mission in the Third Millennium*. He is coeditor of *Peacebuilding: Catholic Theology, Ethics and Praxis*.

Rev. Roger Schroeder, SVD, is a professor of intercultural studies and ministry and holder of the Bishop Francis X. Ford, MM, Chair of Catholic Missiology at the Catholic Theological Union in Chicago. He is the author of *What Is the Mission of the Church? A Guide for Catholics*, and co-author with Stephen Bevans of *Constants in Context: A Theology of Mission for Today* and *Prophetic Dialogue: Reflections on Christian Mission Today*.

Rev. Kenneth F. Thesing, MM, is a Maryknoll missioner who has worked for nearly thirty years in East Africa. He also served as superior general of the Maryknoll Society from 1990 to 1996. After completing a three-year term as Country Director for the Jesuit Refugee Service in Southern Sudan, Fr. Thesing currently works with the Food and Agricultural Organization of the United Nations in Rome.

Rev. John J. Wall has served on the faculty of Niles College and the Seminary of Loyola University and was vocations director for the Archdiocese of Chicago. In March 2007, the Holy See appointed Father Wall as president of the Catholic Church Extension Society, which strengthens the Church's presence and mission in under-resourced and isolated communities across the United States.

Dr. Jean-Paul Wiest has worked for the past eight years as research director of the Beijing Center for Chinese Studies. His primary field of research is the history of Christianity in modern and contemporary China with an emphasis on Sino-Western cultural and religious interactions. He also conducts oral history workshops around the world aimed at preserving the memory and identity of Christ communities. He is the author of *Maryknoll in China* and numerous other books and articles in English, French, and Chinese.

Index

abundance, economy of, 33
Academy of Catholic Hispanic Theologians of the United States (ACHTUS), 192–93
accompaniment, 135
ACHTUS. *See* Academy of Catholic Hispanic Theologians of the United States
adaptability, 13, 15
Ad Gentes (Decree on the Missionary Activity of the Church; Vatican II), 44, 170–71, 185
affability, 13, 14, 15
Africa
  Catholic Church in, 66–69
  Catholic missioners beginning work in, 65
  Christianity's growth in, 44
  conflicts in, 68. *See also* South Sudan
  cultural themes of, 153–54
  HIV/AIDS in, 68
  Maryknoll's approach to mission in, 65–66
  mission units in, 65
  sub-Saharan, Catholics as perentage of population, 65
African Council of Religious Leaders, 20
African Cultural Domains: Cycle of Family and Interpersonal Relationship, 154
African Cultural Domains: Life Cycle of an Individual, 154
African Cultural Knowledge: Themes and Embedded Beliefs, 154
African Synod of Bishops, First, 67
age of mobilization, 40–41, 98
Akashi, Marianna, 18
Allen, John L., Jr., 183–84
Aloysius, Brother, 28

Amaladoss, Michael, 130, 133
American Baptist Mission, 110
American Century, the, 10
American exceptionalism, 9–10, 11, 224
Americans, openness of, to missional issues, 101
Americas
  catechetical process in, 77
  evangelization of, 76–77
  Protestants becoming established in, 78
  republics established in, 77–78
  state support of the Church in, 77
Amity Foundation, 115
Analogical Imagination, The (Tracy), 6
ancestors, veneration of, 56, 77, 107, 111, 114, 119
Andean religion, 77
Anglican Church of Burma, 110
animists, 71
annunciation of birth stories, 145
anti-Americanism, 180
Anzaldúa, Gloria, 22
Arab Spring, 30–31, 225
Arrupe, Pedro, 80
Ashworth, John, 136–37
Asia
  Catholics in, 71
  church renewal movement in, 74
  diversity of, 70
  ecclesiology in, 73
  evangelization in, 74
  homeland to major world religions, 71
  Maryknoll's presence in, 70
  religions of, 71
  religious-cultural experience in, 71
  social, economic, and political conditions in, 72

Asian and Pacific Presence: Harmony in Faith (USCCB), 72
Asian Synod (1998), 70
Asian Christian Perspectives on Harmony (FABC), 133
Augustinians, 114
Aung San Suu Ky, 110
availability, 13, 14–15
Aymara people, 206
Aztec religion, 77

Back to Jerusalem movement, 99
Bangladesh, 5, 70
Bañuelas, Arturo, 192
Bao Dai, 111
Barth, Karl, 95
beauty, 140
Beltrán, Edgard, 191
Benedict XIV, 114
Benedict XV, 82
Benedict XVI, 68, 175–76, 181–82, 186–87, 202, 227, 239, 245
Bevans, Stephen, 7, 126
bishops
    involvement of, in mission, 233
    ordination of, 174
Bishops' Advisory Board, for Maryknoll, 239
Bishops' Institute for Interreligious Affairs, 60
Blaber, Harry, 88
Bolivia, 78, 79
borderlands, 22
Bosch, David, 126, 227
Boundless Faith (Wuthnow), 101
Boxer Rebellion, 114
Brazil, 79, 99
Brueggemann, Walter, 33
Buddhism, 38, 71
Burma. *See* Myanmar
Burma Council of Churches, 110
Byrne, Patrick, 5

Callistus, Joseph, 19
call stories, 145–46
Cambodia, 70
capitalism, as threat to Christianity, 120
Capodanno, Vince, 5
Caritas in Veritate (Benedict XVI), 68, 181–82
Carmelites, 8
Catholic Church
    in Africa, 66–69
    as agent for global unity, 181
    awareness in, of mission, 44, 46
    changing the basic model of, 32
    considering some violent practices normative, 134
    creating, in the United States, 179–80
    demographics of, in the U.S., 30
    future of, in the world, 180–81
    identified with tradition and conservatism, 78
    influence of, in the Americas, 77
    mission of, 166–67
    missionary nature of, 187, 233
    in North Korea, 107
    political standing of, challenged, 41
    presenting, to the United States, 165–66
    privileged position of, in the United States, 78
    redefining its relation to the world, 171
    self-consciousness of, 169
    in Vietnam, 111, 112–13
    women religious in, 23
Catholic Church Extension Society (Catholic Extension), 209–10
Catholic Foreign Mission Society of America. *See Maryknoll*
Catholic imagination, 185–86
Catholic Medical Mission Board, 88
Catholic Missionary Union, 197
Catholic-Muslim relations, 90–92
Catholic Relief Services (CRS), 212, 213